STARTING FROM SCRAP

STARTING FROM SCRAP

STEPHEN H. GREER

Burford Books

Printed in the United States of America.

10   9   8   7   6   5   4   3   2   1

Library of Congress Cataloging-in-Publication Data
Greer, Stephen H., 1968–
Starting from scrap / Stephen H. Greer.
      p.   cm.
ISBN 978-1-58080-160-7
1. Hartwell Pacific (Firm)   2. Scrap metal industry—China—Hong Kong.
3. Greer, Stephen H., 1968–   I. Title.

HD9975.H624H37   2010
338.7'669042095125—dc22   2009050602

To Mei, Hailey, George, and Ashley

A Note to the Reader

Everything that happened in this story is true and the characters are real people. However, as this is a story of my own entrepreneurial adventure in Asia, unless someone has specifically given permission for me to use his or her real name, I made my best effort to protect their privacy by changing names and certain minor details.

CONTENTS

Prologue

This book chronicles the story of Hartwell Pacific, a metal recycling company I founded in Hong Kong in 1993 and sold in 2005.

It's not as crazy as it may sound to end up in Hong Kong at the age of twenty-four, unemployed, having never been to Asia, and deciding to start a business. There's an amazing energy in Hong Kong, as well as in most of Asia's megalopolis cities, and it all revolves around making money. If you have an ounce of entrepreneurial blood in you, it starts to boil the moment you hit the teeming streets.

It was no secret in 1993, as today, that Asia's exploding demographics of low-cost labor combined with the enormous potential of a two-and-a-half-plus-billion-consumer market were converting the region into the world's workshop, as well as its best bet for future global growth. The Western world was also simultaneously suffering from a terrible recession. The combination of these realities along with a sense of wanderlust, desire for adventure, and hunger to strike it rich fueled hundreds if not thousands of ambitious young men and women on their way to Hong Kong.

It seemed like almost everyone was trying to get something going. A twenty-year-old from Kansas was developing a brand of peanuts in China, a fast-talking New Yorker was sourcing promotional items, a sharp-tongued Londoner was trading war-era Harleys out of Vietnam, and a kid from Texas was helping foreign companies invest in Chinese power projects. My roommate had a business arranging for Asian kids to study abroad, while another friend from Massachusetts was trying to set up a stockbrokerage company.

I ended up in the metal recycling industry, but it could have been anything. The what, how, and where were driven by reactivity rather than original vision. As it turned out, though, I did develop a passion for scrap. Waste is one of the most vital raw materials in the world, and it is contained in just about everything you use in your life. Its recovery is also critical to our sustainable development—the only other alternatives are mining, drilling, and deforestation. However, though I am proud today to have been associated with a green business, I would be lying if I didn't admit that the greatest attraction for me was Asia's

enormous and unwavering demand for scrap metal and the potential to make big bucks in a multibillion-dollar trade.

Particularly for recent graduates, a taste for independence as an entrepreneur is life altering and can make it very unappealing to return to the slow grind of working your way up a corporate ladder. Throughout my tumultuous twelve-year career as an entrepreneur, I rarely needed an alarm clock to get out of bed, something many of my college classmates who were slogging through eighty-hour-a-week finance or sales jobs certainly could not say. Being the master of my own destiny was intoxicating.

Unfortunately, most of my entrepreneurial friends gave up this pursuit in favor of something more stable. But for some reason I did not. I may have been young and naive, but I was 100 percent certain that I was going to be successful in the end. Any setbacks or failures, no matter how grave, in my mind were simply frustrating delays on the way to an inevitable positive outcome. Perhaps you can credit my supportive family for this unwavering confidence, but I think such perseverance and optimism are hardwired inside all successful entrepreneurs. As you'll read in my story, I didn't succeed because of a top education, being born with a silver spoon, or having lots of lucky breaks; though luck no doubt plays some role in all business successes. The most important factor was that I just didn't quit. I also had an insatiable curiosity about the world and the way other cultures lived. This no doubt aided in my ability to operate in foreign countries, melding together with business acumen accumulated over years of struggle.

That steadfast commitment is the story of Hartwell Pacific. Regardless of the industry, my dream was to build a great company, live an exotic life, and see the world in the process, and that is exactly what happened on a whirlwind adventure through Asia, the Middle East, Latin America, Europe, North America, Australia, and even Africa. However, that maniacal drive for growth almost led to my destruction, and it was during the recovery period that followed this overexpansion that my transformation into a seasoned businessman took place. I also discovered that building something that can stand the test of time is more important than satiating unbridled ambition.

I hope that by sharing these experiences and the color of my adventure I can encourage a new wave of capable young people to consider entrepreneurial opportunities, and in particular to capitalize on the inexorable shift of power from the Atlantic to the Pacific. Especially for those who are dismayed by the lack of traditional opportunities in the current economic morass, the experience of living and working in this part of the world will be a fantastic long-term asset as well as a hell of a lot of fun. Your life may not turn out exactly the way you plan, but you'll definitely have your own book to write by the time you're finished.

1

THE LAY
OF THE
LAND

The bright neon lights of predawn Hong Kong jumped out from the narrow streets and alleyways, embracing the plane as we banked in low at a surprisingly sharp angle. Kai Tak Airport was carved out of the middle of the city, a single-lane runway protruding into the harbor. As the wheels touched down with a heavy jolt, reality set in. I was twenty-four, arriving in Asia for the first time with no job or specific plan other than to try to capitalize on the economic boom that was unfolding in the most populated part of the world.

Up until six months ago, I'd been working as a financial analyst in the European headquarters of MacDermid Inc., an American chemical company based in a small German town, and had been on a long, slow track toward becoming a financial controller. Fed up, I had left Germany in hopes of finding a power job on Wall Street—only to see those hopes crushed when America slumped into the recession of 1992. But there was a silver lining. As Wall Street and Main Street slashed at their workforces and masses of young graduates joined the ranks of the unemployed, all the business journals were writing of the

great fortunes being made in the burgeoning Far East. Serendipitously, I had also been reading James Clavell's novel *Noble House,* a high-drama story of intrigue, business deals, and romance, all exotically played out in modern-day Hong Kong.

I was now simultaneously running away from failure and running toward something unknown but exciting. A recession in America, some media hype, and a novel I'd picked up randomly had sent me on a journey around the world.

As our plane taxied to the docking station, I was overcome by a pungent odor. A pretty flight attendant, acknowledging my reaction, explained that *Hong Kong* translates into English as "fragrant harbor"; this sweet scent was due to millions of people flushing untreated sewage into the sea.

It was six thirty in the morning and the airport was packed. Representatives of just about every nation in the world were milling about—Africans wearing colorful robes, Indians in saris, Chinese, Europeans, and Americans. I had always naively considered that Asia was a single place and Asians were one people, but I was now starting to appreciate the widely varying features, skin tones, builds, and fashions. I was fascinated by the different faces and studied them all as I waited in the long immigration line. Finally I got to the head of the queue. The officer took my passport and eyed me briefly, flipping through the pages. He stamped it, *kerchunk,* and passed it back without expression. I flipped to the page and looked down: FEB. 22, 1993—HONG KONG.

Baggage in hand, I approached a set of large sliding doors. As they opened, a crescendo of chatter from beyond enveloped me, only to leave me ensconced in silence a moment later as they smoothly slid closed. Taking a deep breath, I staggered through the doors and descended into a sea of people searching for their connections amid a snarled traffic jam of carts. Strange faces stared at me pointedly as I inched, bumped, and jostled through the mob, totally overwhelmed.

I exited the frigid terminal, a suffocating wave of humidity fogging my glasses. I then propelled myself blindly past the taxi line, a herd of people pushing and maneuvering their way along caged aisles like cattle in a slaughtering pen. Avoiding the crush and keeping to the right, I searched for the bus stands per the instructions of Topher Neumann, a friend of a friend who had agreed to put me up when I arrived. I eventually found the A10 that would bring me to Causeway Bay, our designated meeting place.

The thirty-minute journey felt like five as the hydraulic doors gasped open and I was ejected onto the busy streets in front of the Lee Garden Hotel. My fellow passengers dispersed and I stood alone— suitcase and black leather briefcase at my feet, absorbing the tropical humidity on this unseasonably warm day, sunlight dancing off my eyeballs. As I searched the crowd with squinted eyes and a jet-lagged brain, I tried to call up an image of Topher from my vague high school memories and considered for the first time: *What happens if he doesn't show up?* There was no plan B. I'd flown here from my hometown of Pittsburgh on a one-way mileage ticket I had scrounged off my father.

The crowds continued to amass and the temperature steadily rose as I kept searching for Topher with one eye on my bags. Finally a tall white guy with tousled brown hair wearing a T-shirt, shorts, and flip-flops came loping through the crowded streets, his head bobbing above the locals. He was coming straight for me, the sweaty white guy holding a blue blazer. I smiled.

"Welcome to Hong Kong!" he announced exultantly. "You made it!"

❦

I followed Topher through the streets to his apartment. I had imagined that in Hong Kong, a British colony, expats lived in old colonial buildings, where they sat on balconies in rattan chaise lounges under whirling ceiling fans, avoiding the heat while sipping cocktails and exchanging the news of the day. That image started to dissolve as Topher led me through the throngs of people busily worrying around Causeway Bay, one of the most densely populated parts of Hong Kong and in fact the world. We then meandered through a couple of alleys and approached a well-weathered fifteen-story apartment building that took up most of one city block. The entrance was a long hallway coated with peeling white paint and lined with hawker stands selling refrigerated drinks alongside interesting-looking tubs and bins of food. Inhaling a musty mix of fish, cooked meat, and automobile exhaust fumes, I walked by a bucket of shelled raw oysters sitting on the floor, a pile of goop in a plastic pail. I was mesmerized by the sights, sounds, and smells. The locals gawked at us as if we were from another planet while we heaved my bag down toward the elevator. The building was not appealing at all on the outside, but the ninth-floor flat was roomy

and comfortable. I learned that the older buildings like this one are much more spacious and convenient than the newer ones built when land was very dear during the 1970s and '80s property boom, a trend that has continued until today. Topher, presumably with the permission of his flatmates Ian Edgar and Bernie McGuire, had invited me to stay on their couch until I got settled. We sat together sharing a coffee. Bernie was a tall, good-looking Texan who worked in finance for a Chinese chemical company. Ian was a classic New England prep school kid with fair skin and reddish blond hair who worked for the American Chamber of Commerce.

"What's the plan?" Bernie asked with a touch of a southern drawl. As in, *How long are you staying?* Ian sat nearby listening intently, slouched in a comfortable chair, chewing some snuff. *Ahhhh. The plan . . . Good question,* I thought.

"The plan is to figure out the lay of the land, find an apartment, and get a job. Once I figure out what's what, I'm hoping to start a business," I stated confidently.

"Great," Bernie replied. "Here are the help-wanted pages and the *Property Post.*" Ian spit some snuff into an empty Coke can, gazing at the floor. I was grateful for Bernie's assistance, though aware it was a gentle nudge toward the door.

The apartment was located on Haven Street, which Ian, fluent in Chinese, explained is called *Hay Won Guy* in the local Cantonese dialect. If you translate *hay won* back to English it means "promising cloud"; *guy* just means "small street." Ian, a bit of a mystic as well as a Sinophile, felt the name was very auspicious.

It was thus on Promising Cloud Street that I got my start. It was all very exciting though I was totally exhausted. I had somehow made it around the world, met up with a guy I barely knew, and begun a life in a country I knew nothing about. I wasn't sure exactly where I was going, but I was certainly moving fast!

⌒⟨✖⟩⌒

I used those first days and early mornings to wander out into the streets and try to get perspective on the city. One morning, while walking through the crowds, I passed an alleyway between two gleaming new office towers. People wearing shorts, sweaty tank top undershirts, and sandals were sitting on plastic stools underneath an awning,

hunched over bowls of noodles and rice vigorously slurping and stuffing their mouths with their chopsticks. The similarly dressed cook stood in front of his portable burner and wok, shouting grumpily back and forth with his patrons. Everybody chatted loudly in what appeared to be spirited arguments interspersed with bursts of toothy guffawing. I learned this is referred to as a *dai pai dong* (traditional food hawker stand), and that this great local tradition is slowly being crowded out by the expanding city.

The next day I rode the aboveground city tram, a hundred-year-old form of public transportation that is referred to as the ding-ding because of the bell it rings when pushing through crowds of people. I took it from terminus to terminus to try to get a better sense of my new surroundings. Sitting in an upstairs window seat, I watched with amazement as the chaotic city below slowly passed me by.

Though I was spellbound by these new life experiences, the locals didn't really seem to think my arrival was such a big deal. I had expected them to be as curious about me as I was about them. That was a bit naive. I was just another oddity walking down the street, getting in their way. Hong Kong suffers from a fairly understandable phenomenon: Pile people on top of one another, mix in some sweltering humidity, and smiles disappear. I don't judge them negatively for that reason. There are as many good people in Hong Kong as in New York or London and equally as many bastards, sharks, and nasty old ladies. Okay, maybe Hong Kong has a few more nasty old ladies. I once tried to help one pushing a loaded dolly up a hill and she yelled at me. From then on, I considered old ladies fair game in the battle to get where I needed to go.

Now that I was settled and orient-ed, pardon the pun, Topher, Bernie, and Ian introduced me to their favorite neighborhood spa, a Chinese bathhouse named New Paradise. We traipsed down Lockhart Road from the apartment, dodging the drippings from the old air conditioners that cling precariously to the sides of most buildings. Once I took a quick left through the frosted-glass doors of New Paradise, the peppery smell of burning incense hit me immediately. By the base of the staircase that leads guests up to the reception lobby, there was a green ceramic goldfish pond with a fountain in the middle, half a dozen large colorful carp swimming about.

"Goldfish ponds are very important for feng shui," Ian explained. "Fish, or *yue* in Cantonese, represent surplus, and surplus gold is a good thing. Also, water, *soi* in Cantonese, symbolizes money—so gold-

fish ponds are very popular." This pond seemed to be working, as New Paradise was doing a thriving business.

We ascended the stairs, and two middle-aged reception ladies dressed in red cheongsams gave out a startling yell. I wasn't exactly sure what they said but guessed it was something like "FOUR WHITE GUYS!" We entered the locker room and were each given a pair of slippers, a towel, and a locker key. I got key number 14.

Bernie laughed. "Nice number. They would never give that key to a Chinese guy." He explained in more detail. "The number 4, or *say* in Cantonese, is the number symbolizing death. Number 10 or *sup* means 'definitely.' *Sup say,* or 14, means you're definitely dead meat."

Certain locker numbers were reserved for regulars. Eight, 18— any number with an 8—is considered lucky, as *baht,* meaning 8 in Cantonese, also sounds like the word for "rich." I would learn over time that this obsession with numbers is very serious. Apartments on the fourth floor trade at a discount, and people pay huge premiums to get license plates for their cars with auspicious numeric combinations.

We disrobed and moved down a musty carpeted hallway into a tile-clad wet room. It included searing-hot and freezing-cold baths, overwhelming steam rooms, saunas, and a scrub table. This was the real deal, not some sissy spa. We grabbed a quick shower and then worked slowly into the hot tub.

"Dang! It's hot today," Bernie said. "I think we're cookin'."

When he stood up, he had a red line across his chest delineating the water's surface, the red meat below starting to puff out. Ian and I stood and compared matching lines. We *were* cooking.

The boldest locals rolled directly from the hot tub into the freezing-cold tub, exhaling loudly in the form of a moan as their hot skin met the icy water. They then repeated the process back and forth. Bernie, showing his bravado, followed their routine. I was not joining them; seemed like a recipe for a heart attack to me. Ian, ever the professor, explained: "The Chinese have a saying, *Fu how leung yok,* or 'The most bitter medicine is the best medicine.' Pain means that the bad energy is leaving your body. So that's a good thing." I was getting a beginner's education on the complexity of Chinese thinking along with my bath and massage.

Sitting in the tubs and observing the other patrons, it was evident to me that this was not a tourist destination. Many of the guests were heavily tattooed, it was explained, with the symbols of local triads or

criminal gangs. There we sat, four American prep school kids soaking in the tubs with the local businessmen and a few gangsters. We could not have looked more out of place. One other Western guy walked by on his way to the showers. He gave us a knowing nod, as in, *Ah, you found this place, too,* but that was it. This was no place for socializing. I am also not one for walking up to another naked guy and introducing myself.

After the wet room, we put on shorts and robes and headed to the tearoom, where we were served tea and snacks by ladies in tan uniforms as we read the papers and watched horse racing. Ear cleaning was also available, but not even Bernie opted for that. Once we settled in, the mama-san came by to arrange women for our massages. She held a piece of paper with a list of numbers, each representing a masseuse.

"Take numma seventeen. She good massage. Or how bout thirty-two? She available now. Othawise you wait!"

The guys had their favorite numbers booked in advance, but I followed the mama-san's recommendation and we were brought upstairs for a fifty-minute massage, referred to as a one-hour massage. No matter how they did the math, it was cheap—about thirty bucks for the full use of the spa, as well as tea, toast, and massage. The massage was not the soothing Swedish type, though. It involved pinching, kneading, jabbing, and pounding. Remember, pain is important for good health. I was lying there trying to relax when out of the corner of my eye I saw my rather rotund masseuse climbing up onto the table, wood creaking as she prepared to walk on my back. *Must be good business for the local chiropractors,* I thought, exhaling with a mighty sigh as she dug her toes into my spine. The three of us were in one big room and the masseuses were jabbering on, disturbing our peace, so Bernie made the ground rules clear. "Hey y'all. No walky! No talky!"

They got a good laugh out of that.

"Ay yahhh. No walky! No talky! Heee heee heee," my masseuse chortled.

I left the bathhouse that day with my newfound friends, and as we walked back through busy Causeway Bay to the Haven Street apartment I had a revelation. *The orientation week is over. It's time to strike out on my own and see what opportunities are out there.*

2

To Do a
Common Thing
Uncommonly
Well

I soon found a shared flat through an ad in the *South China Morning Post*. The apartment was in the Mid-levels, an expensive neighborhood lined with luxury high-rises halfway up to the Peak on Hong Kong Island, and my little room would cost about $1,000 a month. The Peak, the neighborhood at the top of the mountain, is the most prestigious, but hey, I was halfway there. The clincher was the address: 18th floor, No. 8 Robinson Road. Knowing the number 8 was very lucky and powerful and with 8 and 18 in my address, I felt I was getting a good start. With backslapping man-hugs from Topher, Bernie, and Ian, I set off across town.

My two new roommates and I clicked immediately. One was an entrepreneurial Englishwoman in her early thirties who had a proper accent and was clearly from a privileged background; the other was a wry, Cambridge-educated Englishman in his late twenties who worked for a French waste management company.

It was a comfortable apartment with nice views, not to mention a bed. The only negative was that it overlooked a construction site that did

not break on weekends, and my often hung-over Sunday mornings were greeted with pile driving: *Che che Bong! Che che Bong! Che che Bong!* But this didn't really bother me. On the contrary, the noise and crowds were part of the attraction, and I was invigorated by the ever-present development. I hadn't moved to Hong Kong for peace and quiet.

Beyond business and construction, Hong Kong was also an incredibly social environment. In fact, life was pretty similar to what I had experienced as a frat boy back in Pennsylvania. Rooftop keg parties were regular affairs, and my diet was atrocious. My core sustenance consisted of Domino's pizza, Heineken, Coca-Cola, and Pringles for Western food; barbecued pork buns (*cha siu bao*), pork dumplings (*siu mai*), and Singapore noodles for Chinese food—a healthy East meets West buffet.

Even though I was on a tight budget, essentially living off money I had saved from my cushy expat job in Germany and some funds generously granted by my parents, I didn't feel out of place or out of the mainstream. Luckily, guys in their twenties have similar lifestyles whether they have $10,000 or $10 million. It's pretty much beer, pizza, and girls. I figured I could get by without much income until I hit thirty, when social norms would likely switch to red wine, beef, and women with expensive tastes. One American girl I met complained bitterly, "Hong Kong is the worst city in the world to meet men. In America, men in their mid-twenties are settling down. You guys just want to party and run around like a bunch of teenagers!"

This may have been precisely the appeal of Hong Kong to so many single men from around the world. Hong Kong offers youth a little extension.

Unemployed though I was, I was determined not to be unproductive. I woke up early every morning and did a heavy workout in the gym. I'd spend about an hour on the stationary bicycle, pedaling faster and faster to burn away anxiety and the weight I had gained feasting on Wiener schnitzel and Pils in Germany.

It would be important to be social in order to build a network, so I decided that I would never turn down an invitation.

"Badminton eight o'clock Sunday morning?"

"Absolutely!"

"Lawn bowling at noon on Saturday?"

"Why not?"

I attended the American Chamber of Commerce's Young Professionals cocktail parties, where I walked up to complete strangers and

introduced myself. It was particularly difficult because the typical conversation, yelling over the latest club music, went as follows:

"Where are you from!?"

"Pittsburgh!"

"Where!?"

"PITTSBURGH, PENNSYLVANIA!"

"Oh. How long have you been here!?"

"Two months!"

"Who are you working for!?"

"I'm looking for a job!"

Blank stares. They must have thought, *Oh shit. This guy needs help.*

Most people were quite helpful, though, and happily gave out
contacts and ideas about who might be hiring, even volunteering the
use of their names. Remarkably, the contacts I called were very acces-
sible, much more so than their counterparts in America. Given Hong
Kong's shortage of skilled and trusted employees, it was an "all hands
on deck" situation, so sometimes senior executives would answer their
own phones and invite me in for coffee to discuss opportunities. Hong
Kong was absolutely booming.

I cold-called, sent out résumés, had some interesting interviews,
and at one point felt that a dream job with a Wall Street powerhouse
was achievable. Through one of my mother's tennis partners, I met Jack
Wadsworth, the chairman of Morgan Stanley Asia. After seeing his picture on the front page of the *South China Morning Post,* I promptly
placed a call and was invited in for coffee. Lacking a power suit that fit
my new svelte figure, I rushed down to a tailor perched on the second
floor of a dilapidated building above a noodle shop. Two days later I
donned the ill-fitting, rather itchy $300 suit and headed to Morgan
Stanley—the big time.

Mr. Wadsworth's surprisingly small corner office was within
shouting distance of the dealing room where I, like most greedy young
kids of my generation, aspired to gain a seat. Though not impressive in
size, it had a grand view of the harbor. Barges and loading derricks
rushed to and fro; the office buildings and apartments of Kowloon
stretched out low between the harbor and Lion Rock Mountain,
which loomed in the distance.

Mr. Wadsworth was standing with his back to me, looking out the
window, when I walked in. Sensing my presence, he wheeled around
in an animated manner, strode across the room, and clasped my hand
firmly. He was robust with a healthy build, I guessed in his late fifties.

"Call me Jack," he said in a gruff but friendly voice. Next, he burst into a monologue. "These are exciting times. We're doin' well, but when the Chinese open up the futures market, we're gonna knock the cover off the ball!" he lectured, taking a practice swing with an imaginary baseball bat. "Ya see, Chinese kids have a trading chip implanted in their foreheads at birth. All we've gotta do is train 'em up. Have a seat, Stephen. How can I help you?" he asked, dropping into his chair, eyeing me intently.

"I want to work on a trading floor, but I don't have that experience. Given the chance, I'm positive I can learn quickly," I explained. It was an intense moment but, strangely, I wasn't nervous.

"Well, Steve, our training program is in New York. If we hire locally, we send people back there for training. Perhaps we have something in the research department," he offered. "Joe. Hey, Joe. Come here a second," he shouted over my shoulder and out his open door. "This is Steve Greer. Have a talk with him. Maybe you guys have a position for him in research." This was the signal that my five minutes with the big man had come to an end.

Research? Though the thought of a stable paycheck was enticing, I had always thought of myself as a future Master of the Universe—as described in Tom Wolfe's *Bonfire of the Vanities*—not a research geek. *I didn't leave Germany and the finance track to end up in research. No back rooms! I want to transact business!* I concluded to myself while still smiling calmly on the outside, politely listening to the faceless executive to whom I'd been handed off.

Back at the perch on Robinson Road, I hung up my new suit, put on shorts, and lapsed into a comfortable tropical sweat, cuddling up on the couch with my best friend, the *South China Morning Post*. I was feeling somewhat settled, and for some unknown reason confident. *If not Master of the Universe bond trader, perhaps entrepreneur,* I mused. Now, that had a wonderful ring to it. *I just need to come up with an idea.* I decided to sleep on it.

The next morning I awoke in the early dawn to a lone bird's shrill call, initiating the cacophony of whoops and chirps that every early-morning person in Hong Kong recognizes. Less than a year after leaving Germany and three months after landing in Hong Kong, my mind was clear.

The job search ends today. I'm going to start a business. I'll just have to figure out how.

3

HARTWELL PACIFIC IS BORN

After the predawn epiphany in my bedroom at No. 8 Robinson Road, I got down to work. What's the first thing you should do if you are going to start a business: Develop a concept? Write a plan? Analyze your resources? Understand the needs of your customer? Don't be silly. Incorporate.

For most people, incorporating a company is a clerical task, but for me it was monumental. In coat and tie, I marched down to the offices of McDonald and Murray, an accountancy that specialized in incorporations. Its formal conference room with thick carpeting, a walnut table, and walls lined with prints of nineteenth-century sailing ships was suitable for this great moment. Despite the upscale decor, the partner who helped me was disheveled and appeared utterly exhausted. He explained through a thick Irish brogue, which had me guessing at times, the positives and negatives of Liberian, Tongan, British Virgin Island, Cayman, and Hong Kong companies.

"With British Virgin Island companies there are no required audits," he enthused.

It was all very James Bond to me. I imagined board meetings in the Caribbean under palm trees. I was disappointed to learn that you never actually had to go to the Virgin Islands. In the end, I opted for a plain vanilla Hong Kong company.

It was with great pride that I incorporated Hartwell Pacific on May 21, 1993. I used *Hartwell,* my middle name, so that people couldn't guess that I was a one-man band. I was so proud of that incorporation certificate. It meant more to me than my university degree, when in fact all I'd done was spend a couple thousand dollars on a nice little piece of paper. The registered office and mailing address were in a business center/shared office in the prestigious Prince's Building, not far from Morgan Stanley.

Hartwell Pacific's incorporation and registration process was incredibly easy, taking only a couple of days. There aren't many places in the world as efficient as Hong Kong. I then went down to HSBC (Hong Kong Shanghai Banking Corporation) to open an account.

"I am here to open a corporate account," I announced.

"Very good. May I see your reference?" the girl behind the counter asked demurely.

"Reference? I don't have a reference. I'm here to give you money and business, not take a loan!" I shot back, blood rushing to my face.

"Unfortunately, you need to have a reference from someone who has a corporate account here," she apologized.

"Then I'll take my business elsewhere!" I finished, storming past the other customers waiting in line. I limped next door to another, smaller bank, which accepted my $500 and issued me a checkbook in the name of Hartwell Pacific. I assured the clerk, who couldn't have cared less, that there would be much larger deposits in the near future. With checkbook in hand and officially incorporated, I was ready to begin my journey as an entrepreneur.

Next, I bought a phone/fax machine for my home office and signed up for a pager.

Communication is key! I thought.

A mobile phone in those days would've been a lavish expenditure, and they were the size of a brick. I instead chose New World Telecom's pager service because it was noted for reliability, and more importantly the salesgirl Maggie was a knockout.

Let's see: corporate setup, prestigious office address, bank accounts, communications, dinner with Maggie on Tuesday. What now? Yes: business planning!

I assumed I would start by trading a product or commodity, versus manufacturing or building something, but held a longer-term view that pretty much anything that had worked well in the West could be done in the fast-developing Far East. There was endless opportunity without having to invent a thing, and I was definitely not the mad scientist type. I would focus on the motto of the H. J. Heinz Company, where my father worked for thirty-seven years. It was featured on many walls around the company's offices and in his den at home.

TO DO A COMMON THING UNCOMMONLY WELL, BRINGS SUCCESS.

I sent off a fax (no e-mail back then) to almost everyone I'd ever met of business significance. It went something like this:

Dear Sir,

I am writing to inform you that I have established Hartwell Pacific Limited as a trading company in Hong Kong. We are looking to participate in trade between China and [your country] and hope that we may be of service.
    Please do not hesitate to contact us.

Sincerely,
Stephen H. Greer
President

I figured that was broad enough to have me pretty well covered.
    My first stab was in what's known as the gray market. When the price of, say, Pringles or Duracell batteries is relatively low in one market, such as Florida, due to overstock, and the price is high in Hong Kong or Moscow due to company pricing policy, gray marketeers try to get their hands on the goods in Florida and sell them in Hong Kong, locking in the price gap. I called it "Consumer Product Arbitrage," which had a more sophisticated Wall Street sound to it. This "arbitrage" infuriates the corporates, as they want to dictate where they sell and at what price. I uncovered an opportunity exporting Levi's blue jeans from America to Hong Kong. Utilizing a courier flight, a cheap way to fly if you are willing to carry a mail pouch, I went to the States and closed on a couple of shipments from

JCPenney, but ultimately I found Levi's restrictions on the number of jeans you could buy in any one transaction overly burdensome. I also discovered that after adding in all the transportation and distribution costs—not to mention the discounts required by the Hong Kong buyers to make the deal work—the net margin wasn't so attractive. It wasn't meant to be. I kept moving.

In the hunt for a viable model, I encountered a wacky array of businesses and learned over time that there is someone out there making a buck off just about anything you can think of. At one party I encountered Daryl Patton, the chicken-foot king. That's right, chicken feet. Steamed or braised, they are a delicacy in China. Daryl was head of Asian operations for the largest trader of poultry parts in the world. Clearly this was a niche business, but he explained that they were moving two hundred ocean containers per month, valued at over $500 million per year. *We throw that shit away at home and these guys have built a $500 million business out of collecting it and shipping it to China!*

I was curious as always and grilled him about the business over bottomless glasses of beer as a scantily clad Filipina girl twirled around a brass pole on the stage ahead. Most people in the club had something else on their mind, but I was focused on commerce.

"How do you control quality? How are prices determined? What markets do you buy from? How does the supply chain work?"

The obvious response would have been "It's none of your business and I'm trying to enjoy the show," but Daryl was generous and explained the ins and outs of chicken-foot trading. His employer had created a processing machine that fit on the end of a typical poultry production line. It collected all the feet and in a sanitary fashion removed the nails and other parts that people in China did not consider desirable. They then froze the feet, packed them up, loaded them into refrigerated ocean containers, and shipped them off to China. They had processing lines at most of the major poultry plants in America and also in Brazil, which Daryl explained is a big poultry market.

Convinced I understood the basics, I jumped right on it and through a hot tip learned that New Zealand had a sizable plant. Thanks to persistent calling, I discovered that they discarded their chicken feet as waste. Unfortunately, the business was not to be: The plant slaughtered only about one hundred thousand chickens per week, while a major plant in America would process well over a million. Thus, it did not represent enough scale to justify the investment in processing

equipment. My dreams of becoming the Frank Perdue of Asia went up in smoke, which was just as well. I can't imagine sitting around a conference room discussing ways to kill 'em faster.

In the desperate search for crap to trade, I met a girl named Ivis. It was meant to be Iris, but in her prior job they gave her business cards with IVIS on them and suddenly all her customers knew her by the misspelled version. It's humorous how many unusual "English" first names you come across in Hong Kong—Nigerly, say, or Romson. I even met a prominent businessman named Frankl. Curiously, as I type this sentence, I notice that the L key is right next to the K, so I assume Frankl's secretary had a twitchy right hand.

Ivis worked for a small Hong Kong metals trading company called Tin Wah Metals, which sought to procure steel for China. The state of Virginia, for which a friend of mine, Nick Peterson, worked, received an inquiry from Ivis regarding construction steel. Nick passed it to me and I chased it down, eager to find a deal.

Through research at the Hong Kong Trade Development Council, I was able to find the type of steel Tin Wah was looking for from a company called Russo Ferrous, which was shipping out of the former Soviet Union. Its Hong Kong office was on a high floor in Jardine House, the very headquarters of the Scottish company portrayed in *Noble House,* source of my earliest ideas about coming to Hong Kong. It is a fifty-story building in Central with round windows, giving the feeling of looking out of a ship's portal—a nod to the nineteenth-century China clipper trade. The Chinese, making jest at this architectural anomaly, refer to it as "the house of a thousand assholes." I was excited to be in this building, and imagined the taipan at his desk in a large formal suite on the top floor, pondering the future of China alongside old oil portraits of the former taipans. I entered Russo Ferrous's offices a few floors below, and was escorted into a plainly decorated conference room—no art on the walls, no windows, just a simple laminated table. I thought, *If you can afford this rent, you ought to be able to hang a couple of pictures on the wall.* It all seemed very temporary.

I grabbed the nearest chair and a plainly dressed Chinese lady served some tea, bowing slightly as she placed a paper cup in front of me. A few moments later my counterparts for this negotiation, Vladimir and Sasha, entered. They were an odd couple with long hair tied in ponytails; Vladimir had a straggly beard reaching down to his

chest. In my mind, these guys were textbook stereotypes of Old World Russians. They had rich accents, slowly rolling their *r*'s and finishing their sentences just the way Count Dracula might have. They got out a large map, unfolded it onto the conference table, and pointed out the small Far East Russian port of Holmsk on the Sakhalin Islands whence the steel would be shipped. I loved it. Bond. James Bond. *Or perhaps Greer. Stephen Greer,* I mused. As discussions continued over the ensuing weeks, we would meet in bars to enjoy shots of vodka and let our hair down, both figuratively and literally, while we discussed the possibility of developing trade.

Having found a source of steel, I convinced Ivis that Hartwell was an important trading house specializing in metals. After all, I was from Pittsburgh, the onetime steel capital of the world and former power base of Andrew Carnegie. Whenever potential trade partners would ask how I got into the metals business, I'd reply, "Well, you know, I *am* from Pittsburgh." They'd nod with understanding.

Ivis persuaded me that her boss had strong connections in China and financial power, so payment wouldn't be a problem. Her confidence was very convincing. We negotiated hard back and forth, and once we had a basic framework for a deal—prices, volume, delivery dates, and payment terms—Ivis suggested we meet in person.

"Why don't I stop by your offices this afternoon?" she requested.

Panic set in: My apartment on Robinson Road was clearly not an acceptable office. I would have to rent a conference room at the business center, and I wasn't sure I could arrange it in time.

"Better idea. Let's have lunch. I know a great Chinese restaurant," I countered, thinking fast.

We agreed to meet at Zen, a stylish Cantonese restaurant near Central. I arrived early and took a seat facing the entrance. After a few minutes, right on time, the host escorted a petite Chinese girl toward my table. She walked purposefully in high heels, wearing a pin-striped suit, with long dark hair pulled back off her face and gold-rimmed glasses perched on her nose. She held a folio with papers in her arm and a black leather purse over her shoulder. She looked professional, confident, and also attractive. Keeping focused on business, I stood to greet her. I'd matched her conservativeness, wearing a dark suit, black wing-tipped shoes, a white shirt, and a tie, my hair neatly groomed as usual.

"You don't look nearly as tough as I'd expected," I opened with a wry smile.

Though her restrained dress and calm demeanor were clearly an attempt to seem mature and serious, her baby face gave her away. I guessed she wasn't much older than twenty. I'm sure this feeling of surprise was mutual, but she put her hand forward and said simply, "Nice to meet you."

She either didn't catch my humor or chose to ignore it. *Better keep this straightforward,* I thought, bowing my head slightly as I took her hand with a gentle grip. *Let the negotiating begin.*

She fired the first shot as we perused the menu.

"How do we know that the quality will be right? Which mill is the producer?" Her dark eyes flashed as she stared me down from across the table.

Recoiling from the barrage, I tried to allay her fears and mount an attack of my own.

"Not to worry. We have a great deal of experience with this company and they've shipped well over a million tons of steel to China in the past year," I said, quickly reciting information gleaned from Russo Ferrous's brochure. "Of course I can't reveal my source, but you will have third-party inspection certificates for the cargo. Let's talk about the letter of credit. Will it be opened from a prime bank in Hong Kong?" I inquired, shifting the conversation to her responsibilities and away from my own.

I enjoyed the banter with Ivis. It was exciting to be working on a live deal. I also felt that behind her strong exterior was a softer side. It was in the eyes. There was great warmth once she settled down and relaxed. *This is someone I can work with,* I thought.

The conversation continued in this vein, as we played Ping-Pong with the issues while snacking on tasty baskets of dim sum. This meeting was more about getting to know each other. The final details of the deal could be hashed out later.

We parted with another professional handshake and agreed to wrap things up as quickly as possible. I was impressed with her sharpness and clear command of the details, and was thinking that this was what Hartwell needed—someone who spoke Chinese to help me deal with Mainland China directly.

Though happy with my roommates on Robinson Road, things were getting busier now and I needed more space. Conveniently, I was invited to share an apartment at 37 Caine Road with two young American friends, Ed Silver and Nick Peterson. Ed was a Stanford grad

originally from Boston who worked in consulting; Nick, a Harvard grad from LA, the guy who'd fed me the trade lead introducing Ivis. Though it was in an ugly, run-down building, one block farther down the hill from the Peak, this apartment was a great step forward for Hartwell Pacific. The rent was about the same, but I would now have more space. It had three bedrooms and a wooden box on the roof with a bed in it. The deal was that we'd split the rent three ways and I'd get the smallest bedroom plus the wooden box. I used the smaller, third bedroom as an office and slept in the box, which my friends referred to as "the coffin." I couldn't stand upright in this illegal structure. It was literally perched on the roof, so I had to exit the apartment and climb the common stairs to get to bed. At night, I could hear rats walking around on the ceiling, tripping over old furniture and a chandelier that our landlord stored up there.

I'm not sure this rooftop dwelling was entirely safe. One night I awoke to an electrifying jolt and was frozen for a few seconds, unable to move. There was thunder around, so I was pretty sure we'd taken a lightning strike. Friends were amazed that I slept in the coffin and even more amazed that I was able to coax a lady or two in there with me.

My favorite part of the apartment was the rooftop bougainvillea garden. To manage my stress, I nursed the plants along, watering them and tilling the soil. I was cognizant of the parallel between building a company and growing a garden. Over time it flourished into a high lattice of purples and pinks blocking out the ugly neighboring rooftops and hanging wildly over the edge of our building, visible from the street below.

Settled in, I could now focus on closing my deal with Ivis and Tin Wah Metals. The negotiations cruised along, haggling and arguing, and in a couple of weeks the deal was pretty much settled. It was fairly basic. Her company would open a letter of credit for around $3 million, and Vladimir and Sasha would prepare prompt shipment of the steel per the contract's specifications, or so I hoped. It did dawn on me that I had very little control over the performance of any of this. As it turned out, my intuition was accurate. Ivis's buyer couldn't come up with the money. I also learned through a connection at the US consulate that Russo Ferrous was being monitored by the CIA for flouting the UN trade embargo on Serbia. We were obviously working very hard on a deal that would most likely never happen—and if it did could land me in a heap of trouble.

Realizing that we were not going to get any business done, but respecting her ability, I decided to persuade Ivis to join me as my partner. *Just business for now.* In fact, though I was a bit of a flirt, I felt strongly that I shouldn't mix business and romance.

I came clean with her about the realities of Hartwell Pacific, its pedigree and business scope. She laughed, recalling how she'd called me on several occasions and heard dozens of people in the background taking phone calls and typing. With all the chatter, she'd figured it was a big office. She now understood that it had been a throng of telephone operators working for my paging service in a boiler room somewhere far from Central. Of course, the prestigious office address on my business card had also thrown her off.

With her guard now down, Ivis explained that she, too, had thoughts of being an entrepreneur and felt what I was trying to do was both interesting and admirable. She revealed that she had no respect for her boss at Tin Wah Metals and that her plans for employment there were short-term. *A perfect addition to my team of one,* I thought, *but first I'll have to convince her.*

A day or two later, Ivis agreed to come to my home office on Caine Road, Hartwell's "world headquarters," noting that she couldn't stay long as she was meeting her *boyfriend* in a couple of hours. *That's probably good,* I thought as I waited nervously for her to show up on the sidewalk in front of my apartment. I had other concerns. *What would be her reaction to my home office? Would she lose interest in Hartwell Pacific?* She arrived, again professionally dressed in a suit, but this time with a warmer and more relaxed smile.

"I hope you don't mind a little exercise. It's a sixth-floor walkup. Good for circulation," I joked, offering up an enthusiastic handshake.

She smiled demurely. *Crash!* The metal security door slammed behind us as she followed me up the well-worn staircase. I paused on the fourth floor for her to catch her breath and wipe her forehead. She looked forlornly up the staircase, no doubt wondering whether she could deal with this part of her daily commute. Once inside the apartment and breathing normally, Ivis took a seat in a comfortable leather chair next to a leafy plant and seemed quite at ease with the surroundings. Narita, a part-time young Filipina helper, offered her a glass of water. Because Nick and Ed were at work, the apartment was quiet and spacious—a pleasant atmosphere. She didn't seem bothered, or at least didn't show it.

"Well, this is HQ until we can get some trades going, and then we can consider getting a proper office," I started.

"That's smart. You don't want to have a high overhead until you get some business going," she wisely confirmed.

My fears had been unwarranted. Ivis was also a young ambitious kid interested in giving it a go. She had been born in China and had immigrated to Hong Kong when she was eight years old. Her parents were divorced during the Cultural Revolution and she and her father were struggling, but this did not deter her appetite for risk or desire for success. Perhaps it fueled it. Though working to get her degree at night, she was ready to take the leap. She shrewdly pushed for a partnership rather than an employee relationship, even if it would be a minority stake. Eager to make progress with Hartwell, and grasping the synergy of this budding Sino–US partnership, I was confident that we could come to a mutually acceptable arrangement.

The following week we met in a coffee shop in Causeway Bay to figure out our plan. My nerves were pretty shattered at this stage from overall anxiety about whether I was building a career or wasting my life. As a consequence, my hands shook slightly but constantly. Despite my nervous appearance, Ivis quit Tin Wah Metals and signed up as my partner, agreeing to a survival salary and a share of any profits. In turn, I would have to be the provider of finance, which I convinced her I could muster.

She confided to me later that her thoughts at the time were: *How can I trust this guy? His hands are shaking. He must be hiding something from me.* But upon further analysis, she noticed that I also had thick palms, a Chinese symbol of prosperity. This white guy must have a lot of *fook*—"luck" in Cantonese—something not to be taken lightly.

During one of our initial meetings, I asked Ivis about her life's dream.

"I just want a quality life," she said, recoiling from the question.

"I have big dreams," I countered. "I want to build a world–class corporation and have my own jet! If you could have anything, what would you want?"

"An apartment and a car" was all she replied.

"No problem. Join me and we'll go get it," I stated.

My big dream was a bit naive and unenlightened with regard to the jet, but in the context of business I believe it's important to think

big. I paraphrase Yogi Berra: *If you don't know where you're going, you'll probably never get there.*

I explained further: "You've gotta have big goals. That way if you only achieve half of them, you'll still be successful. What do they say? Shoot for the stars and get the moon."

"Dream, dream, dream," she scoffed. "I'm more practical. The more you have, the more you need. Plain steamed rice can be the most flavorful or least flavorful food depending on your perspective. I just want to build a stable business."

Anyway, she doesn't have to think big. I'm going to be the visionary behind the business. What I need help with is execution, I thought.

What I have found over the years is when you're hunting for one thing, you sometimes unexpectedly find something more valuable. In this case, I'd found my business partner.

4

STARTING FROM SCRAP

S oon after joining Hartwell, Ivis decided to go by her Chinese name, Mei. Chinese have such beautiful names with deep meanings; I often wonder why they trade them in. Ivis explained that her name in Mandarin is Yong Mei or "a tribute to plum flowers," and that her mother gave her the name during the stark communist era, because a plum is the only flower that can blossom in frost. *Powerful stuff,* I thought. *I don't dislike the name Stephen, but I don't really know what it means.*

It was now March 1994, one year after I'd landed at Kai Tak Airport for the first time, and Mei and I set off together: young, ambitious, and full of energy and confidence. The basic idea was to grab on to the flow of products between China and the United States and find a chance to squeeze our way into the middle as hardworking traders. Potential trade leads went something like this: "Looking for 100,000 tons of railroad rail. I need 50,000 tons of rebar delivered CIF Ningbo, China. Prompt shipment!" *CIF* means insurance and freight should be included in the price. These were huge deals that we naively thought

we could put together. I learned later that these inquiries are like chain letters that get passed around the world and are chased by fools like us, talking to other fools. Our focus was broad. A short list of the products we would try to trade included: promotional items, sugar, konjac root, Heinz food products, batteries, Gillette razors, mobile phones, chicken feet and assorted parts, Thai beer, ornamental gift items, a wide range of steel products, plywood, wooden and plastic CD racks, music CDs, glue, army blankets, plastic resin, tuna fish, antique Chinese furniture, gloves, safety products, hairnets, and used Caterpillar equipment and parts. We were open to anything.

In search of opportunities, we went to the Canton Fair in Guangzhou, the major national trade fair for China. This would be my first journey into the Mainland. To save money, we took the KCR (Kowloon Canton Rail) network to the border, crossed on foot into China, and then had to find our bus on the other side. This was a burdensome and intimidating process. At the time the British/Hong Kong soldiers, together with their hired Nepalese Gurkhas, were facing off against China's People's Liberation Army with piles of razor wire between them.

Leaving Hong Kong and the blue-uniformed immigration officers behind, we ventured onto the footbridge that crosses the Lo Wu River, a murky cesspool dividing Hong Kong from China. I paused to imagine desperate refugees from the Cultural Revolution swimming toward a better life. Halfway across the bridge, soldiers in green uniforms, armed with bayoneted rifles, stared us down with steely eyes. No smiles, no *Welcome to China* expressions on their faces. The only signal that we weren't in a war zone was the giant billboard on top of a building on the China side: an unmistakable cowboy, astride a rearing horse with lasso in hand, declaring, WELCOME TO MARLBORO COUNTRY!

Mei and I separated into two different arrival halls, one for foreigners and one for Hong Kong or Chinese passport holders. We would meet up once we completed our immigration formalities. After getting my stamp, I waited and waited as throngs of people hurried by, heading for customs and the exits.

Where is she? I thought with concern. *I'd have thought my section would have taken longer than hers.*

Finally, after about half an hour, she arrived red-faced with anger.

"He let me through, but didn't put a stamp in my passport!" she explained dejectedly, tears forming in the corners of her eyes. It was the first time I'd seen her vulnerability, and I instinctively felt protective. "When we try to leave, there won't be an entry stamp. It will look like I snuck into the country. I could be arrested! These people are so arrogant. He just ignored me and shouted to go away," she continued complaining with exasperation.

Now I was angry. *Who do these people think they are to treat a young woman that way?*

"Okay. Take me with you," I replied, taking her arm and starting back toward the immigration desks. Mei led me to the counter that was giving her the hard time. The officer, a thick-headed bureaucrat with black teeth, a mop of hair, and a scraggly three-day growth sprouting from his chin, was slouched at his desk reviewing someone's papers in front of a long line snaking back into Hong Kong. We were running late and I was annoyed, so decided to make an aggressive move. I took Mei's passport, led her to the booth, and slammed it down on the customs officer's counter, scowling angrily. I pointed at Mei and shouted, "Stamp!"

The guard was taken aback, as were the weary travelers awaiting entry. He looked at me, taking note that I was ready for an escalating argument, and likely considered that this would be a time-consuming challenge requiring his superior's involvement; he clearly spoke no English. He glared at Mei, then grudgingly stamped her passport and tossed it back, uttering some sort of insult in Mandarin under his breath. I grabbed her and we headed for the exits. Mei was pissed; all signs of vulnerability had been replaced by rage.

"These pigheaded communists treat foreigners better than their own people. It's not fair!" she complained as we ran toward the waiting buses.

We boarded in a hurry but then inched our way to Guangzhou, the "three-hour" ride turning into an eight-hour odyssey as the traffic was snarled on the insufficient roads. The other drivers seemed certain that the congestion would be miraculously relieved if only they honked their horns continuously. Exhausted, we checked into our dingy hotel rooms, whose prices were inflated to New York levels in honor of the Canton Fair.

Yet somehow I remained very excited about my first trip into China. I found this very foreign place as I expected and wanted it to

be: exotic and strange. The pollution, griminess, smells, poor service, and even the bizarre food on the menu were in fact all attractions to be enjoyed with a lukewarm beer. They set the mood.

Strange and exotic was cool, but the Canton Fair was just plain confusing. The plan was to look for an ideal product to source for the US market and to find some suppliers. Strangely, the trade exhibition was organized by province rather than product. As we wandered the communist-era concrete slab buildings from hall to hall, or province to province, we found the same samples of the same products. Wicker baskets, nuts and bolts, coat hangers—everything seemed to blend together in a haze exacerbated by swirling clouds of cheap Chinese cigarette smoke.

We also found that each booth was staffed by a government import–export company rather than factory management. The government handled all exports at the time and skimmed off a healthy margin, basically taxing private enterprise. It was impossible to know exactly whom we were dealing with. I was fairly disillusioned and exhausted by the whole process, but returned the second day determined to find something to trade. Though Hartwell's overhead was low, there was a limit to how long my bank account could exist without any income, not to mention a limit to how long my ego could hold out without a legitimate career. We needed to make a move. Everything from brass fittings to Christmas tree ornaments was sprawled out before us with eager salespeople trying to catch our attention. It seemed that most of what could be found in a home in western Pennsylvania was manufactured somewhere in China.

One idea that Mei proposed was the market for "gift items," which is a loose term for the useless junk people put on mantelpieces. I truly hated those little Hummel-type figurines depicting sweet storybook scenes. Before Mei had joined Tin Wah Metals, she had worked briefly in a small enterprise trading these trinkets. She remembered that it was actually quite profitable, and felt this was something we should pursue, but refused to give me the names of the companies she had dealt with. I couldn't understand her perspective; this was about survival, not ethics. Nonetheless, she held her ground and insisted that we could figure it out without stealing her former employer's clients.

I wandered the smoky halls, desperate not to end up in the gift item business, but knowing that I was willing to try anything to keep Hartwell Pacific afloat. We hovered by the booths that seemed to have more activity, in particular the ones with foreigners placing orders. I reckoned that if they had some current business, they would likely be a safer bet. It amazed me to find samples with obvious misspellings: TIS OLE HUSE. *If they can't get the samples right, what happens when you take delivery of ten thousand of them?* I wondered.

I pressed on, pretending to look at samples while straining to overhear the conversations between buyers and suppliers. I noticed that there were very eager-looking people lingering in the background behind the government import–export desks, also craning to hear what was being said. I eventually figured out that these were the actual factory owners. As China opened up to capitalism, private entrepreneurs were allowed to start businesses in nonstrategic industries but not to do business with foreigners except through a government company. *Controlled freedom* is a contradiction inherent in societies slowly relinquishing communist ideals in favor of capitalism.

⸱⟨∞⟩⸱

In the end, Mei and I returned to Hong Kong confident and energized. The genius idea that would lead us to riches? Toothbrush holders with matching soap dishes. We quickly identified both buyers from America and factories in China trading in this type of "ornamental gift item." The next step was to ingratiate myself with a buyer or two while Mei quickly bonded with the local factory owners and collected samples. In short order she was bantering back and forth playfully with them, and I could tell she had that situation reasonably under control. We worked well as a team, and I found her cultural skills invaluable. Our two faces, one Western, one Chinese, both young and energetic, formed a complete picture that could potentially provide a reliable service to skeptical buyers and suppliers. I was focused on Hartwell's survival, and this seemed like a decent short-term chance.

We soon found ourselves touring a factory in Quanzhou, Fujian Province. It was a dingy brick warehouse that reeked of a pungent mixture of cigarette smoke and urine; a bumpy dirt driveway was its only access. I was amazed at what I found. There were hundreds of children, mostly twelve- to fifteen-year-old girls, seated on benches

hand-painting white and black spots onto little cow-shaped porcelain toothbrush holders. I was sad to see them working in a factory, not having the opportunity to get a proper education, but wondered what options they had and supposed perhaps this was the price of progress. Nevertheless, it didn't sit well with me. The factory manager explained that only children could do this job efficiently as "it requires small hands."

I made a decision at that point that if I was going to live and work in the developing world, and play a positive role in its evolution, I would have to deal with the realities I faced rather than run away from them. *There are much sadder stories than young girls painting cows in a factory,* I thought, justifying the decision to myself.

Free samples of trinkets were loaded up and shipped to Hong Kong to show our "buyers"—which we did not yet have. We established a display room in North Point, a neighborhood east of Central, in a fairly new but rather pedestrian office building. It was just a simple five-hundred-square-foot room, the walls lined with shelves from IKEA that we had assembled ourselves to save money. We labeled all the samples, put together price lists, and then attended a Hong Kong trade fair, inviting buyers to come and see our products. Our first visitor, after being dragged away from the conference, remarked testily, "This is last year's stuff." I was devastated.

"At least we have plenty of Christmas gifts for our friends and family," Mei quipped. I shot her a disapproving glance and then we both broke into nervous laughter. Though we had very different backgrounds, we were able to enjoy each other's company and somehow find humor in our escapades.

⌒⟨⟩⌒

As I sat at my desk one hot afternoon, planning a trip to the World Gift Expo in Chicago, a response to a fax I had sent out a year earlier crawled its way onto my desk. It was from a social friend of my parents whom I'd met up with at the behest of my mother while working in Germany. Max Heinecke was the chairman of Nickelmet, a multibillion-dollar metal recycling company. It was a simple fax.

Dear Stephen,

As you may know, Nickelmet is one of the largest recyclers
of stainless steel scrap in the world. We are interested in the
availability of scrap in Southeast Asia and are prepared to pay
you to do a bit of market research for us as you are well
located.
        Please let us know if you are interested.

Yours truly,
Max

    I replied to Max that I was confident we could fit it into *our*
schedule. Luckily Ed, my roommate the consultant, specialized in
doing market studies. He reluctantly helped me to put together the
format, telling me, "It's easy. Just fill in this standard framework with a
load of crap." That's what the company he worked for had done for
Anheuser-Busch and Tropicana, and they'd wound up getting paid
$500,000 for each project. Of course, our study only paid $5,000, with
which I was thrilled, though my roommate was sure they'd forgotten
a zero. I double-checked. No missing zero.

⌐◦∞◦⌐

    We dutifully went through the yellow pages in Hong Kong and
Singapore, looking under *scrap* and finding *stainless steel* alphabetically
nearby. Those sections could be found missing from every phone book
in every hotel room I stayed in from that day forward.
    We cold-called scrap metal suppliers, recycling companies, screw
manufacturers, pots and pans manufacturers, and demolition companies asking how much scrap people generated or traded, prying for
information on the market—sales and shipping data, historical pricing
information, and estimates of market size. Once we'd compiled
enough information to put together an informative and attractive
report, we submitted our product and were paid.
    Max liked our work, and his next request came quickly. This time
he wanted to see if we could buy some scrap from the people we'd
talked to and ship it to England to be melted down. Valuable nickel,

chrome, and iron recovered in the melting process would then be used to produce new stainless steel. Assuming we had a purchase price that was competitive or acceptable to our suppliers, we figured the transaction wouldn't be too much of a problem.

Negotiations were tough, because the Chinese businesspeople I met drove a hard bargain, but Nickelmet's price was very attractive at the time and we were able to outbid the mostly Japanese competition.

Finally, in June 1994, we had our first contract done. It was a trial order for two containers (forty tons) of stainless steel scrap for prompt shipment. There was only one slight problem—we knew next to nothing about stainless steel. All we could have told you was that it is nonmagnetic and can easily be mistaken for iron, which can look the same but *is* magnetic, and is worth a fraction of stainless steel.

Mei and I arrived at the yard with some magnets we had scrounged up, one from the back of an old stereo speaker, and wandered around our supplier's scrap yard inspecting material. I glanced over at Mei as I stifled a yawn while ducking behind a bale of scrap to find some shade. Her brow was furrowed as she diligently scanned each bale with her magnet.

"Ouch. These mosquitoes are killer!" she screeched as she swatted her neck. I couldn't control a snicker.

"Hey, Mei, I think you missed a piece."

"You shut up! I'm moving twice as fast as you! *Hat yan zhan.*" Sweat trickled down the side of her face as she continued playfully cursing me in Chinese. Stainless steel is a shiny and beautiful metal, and in fact is sometimes used by artists due to its shimmering qualities, but its reflective nature also poses a problem. On a sunny day like this one it can turn a scrap yard into a frying pan, magnifying the already intense tropical heat.

I pulled out a camera and took her picture. Wet and tired, she mustered a smile. "I hope we will have someone to do this for us in the future!" she quipped with a wry grin.

My father was coincidentally in town on a Heinz business trip and stopped by to join us for this great moment. The purveyor of our first container, Cheung Hong Hing, a tall, skinny man with an erect posture and a formal demeanor, was a bit aghast when the Mandarin Oriental's Mercedes pulled up and our "chairman" got out to "inspect" the process. Mei and I continued to hover over the cargo with our magnets like bees to be sure we would not be cheated as Dad stood by happily and nursed a Coke, no doubt eyeing his watch pri-

vately. He was very proud to see his son running his business, but a scrap yard is not a nice place to hang around. We agreed to meet him back at the hotel, and Mei and I spent the rest of the day sweating it out. We couldn't afford for anything to go wrong. As it turned out, Mr. Cheung and his company, Sung Yee Hong, though small-time players, were very honorable, and the quality was perfect. They were hard-working, salt-of-the-earth types who no doubt had plenty of money put aside but certainly didn't show it.

That night we had a celebratory dinner with my father at Man Wah, the Chinese restaurant at the Mandarin Hotel. As we entered the restaurant, he put one arm around each of us affectionately and said: "I'm so proud of you kids. Not everyone is willing to do what it takes to get a business off the ground."

Mei blushed. Compliments are dolled out sparingly in Chinese families, and she felt my father's warmth. I could sense his growing affection toward her. He had seen her work ethic and was pleased to know she had my back. I think he truly appreciated that I wasn't all alone in this struggle. Dad returned to America, happy to see that Hartwell Pacific was gaining traction, and left Mei and me behind awaiting feedback from Nickelmet on the quality of our cargo.

About a month later, the metal finally completed its long journey around India, through the Suez Canal, and on to the UK, and Nickelmet was very satisfied. We were asked to continue purchasing for the company, which we did, taking the opportunity to try out various sources while eking out a small income. These low-volume deals taught us a lot about banking facilities and logistics. There are a lot of details involved in a trading business, and we were getting an education in all of them. I also got to develop an understanding of local values, work ethic, and negotiating mentality.

After the warm way Mei interacted with my father, and realizing how much we'd been through over the past year and a half, I was definitely starting to consider her as something more than a business partner. It probably started with a glance that was met and lingered a bit too long. Arguments or disagreements became opportunities for flirtatious teasing. Chinese flirtation is very different from American. In fact, insults such as *Hat yan zhan*—all the people hate you—can be considered sweet nothings.

Mei and I had been working hard out of the Caine Road office when we discovered another interesting character. Narita Sabino, our part-time Filipina domestic helper, had developed into a friend whom Mei and I both liked and respected. She was a very diligent person who worked days cleaning and evenings pulling pints in a bar. A single mother, she sent back the majority of her earnings to Manila to support her ten-year-old daughter and aging mom. But even with such a burden, she always maintained a positive and cheerful demeanor. Narita was also a highly intelligent woman who spoke English, Cantonese, and Tagalog fluently as well as passable Spanish.

My roommate Ed was a voracious reader, and the wall outside his room was lined four feet high and maybe six feet wide with stacks of books that he devoured at night—heavy stuff, not light reading. I noticed one day that Narita was returning a book to the pile.

Surprised, I asked, "What are you reading?"

"It's Nietzsche," she replied sheepishly with downcast eyes, pronouncing it correctly.

"Have you read many of Ed's books?" I asked curiously. I'd never read Nietzsche myself.

She nodded.

"Which ones?" I pressed.

"All of them," she answered with a proud but shy smile as she wiped the top of the stack with a moist cloth.

Evidently she had been working odd jobs all day and reading all night. Narita admitted that she normally only slept a few hours.

Grasping her potential, I told her I wanted to develop business in the Philippines someday and asked if she'd be interested in helping me.

"Of course!" she replied with a big smile, thrilled with the idea of being back at home with her daughter, as well as having an opportunity to do some meaningful work. I made a mental note for future plans. I wasn't sure how I'd use Narita's talent, but sensed I'd find something. A recruiting philosophy was now developing in my mind.

Don't look at surface credentials alone. There is buried talent everywhere. The trick is to identify it and give it the chance to break free. If I could be that facilitator, I'd be rewarded with talent, drive, and hopefully loyalty.

With the scrap business up and running, we considered separating Hartwell Pacific into two divisions; one would be scrap metal, the other gift items. However, in the end we decided to focus on scrap and let the gift business drift happily into oblivion. Though exciting, all of this seemed a far cry from being a Master of the Universe, but I'd left that concept behind quite a while ago. Even if I had wanted to go back to the corporate track, with every month I was away I was becoming less and less qualified for it. I was passing a point of no return. Though this was obviously stressful, particularly for my mother, my pride was now in being independent, living on the other side of the globe, and having my own company, even though that company had not yet made a dime.

⌐✖◦

Though the stainless steel scrap business may not sound sexy to the average person, Max had explained that worldwide these piles of stainless steel add up to an annual trade of around $15 billion. The scrap business was thus a big opportunity, but at this point Hartwell only had one customer, Nickelmet of Germany, and we were clinging to it for dear life.

5

CHINA 101

e were very proud to be associated with a large corporation like Nickelmet. More important than early-stage revenue, it gave us confidence. Stainless steel producers in Asia were ramping up production, investing billions of dollars in state-of-the-art furnaces to cash in on the China party. With these investments coming to fruition, they would now have hot demand for the raw materials to make stainless steel—nickel, chrome, iron, and stainless steel scrap. Nickelmet could smell a killing, and we soon found out that Hartwell's introduction to stainless steel scrap had a greater purpose for them. Given the burgeoning demand of the stainless steel industry in Taiwan, Nickelmet was opening a collection and processing plant there to handle both locally generated and imported stainless steel scrap. Taiwan would need large amounts of it to convert into new stainless steel coils and bars, which would ultimately be made into anything from pots and pans to elevators. Southeast Asia, historically an exclusive source of scrap for Japanese mills, would be a terrific resource for these new Taiwanese producers. Further, the Southeast Asian

economies, and thus the volume of scrap metal generation, were grow-ing rapidly, making it a very strategic and interesting market.

We felt that we were about to make a big breakthrough, so Mei and I eagerly began planning the rapid development of our office and team. Unfortunately, just as we were about to hit our stride, we suf-fered a setback.

One late afternoon as I was preparing to go for a jog, a fax from Max slowly slipped onto my desk.

Dear Stephen,

I am very sorry to say that we will be unable to continue with Hartwell as planned. One of my fellow board members has signed an exclusivity agreement with Caledonia Resources, a well regarded, London based metals trader with offices all over Asia. I was unaware of these discussions until they had been formalized. Of course you can supply to Caledonia and I am happy to make the introduction.

Again, very sorry about this. Perhaps we can find some other business in the future.

Best regards,
Max

It was a very short fax but one that had an enormous impact on us. Caledonia was to supply stainless steel scrap from Asia exclusively to Nickelmet's recycling operations. Up to now, this was our entire business plan, and I was sure there wouldn't be room for two middle-men in the market.

Mei walked into the room and could read the pain on my face. She read the fax over my shoulder.

"Steve. We were too naive! Just cheap market research," she lec-tured. "All this work for nothing!"

"Come on, Mei. On the surface, this is the right decision for Nickelmet. I mean, who the hell is Hartwell Pacific?" I retorted defen-sively. "It's a free market. They didn't promise us exclusivity. We assumed it."

"Well, actually it isn't easy to deal with our suppliers, and we do have good relationships and a strong network now. There is other busi-

ness we can do with these people," she consoled, switching seamlessly from antagonist to supporter, now placing her hand on my shoulder.

Still, I couldn't help feeling like someone had just punched me hard in the stomach. We'd been clinging to this opportunity as our best chance for short-term success, and had already begun to negotiate a lease for a proper office. We were so close I could taste it, and yet one decision, one fax, took it all away. I was totally deflated, but not defeated. I responded to Max's letter while biting heavily on my lower lip.

Dear Max,

As I feel strongly that we provided quality services in the past, and have had a very positive working relationship with Nickelmet, I am obviously disappointed to learn of your board's decision. However, I still believe we can develop a value-adding business relationship with Nickelmet in the future and look forward to that day.

In the meantime, we respect your decision and remain at your service.

Very best regards,
Stephen H. Greer
President

Mei was right. There were lots of trade inquiries out there, and our suppliers weren't just trading in stainless scrap. In particular, there was strong demand in China for nonferrous scrap metals, such as copper and aluminum, as well as a special interest in magnesium ingots from Japan, both of which we thought we could source. We believed strongly that Hartwell would make it in one form or another, and defiantly decided to move forward, signing the office lease. We swallowed the disappointment, but would now shoulder the burden of a higher cost structure.

During this period, it was apparent that Mei and I were slowly becoming a couple. She was conflicted, because she had a stable and loyal boyfriend, but the connection we were forging while building toward our dreams was undeniable. Overcoming the daily challenges and rejections that came our way drew us closer and closer. The more we denied or resisted our feelings, the more they grew, and eventual-

ly we gave up suppressing them. Then one hot summer afternoon on the rooftop among the bougainvillea, a little harmless flirtation in the form of a water battle led to our first kiss.

⚜

Hartwell Pacific was very proud to open its first office on Queen's Road in Sai Ying Pun—Hong Kong's Western District. Sai Ying Pun is Central's poor cousin with shorter, more "Grade C" buildings. The neighborhood is better known for its dried fish and incense markets than for its financial markets. Though it wasn't a fancy area, I was told that many wealthy Chinese businessmen believe their luck started in Sai Ying Pun, and thus still kept their personal offices there and ate lunch in the local restaurants. You could often spot Rolls-Royces and their drivers waiting outside some real dive.

We soon hired our first employee, Li Lee Lee, whom I nicknamed Triple Li. She was a sweet-faced nineteen-year-old whom Mei knew from her previous company. Though her English wasn't so good, and she was a bit inexperienced, she made up for it by being hard-working, eager to learn, and responsible. With Mei and me running around trying to scrounge together deals, we needed someone to hold down the fort, and Triple Li fit the bill. Our monthly rent was only $1,500, but our total overhead, including our cost of living, would now reach $7,000 a month. I was of course not taking a salary.

I could once again practice the ritual I had witnessed as a child of my father suiting up for a day at the office. By going to work, I would join the other morning commuters at the newsstand and coffee shop, feeling somehow like I was part of something, part of a group, not alone.

Working my network, I met a Japanese guy named Fukui-san who traded iron ore for the Hitomi Corporation. Noting that I was in the metals business, and from Pittsburgh, he told me that his company needed magnesium ingots, which it supplied into the aluminum die-casting industry for ultimate use in automobile parts such as engine blocks. Japan didn't have domestic magnesium resources, so it needed to import from overseas. On the other hand, magnesium was plentiful in China. Fukui, who was busy with much bigger business trading shiploads of iron ore, introduced me to Hitomi's Tokyo office hoping that I could handle its inquiries.

Doing research at the Hong Kong Trade Development Council, I found a government-controlled company in China, Henan #3 Magnesium Manufactory, which could supply. Most of the state-owned enterprises, or SOEs, had funny communist-era names like that.

Our job was to purchase and arrange shipment of magnesium ingots from Henan, China, to the port of Yokohama in Japan. The beauty of this kind of trading business was that it did not require capital. We could receive a letter of credit, or L/C, from our buyers, then use that credit to open another L/C to pay our suppliers in a maneuver known as a back-to-back L/C. Mei and I worked closely with HSBC to come up with creative ways of trading off our buyers' finance. We'd forgiven its first-day snub, and HSBC had since become an important partner in our business plans.

With financing organized, the rest of the deal fell into place. There was a bit of haggling over price, but the international market for magnesium at that time was weak and dropping so the Chinese sellers were eager to lock in a deal. As long as we had a firm price from our Japanese buyers, time was against the Chinese, and Hartwell could negotiate a healthy margin. This simple little business gave us much-needed income and, thanks to our low overhead, single-handedly made Hartwell profitable, albeit marginally.

To source the ingots for Japan, I traveled to Henan and Sichuan, at the time very poor and backward provinces. Mining happens where the resource is, and the smelting of mined ores usually happens as close to the mine as possible (as long as there's cheap coal to fuel the furnaces), so we were heading out to the boonies. This gave us a fascinating window into the more rural or inner parts of China and the workings of the Communist Party. I encountered people who it seemed had never seen a Westerner. Children came up to touch me out of curiosity. When we visited, we were definitely the main event in town: motorcades with police escorts, dinners for dozens of people, all paid for by the government. In fact I began to realize that we were a great reason for a party. Every dinner ended up with the entire room stone drunk.

Mei and I set off for Zhengzhou, the capital of Henan, to meet a supplier. The company was actually located about a four-hour drive from the capital in the small town of Tanghe. We were picked up at the airport and chauffeured in a black Mercedes S-class for our journey

along the mostly empty highway. Tanghe was a dismal dust-covered town with no more than a couple hundred thousand inhabitants—quite small for China. It was in the early stage of modernization, with new roads and office buildings sprouting up, but was still a throwback to the nation's "iron rice bowl" period, when villages had been ordered to industrialize. Smallish factories made of brick belched out black smoke and homes burned coal for heating and cooking, coating our mouths and throats with an acrid film. Motorbikes and bicycles were the most prevalent form of transportation, and people gawked at our lavish automobile, unable to see us through the tinted windows.

We arrived at the Hong Shan (red mountain) hotel, where a small group of paparazzi awaited. Our hosts were both gracious and plentiful. About forty people, mostly men, milled about in the cold, stomping their feet and rubbing their hands, awaiting our arrival. When Mei and I stepped out of the car, a greeting line of about ten formed; the rest of the crowd organized behind them. Most in the line were wearing military uniforms. The rest were dressed in what I imagined was their "best suit"—the label on the sleeve conspicuously not removed. Mei introduced me as I slowly worked my way down the line handing out business cards, offering each with two hands, bowing slightly as is the custom. We were told that our room had been arranged; we could leave our bags with the bellman and go straight to dinner. Everyone was included—in total five tables. A stiff white napkin was rolled up and placed vertically in certain wineglasses, signaling that these were power seats. The seat next to mine was kept empty, reserved for our main host, the local mayor, Mr. Zhang.

Once everyone was seated and making small talk, the door to our banquet room burst open and the mayor strode in briskly with a handful of aides scurrying along trying to keep pace. Everyone stood, sending chairs screeching across the wood floor. He was large and stocky in a dark suit, white shirt, and red tie, a Communist Party pin on his lapel. He contrasted starkly with the others, who wore mostly army uniforms or wrinkled business suits. You could tell this was a man of influence. I guessed he was in his fifties, with a graying crew cut and rolls of fat accumulated on the back of his head and neck. He grasped my hand firmly, pumping my arm, and gave me a wide grin, exposing a couple of gold teeth, the rest deeply stained black at the edges of the gums. Mei, acting as my lowly interpreter, relayed my pleasure at making his acquaintance. Once seated, we were all poured a thimble-sized

cup of bai jiu, a clear rice liquor that has a very strong afterburn in your belly and insists on revisiting your taste buds every few minutes. The mayor stood to make a toast, and Mei translated.

"As foreign guests we are very pleased to have you here and you should feel very welcome. China is now opening up and we hope to develop close trade relations with the United States. For us, your friendship is more important than your business." *How nice,* I thought sarcastically. "You can count on us to honor all our commitments."

The United States had nothing to do with this trade and he did not represent the company that was supplying us, but never mind. This was a boilerplate Communist Party toast that I would hear many times in the years to come. He continued, extolling the importance of relations between the United States and China, finishing with a call of *"Gan bei"* or "bottoms up" as we all tossed back the first shot of fiery liquid. It was my turn to speak and I belted it out with gusto.

"Thank you for your welcome and your encouraging words, Mr. Mayor! I am very impressed with the level of development here and also your warm, courteous hospitality. I am extremely optimistic about the success of China and the province of Henan and in particular for the business of exporting magnesium ingots. We look forward to a prosperous long-term relationship with all of you!" Mei smiled as she listened to my words and then translated.

Raucous applause and shouts of *Gan bei!* followed. I was pleased with the reception of my brief remarks and inwardly proud that these diplomatic words had smoothly rolled off my tongue without preparation. I was twenty-five years old and toasting the mayor of a city. At this stage of my career at home, I would have been someone's gofer.

After the formality of the speeches and a couple more shots of bai jiu, everyone loosened up and the party began in earnest. It was at least a twelve-course feast. The food was delicious and the toasting relentless.

"You need to spend more time in China, get a Chinese girlfriend, and learn Mandarin," Mei translated with a smirk.

"I will indeed. The food here is the best I've tasted in China! And the women the most beautiful!" I goaded Mei to translate back.

My gracious host guffawed. "Ohhh. Vely good, Vely good, Vely good. *Gan bei!*"

By the end of dinner, I had a nice buzz going and was truly enjoying myself. I was fascinated by this introduction to the "real"

China beyond Shanghai, Beijing, and Guangzhou. After dinner, the mayor excused himself to attend to some important matters; the rest of us remained for karaoke.

Karaoke is popular all over Asia, and foreigners are always obliged to sing at least one Frank Sinatra tune; "My Way" is a big favorite. In Henan, though, it was a different kind of karaoke. They were all old communist war songs. The background videos, shown on televisions that hung from the ceiling, were of soldiers charging over embankments wiping out their enemies, the capitalist dogs. Not feeling any animosity from our hosts, Mei and I swayed back and forth to the music, cheering the soldiers on to victory. For sure, I was one of the drunker guys because each individual insisted on cheering me with a shot of bai jiu until Mei cut them off, signaling an end to the festivities. Bodies were scattered around the banquet hall in deep sleep. She propped me up as we stumbled back to our room. In fact we had two separate rooms. Mei always insisted on it to protect her honor. The highlight of the dinner had been "Beggar's Chicken," a great dish actually, but unfortunately the chicken would not be fully digested.

The next morning it was time to go have a look at the ingots and the production facility. This was all ceremonial; the deal was done. It had been concluded by fax, and this trip was just a chance to look each other in the eyes and forge a personal, hopefully long-term relationship. Upon checking out of our suite, we were told it was all paid for. We were ushered through the front door to a flight of concrete stairs leading down to our motorcade. There was a throng of photographers and even a guy taking a video of this great moment. As we slowly descended, waving to the assembled crowd below, I started humming "Hail to the Chief" to Mei. Though I was clowning around for her benefit and my own, I admit that I felt a sense of pride at being treated as a dignitary. It felt much better than the way I had felt standing around in our showroom in Hong Kong amid a clutter of clay figurines.

The magnesium business was not high volume, but the margins were pretty good at the time. It was nice, not to mention important, to be able to start putting some money away. We also had no problems with delivery from the Chinese suppliers, as prices had peaked at about $800 a ton and were on a slow, steady decline that would not rest until they had plummeted 50 percent. The Chinese were thus eager to get rid of their metal as the value fell.

Then the market turned back up, and it was time for the Japanese to recoup their losses as prices rose well above those guaranteed in our contracts. Buyers benefit as prices rise, and the Japanese stood to make substantial gains.

"Thank God, Mei. I'm not sure how much more Hitomi was going to swallow before pulling out of this trade."

I had been secretly worried that our only cash stream could shortly disappear. As it turned out, my worry was well placed: The Chinese suppliers stopped returning my calls and faxes. Radio silence.

"What are we going to do? We can't replace the magnesium at the same price," I exclaimed to Mei. "Hitomi is going to kill us. We'll lose over $20,000 based on the current market level. These guys honored all those deals that went against them and we're screwing them on the first deal that goes their way. I'm totally ashamed."

We had no choice but to explain the situation to Fukui-san. I told him straight up that one of our Chinese suppliers in Sichuan was not returning my phone calls and that I was worried about nondelivery on about a hundred tons of magnesium ingot.

I braced for the response, but Fukui just calmly said: "They're not returning your calls because the market has gone up. This is normal. Just offer him today's market price. We'll cover it. Don't worry."

You're kidding me! I thought. *If I were this Japanese guy, I'd be kicking my ass down the road!* As prices rose, all of our contracts with the Chinese suppliers that had not yet been shipped had to be renegotiated in a similar manner. This was clearly a trade that would only work smoothly for us when prices were falling. I was very pleased to do business with the Japanese but unclear about their motives if they were always going to lose money. Apparently harmony was much higher on their priority list than short-term profit. A Japanese friend explained that in Japan, the business is evaluated as a whole. The Japanese trading company's job was to get ingots for their customers with whom they had a web of intermingling business relationships, of which the magnesium trade was only a small piece. Though there is some logic to this, it was now clear to me why Japanese companies, though some of the biggest in the world, were not found at the top of *Fortune* magazine's list of most profitable enterprises.

We set out to clean up our contract problems in China. The largest outstanding obligation that had to be renegotiated was in Sichuan. I decided to go personally and meet face-to-face with these

bastards who were reneging on me. The trip involved a three-hour flight from Hong Kong to Chengdu, and then a three-hour drive to the small town of Deyang. It was very dangerous. We went full speed in our Mercedes, weaving in and out of traffic and barreling down on tractors that were pulling loads of hay at five miles an hour on a major highway. Most of the trucks were not road-worthy, and it was just Russian roulette whether or not we would get caught up in a major wipeout. Chinese roulette, you might call it. I was exhausted but would not allow myself to fall asleep—I was once told that survival rates are higher for those who are awake and braced for impact.

We arrived in Deyang and met up with Jason Chan, a young translator I had hired from Shenzhen. Our hosts were very charming and did not see why the little glitch in our business relationship should have any negative bearing on the future. We were greeted as if we were old friends who hadn't seen each other in years—lots of hugs and backslapping. After the warm greeting our hosts suggested that we begin with a meeting to resolve open issues and then move on to dinner.

We entered a vast conference room; a large rectangular wooden table took up most of it. The middle of the table was hollowed out, and fake flowers were potted along its length. Jason and I sat on one side, and the eight-person Chinese entourage took the other. A heavyset guy in a dark suit, Mr. Wang, took the power seat across from me. The others filed in. It was a freezing-cold day and there was no heat in the room, so I sat bundled in my black overcoat and scarf warming my hands with a cup of hot tea. It was at this moment that my stomach began to grumble. We discussed business, focusing on their future needs and leaving the ugly, nonperformance stuff for last. I tried to focus, but the grumbling was turning into a twisting knot. *Was there mayonnaise on those sandwiches in the car?* I considered. I urgently begged their pardon and was led to the bathroom. Of course, the bathroom was freezing and the toilet was a classic hole in the ground with two slightly raised, treaded foot stands. The stench was unbearable.

How am I going to pull this off without a disaster?

The simplest way of assuring that my nice suit was not soiled was to just strip down, leaving on only my black socks and black wing-tipped dress shoes. I don't know how far I should go with this but I think by now you have a decent mental picture.

I got myself back to the conference room, where Jason and our eight counterparts from Sichuan were waiting. Everyone was concerned, but I assured them that I was absolutely fine.

"Good. Let's wrap up the question of price and get some dinner," Mr. Wang suggested.

I had the contract out on the table and was eyeing all the pages, which were dutifully initialed by both parties, wondering what the point was of having a contract at all. The reality was simple. The cost of recourse would have been more than the value of the contract in legal fees alone, and I would have been arguing my case in a kangaroo court in the middle of nowhere China. I was now experiencing what I had been told on many occasions: "In China, a contract isn't worth the paper it's written on."

Indeed, the contract is just a guideline for future negotiations in the event that the Chinese partner no longer wishes to honor it. Knowing that I had the open support of our Japanese buyer and with my stomach still wrenching, I moved quickly for resolution. The other option would have been to jump up and down, make some noise, and go home empty-handed. I wore a fake smile, swallowed my pride deeply, and offered a face-saving out.

"I understand the difficult situation you are in and that if you could perform the contract, you surely would. What we need to find is some compromise, the best price we can achieve, so that I may save some face for Hartwell as well as for my Japanese buyers. With a view toward our future business together, I hope you can see the benefit of compromise and some shared sacrifice. We need immediate shipment, and are prepared to make price concessions to get it."

Just get the materials out of their hands as soon as possible before the market goes higher, I thought.

The shipment date was set and a price agreed upon, which was more or less the current market price. We then shook hands, as if that meant anything.

It occurred to me that when doing business in China, or in any country with a nascent or corrupt legal system, you need to be prepared to make concessions. From now on I would imagine deals without contracts and how they would work, and then use the contract as a road map for mutual understanding, relying on the strength of a sustainable win—win rather than the local legal system. I had once met an ex-judge from Guangzhou who told me candidly that in China,

judges don't make judgments; they just do what they are told by their superiors. Having influence with the superiors is thus far more important than having a good case. Most foreigners don't have that kind of special relationship. I made my concessions with that in mind.

It was time for dinner. Sichuan food is the spiciest in China. Not hot like Thai food, which burns your tongue, but everything is soaked in chili oil and coated with black or green peppercorns. The flavor is called *ma la,* numbing spice, and it's a slow burn that numbs your mouth and reaches deep down into your stomach. I actually love it, but it was not ideal in my current condition. That night we had a famous Sichuan "hot pot" meal, which is a large soup pot for the table to share. A simmering, chili-laced broth bubbled away with a mix of all kind of meats and vegetables percolating to the surface. I wasn't sure what was what, other than the giant brain that pushed its way to the fore from time to time. Of course, our dear host kept serving me the "special" parts. I ate everything politely, but was anxious for the meal, not to mention this whole trip, to end. That night I called home groaning to Mei that I wasn't sure I was going to make it.

When morning broke and it was time to leave, I was about the happiest guy in the world. But there would be one more hitch. Traffic in Chengdu, the capital of Sichuan Province, was snarled, and it looked like we would miss the flight. *"No!"* I begged the driver to try anything, and he did. We drove the wrong way down a one-way road, the oncoming cars' horns trailing off behind us as we passed. A policeman finally caught on to our scheme and pulled us over. Jason told me to roll down my window so they could see my face, telling the police that I was a VIP and needed to make my flight. The policeman hesitated for a moment and then said something in Mandarin. He returned to his car and proceeded to give us an escort to the airport, lights flashing, continuing down the one-way road the wrong way. There is a valuable lesson here. As a Westerner in China, I was handicapped in some ways and advantaged in others. *Learning how to work with your handicaps and exploit your advantages is key,* I thought.

I boarded the flight and curled up with a blanket, ensconced in the absolute luxury that was Dragonair economy class. As I was looking out the window, reflecting upon the craziness of my first visit to Sichuan, a well-dressed businessman squeezed into the seat next to me, smilingly apologetically.

"Sorry to crowd you, lad," he said in a heavy British accent. "Looking forward to getting back to Hong Kong?"

"You have no idea," I replied.

"So what do you do?" he asked, making small talk.

I flashed back to the many times I had been asked the same question and had squirmed inside my skin as I struggled to find a response. What was I? An entrepreneur? Yes, but doing what? It suddenly came to me. I now had a good answer.

"I'm a metals trader," I stated confidently.

It felt great to be able to say that. The label was as important as, if not more important than, any profits. I was a metals trader, and Hartwell Pacific was a metals trading company. The company had found its niche, and I had found an answer to the question, "What do you do?"

6

HARTWELL HITS ITS STRIDE

O_{ur} magnesium ingot business rode the bust very profitably and the boom very awkwardly and, as with many commodities we would trade, the opportunity just disappeared over time. Still, we were confident that there were more metals out there to be traded.

Nearing my twenty-sixth birthday, I decided it was time to move out of the Caine Road apartment and shed my fraternity house lifestyle. I would miss my bougainvillea but not the coffin. It also dawned on me that I'd been away from home since I was fourteen—boarding school, university, Germany, Hong Kong—but this would in fact be my first apartment, the first time I'd lived alone. Well, that wasn't entirely true; Mei had a drawer, but her father was not at all ready to concede defeat. Mei still lived at home.

I found a small, one-bedroom apartment just a couple of blocks away on Bridges Street—a little side street in Central within walking distance of the office and the bars. My new building was a thirty-two-story needle jutting into the sky, and my flat was on the thirty-first

floor. It had a panoramic view, and there was a fresh breeze when you opened all the windows. However, that breeze could get a little scary when typhoons hit and the window next to my bed was taking direct blasts from hundred-mile-an-hour winds. It was a cozy place, and once again the highlight was the rooftop. It wasn't set up as a leisure facility, just concrete and exposed pipes, but the view of the city and harbor was spectacular. A guy who lived in a nearby building was a bagpiper who would practice on his rooftop some evenings. When I'd hear him starting, I would quickly grab a scotch, sometimes accompanied by a cigar, head up to my lookout, and take in the city while listening to the eerie sound of the piper.

⌒⊂✖⊃ᵒ

On my way to the office the first day, I nimbly navigated the hundred or so steep steps down to Hollywood Road, the first section of my ten-minute walk to work. The downhill commute to the office was far easier than the return trip, which was a solid workout for my glutes. At Hollywood, just below my building, there is a famous Buddhist temple, Man Mo Miu. As I marched purposefully by, anxious about trades, costs, and expansion, I smelled the incense being burned by the local worshipers. At this stressful time in my life it lured me in, and the dark room had a calming effect. I lingered in the background, peering through the smoky haze created by the spiraling yellow cones of incense hanging from the ceilings and sticking out of large brass pots. The smoke hovered around Buddhas of various sizes, shapes, and expressions all positioned throughout the temple. Silently, I observed the locals worshiping. I made this stop a regular part of my morning routine, making a small donation most days. Having learned from the locals, I also started burning three joss sticks and kowtowing three times in front of a random deity—one wish per kowtow. The wish was always the same.

"Success for Hartwell Pacific. Success for Hartwell Pacific. Success for Hartwell Pacific."

Mei gave me a piece of jade, which I wore on a rope around my neck day and night. I got one for my father and was touched to find out that he wore it every day to bring me luck. I can assure you that wearing a piece of jade jewelry was not a natural part of his Midwest American upbringing. Though Dad has a conservative veneer, he is open-minded and curious on the inside. Two men divided by a globe

but deeply connected. I got a piece of jade for my brother, too, but the day after he got it he wrecked his car. He put it in a drawer and asked me not to send him any more good-luck charms.

The concept of luck and the mixing of Western and Asian spirituality and sensibility were becoming interesting parts of my education. I hadn't come to Asia to learn about this but ended up fascinated. I decided that if I was to study these new cultures while reflecting on my own, embracing the good from each, perhaps I could find something ideal.

⚬❈⚬

A couple of months after the fateful fax from Max notifying us that Hartwell's services were no longer needed, my kowtowing started to work. Caledonia, the British company that Nickelmet had chosen as its exclusive supplier in Asia, though good at dealing with large-scale steel mills and mining companies, was not really equipped for the rough-and-tumble scrap business. Metal recycling in Asia was a very local, mom-and-pop industry—no multinationals, no corporations. It would take a lot of determination to build a network and provide what Nickelmet needed, and Caledonia wasn't showing much ability in this area. Consequently, Hartwell was given a second chance to supply, though not exclusively; we'd have to fight it out in the market on our own.

With Nickelmet back on board, we would need to establish ourselves quickly as a meaningful supply source. The longer Nickelmet was in the market, the sooner it would find the bigger recycling companies and establish direct relations. I would try to preempt that by building a network and a healthy volume of scrap, creating a bargaining chip. If Nickelmet ever contacted any of our suppliers, we'd cut them off from the rest of our network.

Thanks to our market study, I knew pretty much everyone in the Hong Kong and Singapore markets but had relatively minimal experience in the rest of Southeast Asia. It was time to hit the road. I arranged for stacks of business cards to be printed as well as a one-page letter introducing our company, which was translated into various local languages. I set up visits to Bangkok, Manila, Jakarta, and Kuala Lumpur. I started in Kuala Lumpur, where I worked the yellow pages and trade associations to establish a list of targets. On most calls, I could barely get through my pitch before they hung up on me. I'd open, "Hartwell Pacific is an

experienced American metals trading company with its Asian headquarters in Hong Kong. We have a strong demand for stainless steel scrap and are prepared to pay premium prices if we can secure a regular supply of high-quality material. Do you handle stainless steel scrap?"

"Wha—?" click, was the most common response. We'd call fifty companies and hope to find five potential suppliers.

Some neighborhoods had high densities of scrap dealers; I could meet ten in a day, banging on metal gate after metal gate. Other times I had to go to remote areas and it would turn into an endless day of sitting in traffic. Either way, I'd arrive well dressed and upbeat, jump out of my heavily air-conditioned car into the oppressive tropical heat, and roll seamlessly into my pitch.

Most dealers were reluctant to talk to a stranger, but once again being a Westerner had its advantages. The obvious presumption was that if I had come all this way, I must have something worthwhile to offer. At any rate, most of the firms I talked to did not have enough stainless to export themselves, but through grilling them and baiting them with valuable pricing information, we could find the larger consolidators who did have enough volume to ship internationally. Once we found the exporters, we passionately made the case that it was in their interest to establish a new marketing channel in order to help them get more competitive pricing. We also gently dropped the names of their suppliers, other small dealers with whom we had met, with the veiled threat that if they would not do business with us we'd offer higher prices to their suppliers and try to build up a new competitor. The promise was, of course, that if they gave us some regular business we would be very careful not to disturb their market and margin. It was thus a carrot-and-stick negotiation.

This is the life of a scrap metal trader . . . hustle, hustle, and more hustle. It may sound painful to some, but for me it was a fascinating glimpse into a world I knew nothing about. I was enthralled by my journey through Southeast Asia, sampling the foods, picking up the nuances of the different cultures. What was once a single homogeneous region in my mind was becoming a gathering of distinctly individual countries. I don't think Caledonia took that level of interest or went through that much effort to establish a scrap business in the area; young and hungry sometimes trumps reputation and brand.

Once we gained a deep enough understanding of the market to become legitimate dealers, we began to squeeze Nickelmet on price.

Nickelmet opened its yard in the Taiwanese port city of Kaohsiung and proceeded to build a $15 million stockpile of scrap. Jimmy Reynolds, a humorous Yorkshireman based in Hong Kong and in charge of sourcing for Nickelmet Taiwan, was under enormous pressure to build this stockpile. He was also not very keen about living in Asia in general and used to refer to Kaohsiung as "The bloody arsehole of the world!" Jimmy, like Caledonia, was not as aggressive as we were in digging deep into the market, and was also skeptical about the quality he might receive or the reliability of contracts from untried traders. He was impatient and dismissive of the locals who lacked the sophistication he was used to in Europe.

⌒✲⌒

Unfortunately for Jimmy, nickel, the primary component of value in stainless scrap and thus its primary price driver, was now being bid up aggressively on the London Metal Exchange, the only exchange where nickel futures and options are traded. I would pop into his office and find him red-faced with anxiety as prices soared and his need to purchase more metal mounted. He was getting high-pressure phone calls as soon as offices opened in Europe asking him how much he'd purchased yesterday. Knowing what we knew about his needs, lack of local market information, and internal pressures, we took full advantage. We gathered up commitments for all the material available in the region at a particular price and, of course, did not inform him of our position. He was now unable to purchase from anyone else but us, as most of the material was spoken for and he didn't know that many suppliers. Having a large volume of great strategic value to Nickelmet, we pressed hard, pushing his bidding price up multiple times, capturing a greater and greater spread for Hartwell.

"Jimmy, the supplier needs another $20 per ton. They can load the containers immediately, but they saw the nickel market jump yesterday and won't sell unless they get another bump." I feigned concern while calculating our profits.

"Bloody peasants! Jesus. Okay, done!" he shouted.

Ka-ching went the Hartwell cash register.

This continued for almost a year with the dollars piling up over at HSBC. We put away close to half a million. Nickelmet hadn't wanted to have an agency agreement, and preferred for us to act and trade

independently, so that is exactly what we did. As it turned out, we
weren't bad at it. We also became experts on freight rates and found
ways of squeezing out extra margin by playing the shipping companies
against one another. At that early stage, I'm not sure it would've been
much fun to be one of our service providers. We were a pain in the ass,
haggling on every bill—freight, bank charges, insurance, accounting
services, even economy-class plane tickets. The business was really
cooking now. I kept my parents abreast of our progress, forcing them to
listen endlessly to the details of the deals I'd made. We spoke probably
five or six times a week. Normally I'd be rattling on and suddenly hear
snoring. "George!" my mom would scold, nudging my dad awake.
"Sorry, dear, your father's very tired." Mom was a real trouper.

᠀᠀᠀

We were now buying stainless steel from local scrap dealers through-
out Southeast Asia, but mainly from Hong Kong, Thailand, and Singapore.
These companies were mostly well-established Chinese, and in some cases
Indian, family-owned businesses. Generally speaking, we found these
dealers to be shrewd and tough but an honorable lot, and though we
struggled to find reliable suppliers in Indonesia, Malaysia, and the
Philippines, we were pleased overall with our coverage of Southeast Asia.
    Building upon our successes, we found some suppliers in
Guangdong, the Chinese province that borders Hong Kong and was
the wild frontier of China's conversion from a communist to a capitalist society. Wherever you find a booming economy, you also find lots of
stainless scrap. There were no major stainless steel producers/scrap consumers in China at the time, so scrap was regularly exported.
    As an added feature, scrap generated in northern China or more
remote territories was also exported via Guangdong. Exporting directly from a northern port should have been the simplest and cheapest
freight, but due to a 15 percent export tax at the time, transshipping
through the south worked out to be the better deal, if you had the right
friends. In fact, a decent part of Guangdong's economic boom can be
credited to the lack of enforcement by customs officials. There is a saying about Beijing: "The emperor is far and the mountains are high." In
a modern-day context, this means the rules are made by the communists in the north and broken by the capitalists in the south. Exporters
were simply avoiding tax through misdeclaration of cargo or under-

declaration of value. This was a business for locals—not foreigners. We bought the scrap once it was free and clear from China's borders, making sure our hands were very clean of any customs hanky-panky.

The southern entrepreneurs were fascinating people. Many of them, particularly in our business, had been absolutely dirt poor only a few years before. Combine their street smarts and a tireless work ethic with a lucky break or perhaps a connection in the customs department and suddenly they were thriving businesspeople. In 1995 they were not yet at the Rolls-Royce or Bentley stage, but they were making profits and plowing the money right back into their companies. They worked their tails off with no consideration for anything other than getting rich as quickly as possible. I respected the hell out of their drive and determination, but not necessarily their table manners. One of our customers, Mr. Chiu, the hard-driving owner of a thriving secondary aluminum smelter who traded stainless scrap on the side, proved himself to be quite reliable, but getting through a meal without losing my appetite was a tough one. I hosted a lunch for him one day at the Shangri-la Hotel in a formal dining room with large, ornate chandeliers and thick carpeting. Chairs with carved wooden armrests and silk-covered cushions were arranged around a round table for four set with crisp linens, high-end silverware, and fine china. A waiter approached, dressed in black tie, and passed out menus. We made some small talk. "What are your favorite dishes? How about something to drink before lunch?" As we talked and waiters hovered, Mr. Chiu, our most honored guest, casually put his index finger against one nostril and started to lean to his left. Before the shock could register on my face, Mr. Chiu cleared his nostril with one long, steady blow right onto the carpet. Mei and I stopped breathing and looked at the waiters, who sort of rolled their eyes. I could tell this was not a first-time experience for them. The businesspeople in Hong Kong and Southeast Asia were much more mature, established, and for the most part couth than those in China. I maintained a solid business relationship with Mr. Chiu but did not bring him back to the Shangri-la.

Though standards varied, Hartwell had now developed strong relationships with the scrap metal dealers throughout Southeast Asia and Guangdong using good old-fashioned street hustle. In the process, we'd developed a book of suppliers that was very valuable to Nickelmet. We were confident that our hard work could not be easily replicated, at least not in the short term.

7

BRANCHING OUT

Hartwell was now solidly profitable, but I felt it essential to develop new product lines and broaden our business scope so we would not be overly dependent on Nickelmet. As we continued our purchasing of stainless scrap from recycling companies in Asia, we found that many of these suppliers also had an interest in purchasing copper and aluminum and having them shipped to China, where the market was hot. We discovered that those metals had been flowing heavily from America to Asia. As an American, I thought, *Piece of cake!* Not only did I feel I could easily find sources of scrap in the United States, it also seemed that selling something to someone I was buying from was a clever way to offset credit and trade risks. If the metals markets fell and they canceled their deal to buy my copper, I could cancel my deal to buy their stainless. It was not a perfect hedge, but better than nothing.

Off I went, touring America and Canada, staying in airport hotels, and tearing out pieces of the yellow pages in my search for suppliers. Under *scrap metal* in the Los Angeles yellow pages, I started with

A: AAA Metals, ABC Metals, and eventually Andara Metals. The latter turned out to be a good cold call. Andara is a one-hundred-year-old family business and is one of the most highly regarded metal recycling companies in the United States. We bought our first container of American scrap metal from it and quickly established ourselves using Andara as a reference.

The next company we got started with in LA was Lincoln Metals, which specialized in aluminum scrap. The president, Larry Bossman, was a tough character with a hot temper, for which I learned he was famous. One of his managers lamented, "Don't worry, he's that way with everyone." We bagged an order for five containers and kept moving.

∾❦∾

While in LA, I took some private time with Mei to show her around. We stayed in a small hotel in Santa Monica and had some nice meals and romantic walks on the beach. Our relationship was blossoming, though she was still uncertain whether leaving her steady boyfriend for this unstable entrepreneur had been a good idea. As a sunset activity, I took Mei down to Venice Beach so I could show her all the nut cases. A tarot card reader was plying her trade on the sidewalk, and Mei insisted on having her fortune told. The woman slowly laid out the cards, watching us intently. She explained in an ethereal voice, "You've recently ended a relationship that was not meant to be. The cards tell that you will marry someone from far away."

Mei smiled. Bingo! I was in. I passed the lady a twenty. With that personal business behind me and a base list of potential and active suppliers, we returned to Hong Kong.

I now needed to establish a steady trade with these American dealers. The price negotiation was complicated by the time differences, but Hartwell was well positioned. After our Chinese suppliers finished reviewing the London Metal Exchange at around 10 PM Hong Kong time (4 PM in London), they gave us firm bid prices, which I used as a basis for negotiation with the suppliers on the West Coast, who would soon be coming to work for an early-morning start in California. "Time Zone Arbitrage," I called it. The suppliers in LA then compared my prices with those of the local scrap suppliers, and began haggling to cut down on my margin. We went back and forth trying

to increase the spread for Hartwell. That often required me to be on the phone in the middle of the night, so I slept with a calculator and notepad next to my bed, waiting for the phone to ring. Normally the margin for us would only be a penny or so per pound. But one container contains around forty-four thousand pounds, and most of these deals were for a few containers at a time, so the crumbs added up! My target was to make a couple thousand dollars every night. Most nights I did.

After finalizing all the terms, we would collect a 25 percent deposit from our buyer in cash and transfer it over to the American suppliers, sealing the deal. However, even after the contract was finalized, it was often very difficult to get paid in full. The buyers felt that since they had already made a deposit, there was no rush to pay the balance; after all, the cargo wouldn't arrive for roughly thirty days. This could turn into a very stressful game, because the metal was on the water and there was no turning back. Even worse, this practice of delaying payment until the shipment arrived really limited the supplier's cash flow, and put us in an awkward position as the middlemen. Nobody is happy when this happens to them, but volatile Larry of Lincoln Metals absolutely blew a gasket. My phone rang one cheery afternoon and I happily answered: "Hartwell Pacific."

Larry's voice exploded into my ear. *"Where's my f---ing money?"*

"It's coming. Larry. Larry. Calm down. I am doing the best I can. You'll definitely get paid."

"You're cut off! No more business till I get my f---ing money!" He cut the line without saying good-bye.

I learned from others that Larry actually liked us very much, but business is business.

Soon we were a well-established trader in nonferrous scrap metals and the cash flowed. The combination of our copper, aluminum, and stainless profits was creating a nice pile in our bank account.

⚬⚭⚬

One of our regular copper and aluminum buyers in Hong Kong, who was particularly adept at the "slippery" importation process into China, told us that the Middle East was another great source of scrap metal that few in China had developed. I think the Chinese buyers were a bit intimidated by the Middle East. They were just getting used

to Westerners—Middle Easterners were another matter. They were also much more comfortable with the US and European markets and their transparent legal systems and business cultures.

One such customer, Mr. Wong Chee Chuk, asked if we'd be able to help his company establish a supply chain from the Middle East to southern China. We were eager to oblige.

"I have very good contacts throughout the Middle East," I promised, despite having never been there and not knowing anyone who lived there.

Once again we got copies of yellow pages and business directories, and set up a grand tour including Dubai, Kuwait, Bahrain, Qatar, and Israel. I admit at this point I was as excited about the travel adventure as I was about the business.

We agreed to bring Mr. Wong with us as he wanted to see the metal and conclude some introductory deals. It is a common Chinese philosophy, with which I agree, to always make some small business when you first meet. It's a great way to open doors and forge relationships. You also weed out the jokers.

He joined us on the Emirates flight to Dubai. We were upgraded to business class, which I felt was auspicious. During the flight, we passed the time playing the Chinese card game *Cho Dai Dee,* which is a bit like Hearts with a lot of loud, theatrical bluffing. I picked the game up quickly, and by the time we were descending into Dubai I'd won fifteen Hilton buffets. Unfortunately, they tore down the Hilton before I could cash in. Beyond passing time, the games were a way of bonding with my Chinese customer, who could not speak English. Dice and card games may seem childish in a Western business context, but they make a great way of bridging cultural divides and breaking the ice.

Everything was going quite smoothly until we started to land. An announcement was made that if you were carrying more than $10,000 in cash you needed to declare it. Our red-faced customer reached under the seat in front of him, retrieved his briefcase, and started pulling out packets of $100 notes and handing them to us. It turns out he had planned to make some deposits on his initial purchases and pay for the whole trip in cash. He had about $200,000 on him. It is quite common for Chinese businessmen to carry a lot of cash, but I was definitely taken aback. Not wanting to offend Mr. Wong, we stuffed our pockets with money and wandered through customs with innocent smiles and frayed nerves—very stupid in retrospect.

After that anxious experience, Mr. Wong asked if I could handle the cash and take care of the expenses. Spending has always come easily to me, so we made the most of our trip lavishly consuming fine food and wine. The diminishing cash pile also reduced our travel stress. I felt like a Mafioso; every time a bill came, I'd have to pull out a wad of notes. Americans use credit cards. I would be surprised if my father ever had much more than $100 on him at any given moment.

We did some business in Dubai but could not find any decent potential suppliers in Bahrain or Qatar. Friday is a holy holiday in the Middle East—it's their Sunday—so we found ourselves with some extra time. Great excuse for some fun and to burn some more money. I chartered a fishing boat to take us out into the Persian Gulf, where we caught a large barracuda—not a prize fish for an angler, but a cause for great celebration. We brought it to a small island and barbecued it, then danced to Arab music with the locals by an open fire on a star-filled night. As it turns out, one of our fellow dance partners was Sheikh Something-or-other, a member of the royal family. He seemed to take a liking to Mei, so it was probably good that we left the next day. I teased her, saying that women disappear all the time in the Middle East and are forced to be part of the royal family's harem. She was not amused.

Though not much got done in Bahrain, or Qatar, we advanced to Kuwait. Entering the country, I made a quick pit stop before reaching customs. The bathroom floor was littered with whiskey bottles. Because Kuwait is a strictly Islamic country, alcohol is banned throughout. The one loophole, as I was told later, is that animal skins aren't picked up by the X-ray machines, so people fill bota bags, animal skin pouches, with booze and dump the bottles. I was also informed the penalty for being caught is flogging, so you must really love whiskey to take that risk. I made a mental note not to get flogged for anything while here.

Our potential supplier, Mr. Al-Wadi of Metal Arabia, met us at the airport. He was everything I wanted him to be—a giant Arab in a flowing gown. He was large in all dimensions, his belly pressing out against the white fabric. He had dark skin and a scruffy half beard that he stroked almost constantly. His rich accent added to the mystique. Mr. Al-Wadi ushered us with a sweeping arm gesture toward his black Range Rover and we were off into the desert to tour his company's scrap yard. I felt like Lawrence of Arabia speeding along, a trail of dust following us as far back as I could see, the flat, desolate desert stretch-

ing out on every horizon. Mr. Al-Wadi's turban fluttered in the breeze created by his cracked window.

Metal Arabia's claim to fame, other than that it was a large metal recycling company, was that it had cleared the "highway of death" after the first Gulf War. Never have I seen so much destruction. Memories of sitting on the couch in my fraternity house watching A-10 Warthogs strafing the retreating Iraqi army came to mind.

The scrap yard was about one square mile of mangled tanks and jeeps, rusted hulks piled up randomly, their gaping wounds exposed to the elements. Electric cables were piled like giant heaps of spaghetti, and spent brass shell casings were stacked neatly based on their size. I pondered the waste of war while Mr. Wong pondered the millions he could make if he could buy all this and process it in China. We went to Mr. Al-Wadi's trailer to discuss business. It was a trailer like any other on the outside, but inside were Oriental carpets and comfortable furnishings. We took seats around a coffee table and were served a heavily sweetened mint tea.

Knowing that Mr. Wong's main interest was copper, Mr. Al-Wadi started. "Let's talk about the copper cables. How much you pay me?" He had roughly three thousand tons of rubber-insulated copper cables from some sort of demolition job, a pile about thirty feet high and thirty feet in diameter.

Mei translated for Mr. Wong, and he got out his calculator. Having checked the London Metal Exchange and spoken to his partners in China, he was fairly confident about the market and prepared an aggressive bid.

"Eighteen hundred dollah pah ton." Mr. Wong spoke for himself, showing off his English.

I injected the obvious on our customer's behalf: "Based on 100 percent copper content! And you'll need to separate the cables into different copper recoveries. Some of the cables are 50 percent copper, others are 15 percent, and they're all mixed together in a giant pile," I emphasized, spreading my arms for illustration. "It'd be impossible to estimate how much of each grade you have!"

"No, no, no. Please, Mr. Stephen. How much for my cables? One price. You take all," Mr. Al-Wadi finished, waving the copper away with the back of his large right hand.

I was incredulous. "You want us to guess? This is a $3 or $4 million purchase, and you want us to guess?"

"You are expert," Mr. Al-Wadi scolded. "You tell me. How much you give me?"

I rolled my eyes, and Mei explained to Mr. Wong what was unfolding. It was pretty clear to me that Mr. Al-Wadi, whom I was told is connected to the Kuwaiti royal family, had no idea what he had in inventory. This would be an opportunity but would also be very risky. If our customer was wrong on his estimate, he could lose hundreds of thousands of dollars easily; if we lowballed the estimate, Mr. Al-Wadi would throw us out on our ears.

"We'll have to think about it and get back to you, Mr. Al-Wadi. But be sure, we're very interested and will definitely bid. Mr. Wong will need to talk to his partners again about such a large and risky deal. Let's try something easier. I noticed you have some stainless steel," I remarked innocently, turning the conversation toward more of Hartwell's interests.

"Yes we do. How much you pay me?" Mr. Al-Wadi asked, leaning forward in his chair and locking in on my eyes.

"Let's try a different approach. How much do you want?" I offered, thinking that it's always better to get the other person to shout first in case you get lucky and they come in with a good price.

"Someone offered me $750 a ton," he replied without much thought.

Okay, this is easier except he is 50 percent over the market, I thought.

"That is very good price, Mr. Al-Wadi," I said, naturally slipping into his vernacular. "You should have taken it because you could never get that today."

"Then how much you pay?" he pressed.

"Mr. Al-Wadi, as we've traveled a long way and it's my personal philosophy to conclude some business in a first meeting, I'm prepared to stretch as high as $500 per ton, delivered to Taiwan."

"Five twenty-five," Al-Wadi announced, taking a sip of tea.

From $750 to $525. Now, that's quite a move. In Asia it would be a total loss of face to bluff so big, only to fold a moment later. This isn't like China, where people fight hard but it's always around a tight band related to a market level, I thought.

"Okay, Mr. Al-Wadi. Let's take what you've got at $525, but we need it shipped no later than the end of this month. We are very pleased to establish business with your good company," I said as I reached out my hand.

"Agreed," Mr. Al-Wadi said, grasping it. As he released my hand, he touched his heart, looked to the heavens, and made a motion with his right hand like releasing a small bird up to the sky. I'd never seen this before, but copied his action. He smiled and nodded at me.

On the way out, Mr. Al-Wadi picked up a burned AK-47 and proudly handed it to Mei. He'd noticed our wonderment at all the munitions in his yard.

"A gift from Kuwait," he said with a big smile. "And get back to me about my copper cables!"

"We will," I said, knowing that we most likely would not. That particular copper deal fell through, but we continued a regular business with Mr. Al-Wadi on a broad range of metals.

We thought the gift was great and planned to have the gun mounted and put on the wall in my office.

⌒◯◯◯◯⌒

Business done, Mr. Al-Wadi took us to a restaurant in Kuwait City and hosted a fine Persian feast, surprisingly served by Filipino waiters. He turned into a very warm and social character, sharing stories of the Gulf War. He had seemed so brash during negotiations, but it had only been theater. I sensed he just enjoyed a good haggle.

The next day in the airport, we put our suitcases through the X-ray machine. When the outline of an assault rifle passed by the security guards' computer monitor, all hell broke loose. The guards ripped open our bag and, astonished, held up the rusted-out AK-47. They nearly threw us in jail. "This is obviously a useless souvenir and I'd have thought that since I am an American, and we liberated your country, we'd be treated a little more gently," I protested to the man in charge. That was not taken well.

Realizing we were stuffed, we made an urgent call to our highly connected friend, Mr. Al-Wadi, who ensured we made our flight. Mr. Wong looked on in dismay, his mouth hanging open. Luckily, they kept the weapon. I'm positive no other country would have found humor in our souvenir. At twenty-six, I was showing my youthful naïveté and stupidity. I can't explain what the hell I was thinking.

On the way to Tel Aviv, we had a quick transfer in Egypt, which I learned was the only Arab country with direct flights to Israel. In the Cairo airport we were introduced to security Israeli-style. The three of

us were separated and interrogated. Then the people who interrogated us switched around and double-checked our stories by asking us to talk about the others in the group. By the time we reached the bullet-proof sheltered boarding gate, Mr. Wong was a bit twitchy, and when we walked out to the plane where a tank was parked he broke into a full sweat. I was having a ball at his expense and could not help pointing out that one of the flight attendants had a pistol strapped to his ankle. I must have really scared him because in Tel Aviv, Mr. Wong refused to leave the hotel without a bodyguard. Now safe, three scrap dealers and their security detail toured Israel, successfully buying containers of scrap metal along the way. In Jerusalem a fighter plane broke the sound barrier overhead, *ka-boom,* and our unnerved customer hit the dirt. Mei and I laughed our butts off, but he'd officially had enough and insisted that it was time to go home. We had no worry that this guy was going to come back and cut out the middleman.

On the way back to Tel Aviv, our driver pointed out that the Dead Sea, the lowest place on earth, was nearby. We spontaneously made a diversion, winding down a mountain road that had no doubt once been an ancient path. We bought bathing suits at the gift shop, stripped down, and waded in. I stood there with Mei, half floating, caked in salt, watching the early-evening light lowering on the mountains of Jordan in the distance across the sea. Scrap metal was a more interesting business than most would imagine.

I gazed down out my window over India as we flew home. It was a clear night and I could see fires burning below, their embers rising high into the sky. Part of my plan had been to see the world and live an exotic life; it was all happening. I was very far away from that accounting room in Germany.

8

STEPPING ON A LAND MINE AND SURVIVING

By 1995, two years after starting Hartwell Pacific, we were a team of four, and the stainless business was getting quite busy. The trading we were doing with Nickelmet was getting bigger and bigger; we were now supplying them with the majority of their imported scrap, close to a thousand tons a month, worth about $800,000 at the time. I understood this was unsettling for them as they were becoming dependent on us, and I was beginning to wonder how long we could keep it going. Then one day in May, we got a phone call. We had sold Nickelmet about fifty containers of metal from Guangdong, and the cargo had arrived with a huge problem. They had found lead ingots packed inside the tight bales of scrap. The bales were shiny and beautiful on the outside, but filled with heavy, relatively worthless lead on the inside. In America, that is fraud and these guys would have ended up in jail. In China, however, it was business as usual. There was no real legal recourse. They just replied, "That's not our scrap!" and stopped taking our calls.

I flew immediately to Taiwan to oversee the slow dismantling of every bale, and watched in horror as one by one the lead ingots were plucked out and dropped into metal barrels with a sickening thud. The final bill came: a $200,000 claim. What a shock! I felt very exposed. This could happen anytime, as we could not inspect the loading of every shipment in any cost-effective or competitive manner. *It could have been even worse,* I thought. *A shipper could put anything in a container. Suppliers are paid in advance, and we only find out the problems when the cargo arrives.* I recalled one of my grandfather's favorite one-liners on business: "Don't lend money to anyone you can't send the sheriff after!"

The sheriff in China would not be helpful. He works for whoever is paying him, and unless we wanted to get involved in bribing government officials, we were out of luck. We had become a cheap insurance company for Nickelmet, and had little protection against the high risk of receiving inferior-quality scrap.

Nickelmet's chairman, Max, was in Hong Kong and called me to his $1,000-a-night suite at the Peninsula Hotel. He then explained that the Southeast Asian market was just too big, and that internal pressure was mounting to cut Hartwell out of the program, pushing directly into our market in competition with us.

"We respect what you've done but it's just not sustainable. Anyway, as you now see, this is can be a very risky business," he offered sympathetically. The proposal he had in mind was simple. "Forget the $200,000 claim and come work for us. We'll hire your whole team; you will become managing director of Nickelmet Asia and Mei will be head of trading. It's time for you to become a proper executive," Max concluded with an encouraging smile.

Even though I would be giving up Hartwell Pacific, ending my run as an entrepreneur, it was a tantalizing offer. In addition to having access to the infrastructure of a global corporation, we would be paid very well, given good bonus opportunities, and afforded a housing allowance. With this deal we'd also be shifting the risk of fraud over to Nickelmet, a company much more capable of shouldering it. We had put a decent amount of money aside by now and wanted to hang on to it. Further, I recognized that Hartwell could easily go bankrupt in one bad deal. The margins on our copper and aluminum businesses were also dwindling due to growing competition as more Chinese searched the globe for these valuable raw materials and started con-

tacting our suppliers directly. Another consideration was that Nickelmet, our only stainless buyer, with whom we had no exclusivity agreement, was threatening to go into competition with us. We'd done some successful trading, but Hartwell's value was minimal without Nickelmet as a customer and much less than that with Nickelmet as a competitor. With those thoughts weighing heavily on my mind, being a corporate executive of a large company felt like a warm blanket on a cold night. Although my entrepreneurial spirit remained, I was sick of living in a shack and working my tail off while flying economy and staying in dumpy hotels.

Mei and I accepted Nickelmet's offer and celebrated together with Max over a Bordeaux-filled dinner at Gaddi's, the French restaurant at the Peninsula. I staggered out of the cab with Mei, went straight to the roof of my apartment block, lit a cigar, and called my parents. At twenty-seven years old I was now the youngest managing director in a multibillion-dollar corporation and it felt great.

⚬⚭⚬

At Nickelmet, we moved into the forty-first floor of the luxurious Convention Plaza office complex. It was obviously not a lucky floor number, but my private corner office had two walls of windows with a stunning harbor view. I would be very proud to show it to my father when he came to visit. This is how I'd imagined my surroundings should be. I loved sitting in my office at night after everyone had left. I would turn off the lights and look out at the sparkling city reflecting on the harbor. I had arrived. Life was now luxury, and Mei and I were finding it easier to enjoy each other without all the anxiety of being entrepreneurs.

Unfortunately, all did not go smoothly. The first sign of trouble appeared when I sat down at a meeting with the head of finance for Asia, a German, and the head of the Taiwan business, a Brit. We exchanged business cards and, to our dismay, found that we all had the same title—managing director Asia. There was a chorus in almost perfect harmony of "What the f---?" As it turned out, three board members had each promised the managing director Asia title to their own man! This was a recipe for disaster and panicked calls to Europe were made, but eventually we accepted the situation as we all sensed we were on to a good gig. Our job responsibilities didn't really intersect,

so we stayed out of one another's way and got on well. The other choice would have been war, and none of us seemed up for that. *Titles aren't that important. Hell, at the banks it seems even the tea lady is a vice president,* I consoled myself.

Anyway, I had a better office than the finance guy. He had one window and no sea view, so in my mind it was clear to everyone which of us was more senior. *Ahh, the bitchy corporate world.* The politics among the board in Germany was also unbelievable. They were at one another's throats about everything.

The second disappointment was that the business was a disaster. Nickelmet had entered the Taiwanese market in hopes of becoming the leading domestic collector and importer of stainless scrap. However, not only did it not yet have a sales relationship with the Taiwanese steel mills, its entire business plan was against the mills' wishes. They viewed Nickelmet's purchasing activity in the local market as inflationary and bullying. Actually, they were right. Nickelmet had built a $15 million inventory of scrap in a fast-rising market as a pure and timely speculation. The sentiment was that if it controlled the material, everyone would have to buy from it. In turn, Nickelmet now wanted to sell the metal at a big premium and on its precise trading terms, which were considered foreign and unacceptable. I remember sitting in a meeting with Max and the owner of a very large Taiwanese conglomerate. Believing I was a smart kid, I suggested to the elderly chairman, "Nickelmet can be your partner. We're here to help you solve your raw material problems."

"I don't have a problem. You do! We'll never buy from Nickelmet as long as you have a yard in Taiwan," he shot back.

Max looked at me with outright scorn. I had teed the ball up for the chairman to smash it down our throats. I learned a valuable lesson that day, and my grandfather's rusty voice echoed in my ears yet again, this time paraphrasing Abraham Lincoln: "He who is silent is thought to be a fool. He who speaks out removes all doubt."

The rising market had been our friend and Nickelmet was sitting on a significant appreciation of inventory value, but had nowhere to sell it locally on their traditional terms. Exporting our stockpile, on the other hand, would be seen as outright aggression, as most mills consider their domestic scrap generation a strategic national asset and Taiwan had an acute shortage at the time. We faced a serious issue with our target customer.

Other than the strained relationship with the mill, we also struggled on the local purchasing side. The scrap metal business is an aggregation business, and large scrap dealers sell their metal at a premium to cover their collecting and handling costs. Therefore, all metal recycling companies prefer to buy from smaller dealers to avoid paying high prices. Unfortunately, we could not buy from the small suppliers because they would not provide us with proper government-required invoices for our purchases.

I flew weekly to Taiwan to sit together with the team racking our brains, trying to figure it out. In Taiwan, businesses were required to have supplier invoices for all transactions. The problem is that once you issue an invoice, you exist in the eyes of the government and have to pay tax. Nobody likes tax, so the small companies just didn't pay it. In fact, it was very common for companies in Taiwan, and throughout the developing world, to have two accounting books—the break-even one, which they showed the government, and the one with all the cash. Without invoices from our suppliers, it would look like our revenue was 100 percent profit with no costs, creating a huge tax liability. Our competitors, on the other hand, the big aggregators of scrap, must have had a creative solution because they bought from all those small suppliers.

We hired a top consultant to help us understand what our competitors were doing and how they got away with it. He explained that the standard practice in our industry seemed to be to create a labyrinth of trading companies owned by a mysterious web of nominee shareholders. These companies would issue invoices matching the scrap volumes that were purchased, thus, in effect, pretending to be the supplier. If one of these companies fell afoul of the regulators and could not sing and drink its way out, they would simply liquidate the assetless company and the nominee shareholders would just disappear. In some cases, the directors of the company were simply field workers who had been paid to "just sign" a piece of paper, not knowing what they were doing. As the high-paid consultant explained, rolling his eyes, "There is the law and then there is the common practice. If you're going to invest in a foreign country, you'd better understand the common practice and be sure it's acceptable to you before building your business."

The common practice was obviously not something we could participate in. We were discovering the hard way that being in business is one thing, but being competitive is another.

As we pondered the conundrum Nickelmet was in, the nickel market went into a free fall, causing a loss of millions of dollars against the value of our stockpile in Taiwan. The resistance of the customer, the complicated tax problems, and this multimillion-dollar hit put Nickelmet's Taiwan operations at great risk. We worked very hard to find a solution, but the reality was that there wasn't one. In my opinion, it was obvious: Nickelmet needed to pull out of Taiwan.

Following the nickel market's collapse, I was asked by Max to fly to Germany to give a survival plan for Asia. As I prepared to board Cathay Pacific's flight to Düsseldorf via Frankfurt, I considered that Nickelmet's days in Asia might be numbered and that this could be one of my last business-class flights for a while. I polished off a good part of a bottle of champagne before the lights went out and was a little groggy by the time I got to Düsseldorf, but a cup of strong black coffee and a sweet roll slapped me back into the game while I waited my turn outside Nickelmet's boardroom.

I was called in to face the five directors, who were spread out around a large oval table. Everyone offered closed-mouth smiles and nodded their welcome. Max gestured for me to take a seat near him. I wasn't nervous. I was confident and pleased to be addressing such senior people. Though it was a precarious situation, I loved my high-level moment. This is where I had dreamed of being—the boardroom.

"Tell us, Stephen. What would you do with Asia?" Max opened, encouraging me to lay out my plan.

I organized my papers, took a deep breath, and stood to address the board, taking a moment to make clear eye contact with each of the members.

"I know you're all frustrated with the situation in Taiwan and are very uncomfortable with the losses," I began. "But if you boil the problem down to its essence, the issue is a simple one. We should never have set up a domestic recycling facility in Taiwan. The local tax system there prevents us from developing a grassroots collection business, and thus we are unable to add any value. We have been left to play the role of speculator, a role that saw us sitting on a windfall profit that has turned into an ugly loss. The question we must ask ourselves is this: How can we add value for the stainless steel consumers in Asia?" I paused to let each board member consider the question.

"One option would be to fire me and shut Asia down; you can continue doing what you already do—supply them with scrap from

America and Europe. But my plan is to build metal recycling operations throughout Southeast Asia. Not only do these countries lack stainless scrap consumers to compete with us, making them 100 percent export markets, they don't have Taiwan's invoicing problem. They are also fast-growing economies, so we can expect organic growth in the future from market expansion alone. We will be able to offer high-volume, high-quality supply contracts from the region, which should give us competitive pricing compared with the other local scrap dealers, who are for the most part unprofessional mom-and-pops. The answer is clear to me: Shut down Taiwan, keep the headquarters in Hong Kong as an international trading hub, and start building out this regional footprint in the export-oriented developing world." I stood tall, projecting an air of confidence.

"Let's not look back. It's time to look forward," I closed, taking my seat, feeling the moisture in my armpits for the first time.

"Thank you, Stephen. That is a very interesting plan," Max noted supportively.

The head of finance shifted awkwardly in his chair. The head of the UK eyed the papers in front of him, and the French director bounced a pencil on its eraser. Dead silence.

"Well, let us discuss it, Stephen. Thanks again for coming all the way from Hong Kong. Well done," Max said, nodding at me while eyeing the other board members with frustration for their lack of questions.

Everyone stood and shook my hand as I worked my way to the door. It was all just a bit too warm. If we were facing a turnaround, this would've been an intense meeting full of tough questions, but instead everyone was sullen and flat-footed. People said "good-bye" with a pat on the back and a wink, not "see you soon" or "we're excited about your proposal." I started to realize that the gig was probably up. *No matter how slick my presentation, persevering in Asia is probably more than the board would be able to take,* I thought.

I arrived in Hong Kong with a fax waiting, informing me that Nickelmet had decided to close up shop in Asia but was offering me a job in Germany and Mei a job in France. *Germany? France? What the hell!* I quickly realized that this honor was in lieu of paying us out on the remaining two years of our agreement. They had insisted on three-year employment contracts with stiff noncompetes to lock us up, and were now looking to break up the team and banish us to Europe. I was

pretty certain I was not going to be MD of Germany and was not clear how great a trader Mei would have been speaking French. Not to mention, Mei and I were now a serious couple, though most people, including our colleagues at Nickelmet, were probably unaware of it. I believe we were tougher on each other in front of others just to mask our relationship; most evenings we even left the office at different times even though we were now living together full-time.

Mei and I rejected the employment offers and insisted on being paid out. Nickelmet's lawyers then informed us that our contracts were with the Hong Kong limited liability company, which had a couple of dollars in paid-up capital, and we were welcome to sue it. Unfortunately, they forgot that my contract had actually been with the German company. There was a big brouhaha that dragged on for a couple of months until a settlement was finally reached. I had just learned the most important lesson in contract law: It doesn't matter which corporation you are doing business with, it matters who your contract is with.

My relationship with Max was strained a bit over all this, but I also knew that he was personally against the board's decision to pull out of Asia and did not begrudge us our settlements. Anyway, I was very excited about rebuilding Hartwell. The corporate experience had not been all that I thought it was going to be; it was comfortable, even luxurious, but on the whole unsatisfying. Max and I kept in touch, sharing nice meals, fine wine, and valuable market information. As awkward as the situation could have been, Max and I remained on good terms.

We canceled the lease on the unlucky forty-first floor of Convention Plaza, shut down the office, and prepared to beat a retreat back to Sai Ying Pun together with our team. As we moved out of Nickelmet's office, a feng shui master was checking the place out for the new tenants. He explained to me that the wonderful harbor view was good because water symbolizes money and the window let the money come in. Unfortunately, he noted that we had a window in the back of the office, and the money was slipping right out. He was actually quite accurate. If only I had known, a simple window shade could have saved Nickelmet a fortune.

Having enjoyed the good life of a senior corporate executive, I was now a belt-stretching fifteen pounds heavier. Still, my brief tenure at Nickelmet gave me a chance to mature a bit and observe the leader

of our industry in action. I had toured all the major mills in Asia and learned who the players were, as well as their relative strengths and weaknesses, and a picture of how I could add value in the marketplace had emerged. The problem for Nickelmet was simply that it had created the wrong platform for the region and no longer had the patience to rebuild from scratch. It had lost its appetite for Asia, moved on, and this created my opportunity. If Nickelmet didn't find merit in my business plan, we would.

9

THE ROOT
OF THE
TREE

Though we were back on our own again, facing the uncertainty of being entrepreneurs, I reached a significant personal milestone. With my share of accumulated profits from Hartwell combined with the Nickelmet settlement, I snuck across the million-dollar mark. I was twenty-eight years old. Someone had once joked—making light of the currency exchange of roughly eight to one between the Hong Kong dollar and the US dollar—"The best thing about Hong Kong is that it's eight times easier to become a millionaire."

Although this is technically true, my status was a real one using good old-fashioned US dollars. This moment should have been hugely exciting, and I had been quietly measuring my money with eager anticipation, but in fact it was a wholly disappointing experience. I remember standing on my perch on the roof of the Bridges Street apartment with a scotch and a cigar. I called home to tell my parents about my achievement. They were very pleased and offered their congratulations, but when I got off the phone I felt empty. I thought it would have given me more self-confidence and contentment, but

it did not. It had been a hollow goal. I vowed that even if I had personal financial targets going forward, I would never again expect the achievement of them to give me any deeper fulfillment. I luckily realized at a young age that chasing wealth for its own sake can only end in depression. Wealth helps make some things possible, but magnitude of wealth is just a number. I had to attain some before I could realize this.

While the milestone did not give me the peace and serenity I had expected, it was a decent point in time to take stock of the past, reflect on my life, and consider how, at twenty-eight, I ended up standing on the roof of a building in Hong Kong with a scotch, a cigar, and a million bucks in the bank.

❦

Ever since I was a young boy, I've had an entrepreneurial spirit. While other eight-year-olds were playing cops and robbers, I was organizing lemonade stands and garage sales with my brother Andy. While my classmates were having snowball fights, I was managing my snow-shoveling business. At the age of ten, I took over the neighborhood morning paper route. I was probably the youngest paperboy in Pittsburgh, not even big enough to carry a full bag, but I was also the best. My customers loved me. I made deliveries based on when people needed them, not where they lived. Mr. Levinson was always first. I never threw the papers like the other paperboys. Instead, each was hand-delivered and put behind the customer's screen door to protect it from rain or snow. My reward for this extra effort was lots of good tips, and thus at ten years old I had my own money and my own checking account. I loved playing the salesman, talking to strangers, hamming it up and closing the deal.

I found great enjoyment watching my dad put on his smart suit to get ready for work. Thanks to his peacetime military service in Germany, he was always immaculately dressed: his shoes perfectly shined, the knot on his tie precisely centered. He would march around the house nervously preparing for his ritual commute, bolting out the door at 6:30 AM. Most days I would put several calls into his office, so I was on a first-name basis with his secretaries Gladys and Judy, who fawned over me.

"Morning, Gladys. Is the big guy around?"

I can't remember a time when Dad sent a message through that he was too busy, unless he was on the phone. He always took my calls, even if just to say, "I'm a little busy here, Stevie, make it quick." I was a part of Dad's business world, not just his home life.

Sometimes over summer break, after a little begging and pleading, he would let me come to the office for the morning. The H. J. Heinz Company had a doughnut lady who pushed a cart of coffee around, and my father would stick me with her. I would do the circuit, meeting the other executives while helping to serve. Once, Dad got caught up in a meeting and had Judy send me to the executive kitchen to grab my lunch. He must have figured the chef would make me a peanut butter and jelly sandwich, but we hit it off pretty well and Dad was shocked to find his son in the boardroom dining on lamb chops, the tips of my toes barely touching the floor. I was refining my taste buds, getting an eye on the business world, and learning to use my charm to get what I wanted.

My business acumen did not go unnoticed by my family and I received special encouragement from my grandfather, with whom I was very close. He always called me Stever and told anyone who'd listen, in his grumbling, deep storyteller's voice, "That Stever's a good little businessman."

Every time he'd see me he'd call out, "Hey Stever! You a good businessman?"

"Sure am," I'd reply.

"Good. Now make sure you turn out the lights in your house. Your parents are lighting up half the city! I don't mind, of course. I have shares in the Allegheny Electric Company."

My parents would think he was babysitting but we'd stay up late talking. It was bourbon and bullshit. He'd drink the bourbon and I'd soak up the bullshit. He loved to tell stories about the Civil War, on which he was an expert, or read *Huckleberry Finn* to me. He had a different accent for each of the characters. Huck Finn was one of my childhood heroes: always on an adventure, always getting in and out of trouble.

We would sit around watching the news and I'd listen to him bitch about the politicians. "Bunch of bums! Never trust a politician, Stever!" he'd warn.

Years later, after CNBC created the greatest invention in the world for my granddad—the live ticker feed—we'd sit together and stare at it for hours, Grandpa stretched out on his La-Z-Boy recliner

and me squatting on the floor next to him. Granddad treated me like a peer, not a child.

"Beatrice Industries! What a bunch of bums. Management made millions and the shareholders got nothing. Bunch of bums!" he'd call out. Then he'd look at me, smile, and giggle. Pretty much everyone was a bunch of bums.

"Most of these corporate execs are crooks, Stever, except your dad of course."

He was always goofing around but at the same time had underlying messages of integrity, frugality, and industriousness. Later, during my business career, I encountered a lot of the dishonesty that my grandfather, the sage lawyer, had warned me about. I was determined to honor him and not be one of the crooks.

Although as a child I felt ready for the business world, my education was as yet incomplete, so at fourteen I went off to Pomfret, a boarding school in Connecticut. I say *went* rather than *was sent,* as it was in fact my idea. Though Pomfret has a great academic reputation, this was not my motivation for attending. I had read *Catcher in the Rye* and was enamored with Holden Caulfield's adventures at a Pennsylvania boarding school. I arrived yearning for my parents but proud of my independence. The school assigned me a roommate from Boston named Mark Walsh, who would become my partner in crime. We had a common disrespect for the rules and a great time seeing what we could get away with. We also learned quickly to watch each other's backs. Bullying by older students was a fact of life at the time, so we founded the Freshmen Raid Committee, or FRC, and went on the offensive. I believe it was a Pomfret first for the weenies—as they called freshman—to be raiding the older kids. Still, our ingenuity and battle tactics were not admired by our teachers; my grades suffered. That year my father had a parent–teacher conference with the vice principal, who explained, "Someday your son will make a great CEO, but he needs to graduate from high school first."

I never forgot those words of encouragement, focusing on the positive part of the message. I was excited that someone saw greatness in me. This was my motivation to turn things around academically, and I ended up my junior year on the honor roll. Unfortunately, other antics would cut my academic career at Pomfret short.

At the age of seventeen, Walsh and I were unceremoniously given the boot after four years of getting away with murder. We'd had a fully

stocked bar in our room, and our dormmates would often come over for cocktails before dinner. It was very civilized. Our dormitory was named Pyne dorm, I suppose after a Mr. Pyne, and hence the Pyne Spritzer was born. Two parts vodka, two parts cranberry juice, and topped off with soda water. Ironically, after such an obvious and constant infraction, we were expelled after being caught bringing a six-pack of beer up from Mark's car during study hours.

At that age, you are defined by the institutions with which you are associated—high school, university. People always asked, "Where are you in school?" or "Where are you going to school next?"—nothing else, much the way people asked, "What do you do?" when I arrived in Hong Kong. The period of time after being kicked out of boarding school was a critical stage in my development. Suddenly I wasn't in high school and not yet in university.

Whatever I thought about myself or my future, one thing was clear. I needed to go to college and I could not go without a high school diploma. In Pennsylvania, as in most states, you can take an exam to get a GED, or general equivalency diploma. I slunk down to a municipal building in one of the worst neighborhoods in Pittsburgh to take the exam, a far cry from walking out of the Pomfret chapel on a sunny June day in Connecticut. My situation was terribly disappointing and stressful for my parents. I walked into my mom's bedroom one evening and found her sobbing.

⌒⨳⌒

No matter how disappointed they may have been, my parents, particularly my father, were very supportive. Rather than grounding me or putting me to hard labor, he made a great management decision and decided not to let this error or failure define me. Instead we picked up the pieces and moved on deliberately together. He gave me my freedom, and my prime teenage years were not wasted.

Finally, after much strain, my ship was fully righted. Dad had pulled hair and teeth, not to mention every string he had, to get me into Penn State. I was now back on track, but the scars from my abrupt disassociation with the mainstream and my acceptance and handling of that situation made me a much stronger and more independent person. The other thing it did was drive me like mad to get back to being "Stever the good businessman" rather than "Steve the bum."

By the time I arrived at Penn State I was ready to hit the books, and majored in economics with an emphasis on emerging markets. Penn State is a huge university with over forty thousand undergraduates. Great place to learn and fabulous professors, but it was entirely up to you to demand attention. I did reasonably well and was president of my fraternity, Sigma Alpha Epsilon. I took great interest in my major and the interconnectivity of global economies, and was particularly proud of the A that I received in my senior course on emerging markets. My thesis paper was well written and well thought out but perhaps not visionary. The title: "Zimbabwe: A Shining Example of the Potential of Post Colonial Africa."

Things were looking up.

⟡

By 1992 I'd been out of school for just over a year, and I was fortunate to have found a job as a financial analyst in the European headquarters of MacDermid Inc., an American chemical company based in the small German town of Bruchsal, near the French and Swiss borders. I was having a ball tearing up the autobahns in the company Mercedes, skiing in Verbier on weekends, and playing blackjack in Baden Baden. I was also building a solid understanding of the fundamentals of accounting and finance. But the thrill of Europe was wearing off and I itched to be on a more commercial track—meeting businesspeople, not toiling in the back office. *How did I end up working in the accounting department of a hazardous chemical company in a small town in Germany?* I thought. *I want to be a player, not a "shiny-assed bookkeeper"*—as my grandfather kept calling me.

Over the next few months, I formed a plan. I would leave MacDermid, return to the States, and get a job on a Wall Street trading floor. This dream was based soundly on having seen the movie *Wall Street* and having read *Liar's Poker* by Michael Lewis and *Bonfire of the Vanities* by Tom Wolfe—a movie and books that set the tone for a generation of greedy and ambitious young men.

I arrived back home to the rolling, green hills and pristine golf courses of western Pennsylvania to try to find a job with one of the large-scale investment banks in New York. Some of my job-search methods were highbrow: My father's boss at the time, H. J. Heinz CEO Tony O'Reilly, was on the board of Bankers Trust and got me

interviews with their top traders. I arrived to discuss my ability and ambition, but was first asked to solve math equations. I was able to get by, but was hardly competitive with the best and brightest math scholars. As my grandfather, who could never resist a good one-liner, would have said: "I went over there . . . like a lead balloon!"

The other approach was more street-level. I stood in the lobby of the World Trade Center with a *Wall Street Journal* in hand and started calling the phone numbers of the firms in the investment banking advertisements that touted the latest deals. These are known as the "tombstones." I got the main numbers from directory assistance and started dialing for dollars.

"Good morning. Merrill Lynch. How can I help you?" the receptionist purred welcomingly.

"Give me the equities desk!" I'd bark. Being polite in New York gets you nowhere. The naive and nervous receptionist would usually transfer my call without further question. Someone would pick up the phone and yell "Convertibles!," "Syndicate!," or something like that.

I'd jump rapidly into my pitch. "I'm in New York today for an interview with Goldman Sachs and happen to be in your lobby. Can I come upstairs and talk to you about job possibilities on your sales, trading, or syndicate desks?"

Click was the normal response.

That's okay. This is a low-percentage game. It's all about volume. You can't be too proud, I thought. Though most people cut the line, the guys at Oppenheimer & Co. thought it was so funny that they asked me up. We had a good chat, but unfortunately they weren't hiring and didn't have a training program.

I always got a kick out of cold-calling. Even when I was a little kid I used to make all of my mother's pain-in-the-neck phone calls for her: checking bills, returning goods that were unsatisfactory, anything that let me get on the phone with a stranger. Most people hate it, but for me it's a game—maneuvering your way through a bureaucracy, finding your target, and getting what you want.

❦

Somehow, I got a contact at Salomon Brothers, and I presume they found my European experience interesting enough to give me an interview for the Sales and Trading Training Program made famous in

the book *Liar's Poker*. This was the dream spot for me. My interviews went well, and I went on to have three rounds of them over five months. Plus, they were flying me to New York so I knew they were serious. Unfortunately, nobody was hiring on Wall Street in 1993, and a class that normally took in 250 people was only taking 35. The interview process dragged on.

There were seemingly endless periods between interviews, but rather than relaxing and using this free time to work on my golf game, I quickly lapsed into a depression. I wanted to be moving, making progress, yet with the passing time I felt as though I was falling behind. The days and nights seemed interminable. Though I had every creature comfort, I was at my lowest. The only productive thing I achieved between interviews was quitting my pack-and-a-half-a-day Marlboro habit, which I'd started at boarding school and Penn State and developed with zeal in the dark halls of the accounting department. I also happened to devour most of James Clavell's series of books on Asia, starting with *Tai-Pan* and ending with *Noble House*. The energy and intrigue contained within lifted my spirits and got me thinking of the Far East. Not to mention *Fortune, Forbes, BusinessWeek,* and the rest of the news journals were touting the economic boom on the other side of the globe.

As it would happen, my boarding school friend Scott Kalmbach told me about a childhood friend of his, Topher Neumann, who was living in Hong Kong. We'd met briefly during my teen years, but I had no visual memory of him. Topher was taking the world by storm out in Asia and having the time of his life. He was exporting cameras from China and a leader in the young expat community. I rang Topher one Pittsburgh night (Hong Kong morning). Determined to at least drink like a successful businessman, I filled a crystal tumbler from my father's bar with ice and poured myself a single-malt. Topher answered the phone, pumped up and energized for the day ahead.

"Mornin', Steve! Scott tells me you are thinking of moving out here. What's on your mind?" he asked.

I regurgitated my background information and explained that I was seriously interested in the opportunities unfolding in Asia. Topher, a borderline hyper guy, downloaded the energized stories of being a twenty-three-year-old single, successful male in Hong Kong. The conversation lasted for two good-sized scotches, and I was hooked.

He boomed into the phone, "Get your butt over here! China, Vietnam, Indonesia: It's all happening now! Forget about New York! You can crash on my couch until you get settled. Asia is a whirlpool of opportunity, but if you want to grab it you've gotta jump in it!"

This is for me! I thought, my imagination running wild. Hong Kong sounded exciting. Even Vietnam had an amazing feeling of adventure to it—*Apocalypse Now!* Wagner's "Flight of the Valkyries" swam through my brain. *Dan da da dan dan, dan da da dan dan, dan da da daaaa!* I hummed to myself, taking the beachhead with Robert Duvall.

But first I would play out my hand with Salomon Brothers. As I waited for my third interview in the drab anteroom off Salomon's main trading floor, I decided to make friendly conversation with a few guys silently sitting next to me.

"Where are you guys from? Are you all interviewing for the training program?"

"Yes. Just graduating from Chicago, Wharton, Harvard," came the answers.

I can still hang even though I came from Penn State 'cause of my solid European work experience, I thought, reassuring myself as I prepared for my interview. That was until I discovered through further inquiry that they were graduating from business school, not undergraduate, and all had prior Wall Street experience. Even with such tough competition, I charmed my way through the process and was not rejected, but put on the waiting list. In other words, if enough people rejected Salomon, I might get a chance. With *Liar's Poker* and its exultant tale of the Salomon Brothers' trading floor a recent memory for all young bucks, I doubted that this would be the case, so I decided to pull a play out of the poker handbook—bluff big.

I rang the HR department and told the woman in charge of recruitment that I had an opportunity in Hong Kong and if they didn't have a place for me I was going to take it and leave next week. There was a brief pause, during which I could hear the sifting of papers. I figured she would have to check with the bosses and get back to me. *Those guys who interviewed me will put in a good word. We hit it off pretty well,* I thought.

The pause ended when she simply responded, "Best of luck to you, Stephen. We can't guarantee you a spot." *Click.* The dial tone was deafening. Lesson learned and experience lodged in brain: If you play a pair like a full house, be prepared to lose.

I went upstairs where my father was watching TV and told him the "good news": I was going to Hong Kong and would bring back glory for the Greer name as our Scottish ancestors had done—the ones not related to us.

"Dad. I have just one favor to ask. Can I have some of your frequent flier miles for the ticket?"

No doubt concerned, but at the same time eager to see his son getting going on something, he gave his blessing. I got right on the phone with American Airlines and discovered that a round-trip economy ticket would require eighty-five thousand miles. However, I also noticed that a one-way business class ticket was only ninety-five thousand. This begged the obvious question: If I was definitely going and was definitely going to be successful, what need did I have for the round-trip part of the ticket? Anyway, I surmised, *I'm not backpacking. I'm going to do business and I should have that attitude.* A one-way first-class ticket on American Airlines to San Fran and on to Hong Kong in business class with mileage partner, Singapore Airlines, was procured.

Ten days after I was rejected by Salomon, my father gave me a hug and a reassuring smile, his blue eyes fixed on mine as I stood on the curbside of the Pittsburgh International Airport. This is my father. His son has no job, is flying one-way to Hong Kong, using his mileage, in business class, and yet he's beaming with pride and confidence. As he pulled away in his burgundy Volvo station wagon with my beloved dogs Willy and Gypsy pining for me out the back window, I welled up. I suppose it was caused as much by trepidation as by the feeling of saying good-bye and not knowing when I'd see my family next. *What am I getting myself into?*

When my grandfather heard about my plans, he just deadpanned in a deep grumble, "Don't you think you can find a place that's *farther* away?"

The melancholy feelings didn't last long, though, and I was soon cruising across the United States dining on beef Wellington and sipping a decent Cabernet in first class. An older gentleman sitting next to me, wearing a crisp white shirt and tie, asked where I was going.

"Hong Kong," I replied.

"Business trip?" he pressed.

"Moving," I concluded with a strong sense of certainty.

"Really, what do you do?"

I stammered for a moment, trying to come up with a good answer.

"I'm planning to set up my own company out in Hong Kong. Not sure what exactly it will be, but Asia's booming and there's bound to be a lot of opportunity."

He turned toward me, meeting my eyes, and replied firmly with a relaxed smile, "I envy you."

What was there to envy? I don't know. I suppose it was the adventure. For most people life is a routine that is established with the purpose of achieving an end, which in turn will help achieve another end. Every action is logical, and heavily influenced by friends, family, and societal norms. I was wandering off that well-worn path.

10

THE REBIRTH OF HARTWELL

Hartwell Pacific was reborn with minimal seed capital of $100,000. Good-bye Mandarin Oriental, hello Holiday Inn. I was thrilled, and the original Hartwell team of Mei and Triple Li were excited to stick together. After closing down Nickelmet Asia, we set up on Connaught Road West back in Sai Ying Pun (Western), but now with an open harbor view. This time, I made damn sure the back door was well covered to keep the money from flowing out. Our office was also on the lucky eighteenth floor so I had all my feng shui taken care of, not to mention the rent was one-fifth of Nickelmet's. We were quite happy to be a little more cramped and, with a cheap-as-chips overhead, were ready to go.

It was November 1996, and we put together a formal budget and business plan. Mei and I agreed that if we could not develop initial trading income or land a major steel consumer as a client in short order, we would shut the business down. We gave ourselves nine months. Mei and I had safety nets in our bank accounts, and we didn't want to throw them away on a failed idea.

The major problem we faced was that we had no sales customers. Who would want to buy stainless scrap from us? The Japanese disliked us for disturbing their market, and my relationship with the chairman of the biggest mill in Taiwan was, to put it mildly, tarnished.

Korea-based POSCO, the fourth largest steel company in the world at the time, was also one of the biggest producers of stainless steel. It did not buy scrap in Southeast Asia because it wasn't comfortable with the "local" dealers, and it would also only buy in large minimum volumes to reduce the logistical headaches of fulfilling its vast needs. Currently, no company in Southeast Asia was able to consistently meet this volume requirement, so I sensed an opportunity for Hartwell. I'd also met some of POSCO's senior management while working at Nickelmet with Max, so I had an intro. *My former title of managing director will give me some credibility,* I hoped.

I set up a meeting with Y. K. Song, head of raw materials trading for POSCO Asia. He was a very serious guy who asked a lot of questions and took copious notes while chain-smoking. I explained that Southeast Asia, in aggregate, was a meaningful resource for POSCO, and estimated that the market contained as much as one-fifth of its overall stainless scrap needs. Also, we could easily fulfill its minimum volume requirement by supplying from the various markets in the region. I gave Mr. Song my pitch.

"POSCO can count on us to be a reliable supplier. I'm going to build the first professional recycling corporation in Southeast Asia, not a mom-and-pop scrap business," I explained. "We're going to be the Nickelmet of Asia!"

Mr. Song told me flat-out, "We don't buy from brokers. Where are your yards, your physical operations? As a broker you don't control the situation, and the recycling companies in Southeast Asia are not reliable, as you have pointed out."

I understood this point well from my previous lead ingot experience. POSCO would want to see cranes, forklifts, and workers. I told Mr. Song precisely where our operations were "going to be."

"It'll just be a matter of time," I pleaded.

I went back to see him over and over again, making our case. I was determined to rebuild Hartwell with the support of an important customer. One late afternoon, standing in the waiting room of POSCO Asia's fifty-fifth-floor offices, I recited a mantra to myself as I stared out the window.

"It all comes down to moments like this. Don't take no for an answer!"

We'd left Nickelmet to take this gamble and our fate, not to mention my pride, hung on the success of this sales pitch. Unfortunately, this would be a committee decision, not the will of one man. Nobody at POSCO would want to take singular responsibility for the potential failure of a start-up. Therefore, during the courting period I made several trips to Korea to try to cross the cultural divide, gain their trust, and build relationships with all the key decision makers. Korea is a very formal, Confucian society that is quite xenophobic toward its regional neighbors and very nationalistic, but the good news is that once you earn their trust and are on the inside, they really value the relationship.

I thus became a student of Korean culture. No one can possibly learn all the spoken languages of the world, so I thought it was more important to become a student of body language. How do people express pleasure, displeasure, agreement, or disagreement in a given society? Korean social cues are too subtle for most Westerners to perceive. For example, Americans express displeasure very openly, while Koreans feel direct conflict would be shameful, and rarely display overt anger in discussions with their international counterparts. Foreigners often brag about all of the "good meetings" they had in which no one dissented, yet are shocked when no deal gets done. For the most part, this can be boiled down to misread signals often influenced by wishful thinking. This is a problem throughout Asia, not just Korea.

As part of my education, I tuned in to a television program in Hong Kong called *Korean Hour,* which was a family drama. I couldn't understand what they were saying but watched the show every week to try to gain a sense of their value system and body language. I learned to divert my eyes from senior or older people as a sign of respect. "Look 'em in the eyes and give 'em a firm handshake" is what most young American boys are taught; not in Korea, and in fact not in most of Asia. Most importantly, I learned to be very careful not to offend the older and more senior managers. Noticing my baby face, POSCO executives would frequently ask my age, to which I would reply "thirty-something" with a smile that said, *Don't press me on this one,* though I was only twenty-eight. Luckily, prematurely graying hair supported my case, along with a very humble approach. It was an awkward situation as Mr. Kwon, my equivalent in title and decision-making authority, was about fifty years old, so I had to treat and respect him as a father figure, not a peer.

During those months of anxiety and effort trying to develop a relationship with POSCO, Hartwell had zero revenue—only expenses. Though I knew my pitch was logical, I wondered if I was ever going to get them to take the bait. As the slow wheels of bureaucracy turned, the calendar was working against us. Our overheads, including an office, a team of four, all the entertainment and traveling expenses, and my apartment and personal costs, would not be sustainable. My hands began to tremble again from nerves that had only had a brief respite for the past year and a half. I was back to smoking a pack of cigarettes a day, a habit I picked up again while trying to assimilate with my heavy-smoking Korean customers. I knew this kind of stress was unhealthy, yet my lifestyle of coffee, alcohol, and cigarettes did nothing to counter it. Mei was concerned, so she secretly switched my coffee to decaf and heckled me constantly about the butts.

One morning I called Mei into my office.

"It's getting down to the wire. We're going to have to decide whether to pony up more capital or cut costs," I began.

"Well, what costs can we cut? We're not even taking salaries," she replied with a concerned look.

"I don't know—the office, staff? I'm just saying it looks tight. I guess we'll have to dip into our savings," I said softly, understanding that she wouldn't really want to do that.

A few days later Triple Li, recognizing that times were tough, came forward and offered to work for free until we could get some business going. Mei choked up and gave Lilly a big hug. "That won't be necessary. We'll be fine," she assured.

Though there were warm moments of mutual support during this anxious period, the stress also manifested itself in colossal blow-ups. We did the best we could to avoid conflict in front of our staff, and that usually resulted in my doing a couple of laps around the block to cool down. On the one hand, the stress and strain were a burden on our relationship, but on the other we were becoming well trained in the art of healing battle wounds.

We were ready to face Armaggedon, but luckily it didn't come to that. My cultural knowledge had enabled me to successfully navigate the complex Korean business landscape, and I ended up having a very good relationship with General Manager Kwon, the most senior decision maker. Then one day in May 1997, POSCO's purchasing team said it would back us on a trial basis. It was nothing dramatic, just a

calm phone call requesting that we make an offer to supply five hundred tons of scrap from Southeast Asia. We made that first sale within a couple of months of giving up, literally saving Hartwell from the brink of extinction.

As we reached this critical turning point, we had an opportunity to take part in a moment of broader historical importance. The British would hand over Hong Kong to the Chinese on June 30, 1997, my twenty-ninth birthday. We planned a black-tie celebration at the Dynasty Club, which is located directly in front of the convention center where the ceremony and the fireworks would take place. Mei and I were celebrating history in the making as well as our own survival. Once again we were a success, and I was proud of it, but clearly realized that my life had been a series of tumultuous ups and downs thus far. I noticed that most of my friends' careers had steadily progressed without all of this seemingly endless strain and anxiety, and that their youthful faces had a serenity mine sorely lacked. Nonetheless, I wouldn't have traded places with them for anything.

As Prince Charles stood mournfully in a torrential downpour watching the Union Jack lowered in favor of the red flag of China, I felt excited to be living in such an important and relevant city at a great moment of change—the peaceful handover of a capitalist society to a communist country. Having grown up during the Cold War, this was almost an unimaginable event and in my view a harbinger of good things to come. In my mind, change equated to adventure, and adventure is what life is all about. I turned to Mei.

"This is all going to work out."

"We're not out of the woods yet," she replied looking into my eyes. We held hands as we entered Hong Kong's new Chinese era.

⌒✖⌒

Through our global trading business, we had discovered another type of scrap metal: reusable. Reusable stainless steel is only slightly damaged and with a little processing can still be made into anything from lower-grade kitchenware to industrial machinery. Even better, the Chinese were willing to pay large premiums over scrap for it. *This is our ticket into China,* I thought, *not to mention a gold mine of an opportunity.* Mei and I were very eager to find an opportunity in the Mainland. We were well aware of the cautionary tales about investing

there and had our own experiences doing business with China, but we were brave and determined to elbow our way in. *This is going to be the biggest market in the world someday. We have to get started now!* I thought enthusiastically.

The idea was to set up a small factory across the border from Hong Kong in Shenzhen. There we could import reusable stainless steel and then, using some machinery, cut damaged sheets and coils down or hammer out dents, upgrading the material to a more valuable product. Downstream customers abounded in the booming Guangdong economy, so selling our inventory would be easy.

We quickly analyzed our global distribution network and discovered large amounts of reusable available for export in Thailand, Mexico, and Romania. Though I yearned to visit Count Dracula's castle, we decided that Thailand and Mexico would be easier to handle. Thailand was in our backyard, and I had some contacts in Mexico. I jetted off to Mexico to establish a supply chain there, having found a cold rolling mill from which I could buy both reusable scrap for China and melting scrap for Korea—a double whammy! A cold rolling mill does not have a furnace. It processes steel but does not melt scrap, thus any scrap generated by its processes is available for sale rather than being remelted.

I was very pleased when my black Cadillac pulled up to the entrance of this Mexican steel mill and saw a large sign outside its offices declaring:

WELCOME
STEPHEN HARTWELL GREER
PRESIDENT OF HARTWELL PACIFIC HONG KONG

My name in lights! The receptionist quickly introduced me to the head of scrap sales, Sergio Ramirez Sanchez—great name. He was about the same age as me and very curious about my young entrepreneur story. We got on well, and over some *queso fundido* and a Tampequena beefsteak I was able to secure a nice piece of reusable business for China as well as get some melting scrap for POSCO. I left Mexico confident that I had secured a good new customer.

Next, I dove into China. Finding warehouses and machinery didn't concern me, but getting all the licenses and permits was very complicated and, by Chinese law, required a local joint venture partner. JV

partners, usually highly connected individuals, also came in handy because of their ability to reduce red tape and allow business to run with minimal censure from the government. Luckily, Bernie, the tall Texan who'd been my first roommate in Causeway Bay, now worked for a large private equity investment company, ASIMCO, based in Beijing. He referred me to one of its investee companies in Shenzhen that could potentially be a good partner.

"They haven't ripped us off yet," Bernie commented wryly.

The company was called Li Yuen—"beautiful garden" in English—and its owner, Madame Yuen, was the daughter of an important and powerful government official in Beijing. She was what Mei refers affectionately to as round-round. Plump in all areas. She was pleasant and put on a warm and trusting smile, but she also played the role of important Chinese power broker very well. She would sit tall in her big, black chairman's chair with her elbows on the table, chubby fingers intertwined, and a furrowed brow showing her focus and determination. Her large and opulent office, with leather furniture and fine wood tables, also had a trophy case filled with medals, certificates, and photos of her standing with various dignitaries who were unknown to me. Lu Lu and Bo Bo, a pair of tiny white Lhasa Apsos, would scurry around the room yapping as we discussed business. Madame Yuen would bark, "Lu Lu! Bo Bo!" and they'd scurry under her feet and sit panting. It was quite a distraction.

Madame Yuen was backed up by a curious-looking brainiac named Clifford. Clifford was her opposite, tall and lanky, with a deep scar below his eye from some sort of accident. He was soft-spoken and cautious. If Madame Yuen, granddaughter of peasants, had benefited from the Cultural Revolution, her family rising to power, influence, and affluence, Clifford, son of math professors in Beijing, had suffered from it as his parents were knocked from their intellectual elite pedestal. He was torn away from his family and sent to work the distant fields on the Burmese border when he was only thirteen years old. Clifford was one of those broken men that are so common among the generation born in China during the 1940s and '50s—afraid of everything, trusting nobody. They made a curious pair, but we decided to do a JV anyway. Li Yuen would get a 25 percent share, handling the permits, licenses, and customs clearance, but we would run the business.

I had learned along the way that relationships in China are of vital importance, and the best way to build a solid one is to make it

personal. In Asia, a personal relationship begins when you are invited home, so Mei and I invited Madame Yuen and Clifford to visit Pennsylvania and meet my father. They agreed, and we teed up the big VIP visit: a black stretch Cadillac limo, a tour of Pittsburgh, dinner at the exclusive Falling Pebble Club, and a visit to my parents' home. They were duly impressed though disappointed that there was no steamed rice on the menu. Madame Yuen particularly took to my parents' hundred-pound Bernese mountain dog, Willy. Willy cuddled right up to her round-round leg and took a seat, warming her feet, looking deep into her eyes, and melting her heart as only he could do. What a salesman. The deal was done. With the partnership bonded, Madame Yuen relaxed and went into holiday mode. We even toured eighteenth-century Fort Ligonier taking plenty of pictures, including a portrait of the two of them in colonial outfits. God I wish I had a copy.

Madame Yuen quickly made herself indispensable. She not only promised to get all the permits and handle the notoriously opaque and corrupt customs department, but also found us a warehouse, which she owned, and a supplier of several industrial machines at a fraction of international prices. *Who says doing business in China is so hard?* I thought.

After organizing the basics, it was once again time to incorporate. Ever since the old days when I started Hartwell, I always got a special thrill out of officially founding a new company. We incorporated as Grand Metal, one of the few acceptable company names that was available for immediate registration. The next best options were Lucky Gold Rich or Happy Bullion, which were not going to fly. *We can change the name later,* I thought.

To cash in on this fantastic opportunity, Hartwell just needed a general manager to run the day-to-day of Grand Metal. We also hoped to eventually grow scrap metal collection/recycling facilities throughout Guangdong Province, of which Shenzhen was an important part. I met an American guy named Roger Holland in a bar in Hong Kong who had been working for IBM in China and was now between jobs. He spoke some Mandarin, was enamored with my life as an entrepreneur, and best of all was willing to work for "at cost" pay if he could get a piece of the upside. Mei and I believed the Chinese people would like and respect Roger, thus we were comfortable with our choice. Why a Westerner? Our view was that, unfair as it may be, a Western face opened doors in Asia. As long as you had strong local backup to handle cultural issues, this could be a good management

cocktail. We also thought that with Roger we at least had less risk of being defrauded. If we appointed a powerful local like Madame Yuen, we'd have little recourse if business ever turned bad.

We set out to organize our warehouse, hire a team, and get everything prepared to start business. Unfortunately for Roger, it became clear to everyone after only a few weeks that it was never going to work. Even though he spoke passable Mandarin, Madame Yuen was out to destroy him so that she could get more involved in the business. She felt she outranked him no matter what and would not tolerate any arguments or dissension on his part, making his life a living hell. Mei and I had to constantly adjudicate the battles, and Roger eventually just gave up and became passive. The hardest part for him was that the battles were never overt. Madame Yuen was personable and even warm to him, but vicious behind his back. This obviously set off alarm bells. Why was our partner so aggressive about who would run the business? After all, Madame Yuen's company would be collecting rent and hadn't invested a penny. We were starting to understand that even though we had a majority share of the company, we did not control the situation in China, because she controlled the warehouse. We would now have to make a decision about whether to go to war with Madame Yuen, or let Roger go. The choice wasn't difficult. We had a friendly dinner one night with Roger and parted amicably. He seemed relieved not to have to deal with Madame Yuen or Lu Lu and Bo Bo anymore.

We had given Madame Yuen what she wanted, but we also gave her a surprise she may not have expected. Mei, who was primarily stationed in Hong Kong, just two hours away from our site, would now take charge of the joint venture. Madame Yuen had the power and authority of presence, but she was no match for Mei's intellect. She'd grow red-faced as Mei smoothly maneuvered around Madame Yuen's own arguments. Madame Yuen was always trying to squeeze us. She would whine, "We need some extra money this month to resolve licensing problems."

Mei would deftly reply, "But your father is so powerful. Won't they give him face and not cause our company any problems?"

Madame Yuen was trapped. She either had to admit that her father was weak or handle the problems herself. It was a perfect defense. Mei remembers everything anyone has ever said and relentlessly wears them down. She has a brilliant mind. With her in charge, we were ready to roll.

We also increasingly had problems with Madame Yuen's sidekick Clifford, who in classic Chinese style was the buffer, or forward negotiator. When negotiating in China, we learned over time that nothing the people we were dealing with said meant much, as they could simply tell us later, "Sorry. I know I said that, but Madame [my boss, my board, my father] rejected it. She is the boss. She can be very difficult sometimes but don't worry, everything will be fine." Madame Yuen would make herself scarce anytime a serious discussion was to be hashed out. This is actually common in China. The principal concept, which has been played out no doubt over thousands of years, is that bosses should never be involved in detailed negotiations, as it is beneath them. Behind the scenes, they are involved in even the smallest detail, you can be sure of it, but they will never give their chop of approval until the cement has dried. In America, the decision makers always want a seat at the table. The theory, which is correct, is that things will get done much faster and more clearly if those responsible do all the talking. You can do it either way, and the American way is clearly more efficient, but it doesn't work well in Asia. Mei had the decision-making authority, but she would pretend to be the buffer and say, "I agree, however I need to confirm with Steve on every major decision," both buying us time and giving her a face-saving out.

In anticipation of Grand Metal's opening, Hartwell had purchased about a thousand tons of stainless steel reusable, worth about $1 million once it was upgraded. Though Madame Yuen was difficult at times, I believed wholeheartedly in our prospects. All our licenses were in order, equipment was in place, and we were ready to take delivery. Our incoming inventory had been purchased at very good prices, and it would be at least a few weeks before the first shipments started arriving and clearing customs. *Things will be fine,* I thought.

It was now time for the official opening. The lucky date had been carefully selected from *Tong Sing,* a book about Chinese traditions. We put on our best suits and schlepped into Shenzhen the night before to attend the grand opening dinner for around a hundred dignitaries, hosted at a fine restaurant owned by the local police. Madame Yuen's very powerful father came down from Beijing, so there were lots of big shots in attendance to give him face. A fleet of Mercedes and other luxury cars lined up at the entrance, looking much like a funeral procession. The banquet was a classic—every seat and position carefully selected. I was placed next to a particular gentleman, I was told,

because he had gone to Harvard Business School. *Wow, from Shenzhen to HBS. Well done!* I thought. I jumped right in.

"I understand you went to Harvard. That is a great achievement. Don't you love Boston? My brother lives in Boston."

"Havard. Havard. Yes, Havard," was his reply.

This guy didn't speak a word of English. He certainly didn't graduate from Harvard. I am not even sure he could have managed to buy a Harvard T-shirt on his own. He obviously was telling a big lie to his Chinese-speaking friends. Realizing he was busted, he excused himself from the table and switched seats with someone on the other side of the room.

Chinese tradition requires that there be too much food for everyone or anyone to consume. At home I was raised to finish everything on my plate, but in China if you can finish everything it means that the host did not serve you enough. No one was going to go home from this banquet hungry. We moved from shark's fin to abalone and on to beautifully steamed pink garoupa fish. At about course number six or seven a plastic hand glove was distributed to each of the guests. This was a first for me. Everyone put on a glove and the next course was delivered: giant braised goose webs. The way to eat these is ice-cream-cone-style. Using your gloved hand, you grab the web by the ankle and then gnaw the skin, tendon, and minimal flesh from the bones. Nibble the small fingers from their joints, suck the juices, and then spit the cleaned bones onto your plate. It actually tastes pretty good. If you like chicken skin, you'll love this, especially the webby part.

The next morning we proudly greeted our guests at the new Grand Metal facility. Everyone milled about outside the warehouse, where we were pinned with gaudy red corsages. Then the music began, signaling that it was time to enter. I was prepared for everything and anything but not the music; the chosen piece was Mendelssohn's "Wedding March." Mei and I strode down the aisle between the seats in disbelief.

Inside the warehouse there was a stage where flowery speeches would be made. A giant de-coiling and cut-to-length machine, shrouded in plastic, was perched on wooden pallets off to one side, a bright yellow forklift parked next to it. Dignitaries in the front two rows were to be seated in metal folding chairs covered with red silk.

I had a big speech well prepared and rehearsed, the timing for Mei's translation planned out for a smooth delivery. Madame Yuen

made some introductions, and the vice-something-or-other from the something-or-other section of the Communist Party was the first to speak. She was a diminutive but highly confident woman who delivered both a voluble and voluminous monologue, pointing her fingers and pounding the lectern, emphasizing points in shrill, high-pitched Mandarin. I kept elbowing Mei, demanding to know what the lady was saying.

Frustrated, Mei just replied, "She said that anybody who messes with this business will be crushed by the Communist Party"—a typical one-line summation. *Wow, that could work for us or against us,* I thought.

The long-winded speeches, which lasted about an hour, were finally concluded and, again to the tune of the "Wedding March," we were ushered out of the warehouse and lined up in front of the entrance gate. Firecrackers by the thousands were strung together and hung from bamboo poles, looking like giant red beehives. A long red ribbon with a bow in the middle was strung across the entrance gate, and Madame Yuen and I were each given a pair of scissors to ceremoniously cut it in front of a throng of cameramen and guests. The photo session went on for quite some time until we were finally allowed to cut the ribbon. At this moment my world went into slow motion. Both hives of firecrackers were simultaneously lit and the resulting explosion sent me out of my skin. The deafening popping and cracking had me on my toes, back arched, for at least thirty seconds. In the deafening silence that followed, we were engulfed in acrid smoke. When it finally cleared, like mist from a valley, Madame Yuen and I were doubled over coughing, gasping for air, and the crowd had moved back a good thirty feet. With that, we were in business.

11

JOINT AD-VENTURES

Although Grand Metal looked promising, we still needed a fast solution to POSCO's requirement that we open our own recycling yards. The company again made it very clear that we could not count on its support unless we achieved this. We showed them our Grand Metal facility and put on our best show, but this offered little benefit or assurance of supply and POSCO was not impressed. It was a reusable business, not a scrap metal business; POSCO's patience was limited.

To fast-track this development, we decided to put together joint ventures with our existing suppliers. By leveraging their infrastructure, we could eliminate most of the hassle of setting up a business and get right down to trading. In return, our partners could get the benefit of my knowledge of the impending changes in the stainless steel market, of which we would be the main driver. Nickelmet had also taught us a margin-enhancing process called blending, whereby inferior-quality scrap can be utilized without detriment to the customer, but we were not prepared to share our knowledge with a partner until the ink had

dried on any JV agreements. Our trading relationship with most of these suppliers had been very cordial and successful to date, and I was now proposing to take it to another level.

Searching for potential targets, I spoke with the key players in Thailand, Hong Kong, Malaysia, Singapore, and the Philippines, but decided to skip Indonesia due to political, economic, and religious instability. Mei and I created a battle plan. We would systematically work our way through each country and try to close a deal with our preferred supplier. If it fell through, we would move on to the next country.

～∞～

First up was Thailand, the biggest market in Southeast Asia. Our prime target was a company called Sun Tak Metal that employed about fifty people, but the sole driver behind the company was Mr. Ho Yu Wan. I used to joke that people must be confused when he answered the phone, "Who you wan?" Mr. Ho is Taiwanese, and I was told he spent his early years as a laborer for the largest recycler of stainless steel there, before establishing his own business in Thailand. He had quickly become the leading stainless scrap company in the Thai market, and Hartwell was his biggest customer. We knew that Mr. Ho had recently lost a lot of money speculating on real estate during the Asian economic crisis, and hoped that it might be the right moment to negotiate a JV with him.

Despite the rumors of financial troubles, Mei and I had a very stable business relationship with Mr. Ho, and million-dollar deals were done on a handshake. Keeping it casual, we decided to discuss our idea with him over a round of golf. I was a little taken aback, however, when nine caddies joined us at the first tee to escort us around the course—one each to carry our bags, one to carry a chair and massage our shoulders between shots, and one to carry an umbrella. *Hell, I'll carry his bags and massage his feet if he'll do a JV with us,* I thought, while shanking another ball out of bounds. Time was awasting. We urgently needed to get a partner before the Koreans bailed on us. It even crossed my mind that perhaps POSCO might reach out to a guy like Mr. Ho if I couldn't deliver, and that would put an abrupt end to our Thai aspirations. Not to mention, without Thailand our Southeast Asian strategy would be halved. Strolling down the lush fairway, our battalion of caddies in tow, I broached the subject of a joint venture.

He asked calmly, "Why should I do that?"

I jumped into my prepared pitch. "We're obviously good enough at marketing to be able to buy from you, and we would purchase exclusively from the joint venture in Thailand as partners. Up to now we have around five suppliers in Bangkok. We'd drop the others," I explained.

Mr. Ho had always been complaining that we supported his competitors. I further explained that he would gain the strength of our regional market knowledge.

Mr. Ho nodded and smiled, acknowledging our attributes, but I could tell he was not convinced. I pressed on, highlighting the value of our blending technology. This really piqued Mr. Ho's interest—no more smile. He was well aware of Nickelmet through his Taiwanese contacts and also aware that they had technological methods that were quite advantageous. We explained that we couldn't tell him more about it until after the JV, but he should understand that this would be part of the package.

Discussions continued for several weeks, and although Mr. Ho expressed great interest in a JV and even greater curiosity about our technology, I was starting to have my doubts. Beyond the fact that he was clearly trying to pump us for information on blending without signing a deal first, I began to notice that the business depended wholly on Mr. Ho. He made all the decisions, not just the important ones, and signed every check. Other than him the next level of staff seemed to be young girls who were just out of school. There were no computers. Accounts were done by hand in ledger books, and cash was kept above the false ceiling over his desk. The closer I looked, the more unprofessional I realized the company was. But I still persisted, believing that in a JV with Mr. Ho, we would be number one in Thailand overnight and that I could eventually bring him into the modern world of business. Negotiations continued to drag. In the meantime, we decided to move on and try our luck elsewhere. We left on good terms, but were still no closer to a deal. I was concerned. Getting into Thailand was critical, and I understood well that I would have to either partner with Mr. Ho or go to war with him, and the latter would be bloody.

With Ho on the back burner, we moved on to Malaysia. Although the Malaysian market was strategic in terms of scrap availability, most of the big dealers had pretty bad reputations. They were

sizable operations, but I personally felt and was warned that they would not be ideal partners. I'd had many bad experiences with these people with regard to contract performance as well as quality, and I also noted something important: *Why haven't the long-standing and successful Singapore metal recycling companies entered the much bigger neighboring Malaysian market? Proceed with caution.*

I had an introduction to one company in Kuala Lumpur named Hing Wah. It was a medium-sized company dealing in iron, but not stainless scrap. The owner, Mr. Koo, a Chinese businessman whom I estimated to be in his forties, had a strategically located piece of land with plenty of extra space and modern equipment that was well organized. I believed I could put a stainless business on his site and pay him a monthly rent for his facility and any shared equipment such as the weight bridge. My view was that this was a perfect win–win: Mr. Koo's ferrous or iron business would get an obvious cost cut and also share in the profits of a new business line. For Hartwell there would be a dramatic reduction in setup costs and an immediate introduction to Mr. Koo's customer base, who in the business are known as gypsies—small dealers running around the country collecting scrap metal.

Mr. Koo and his wife loved the plan. They were a husband-and-spouse team much the way Mei and I were unofficially becoming. We got right down to discussions and together did a survey of the entire market, driving tip-to-tip and coast-to-coast around Malaysia at mach speed in Mr. Koo's shiny new black S600 Mercedes. I was impressed by Malaysia's first-rate highways and tunnels, and started getting excited about our prospects. *Malaysia's level of development is the most advanced in Southeast Asia. It must be doing something right,* I thought.

Negotiations quickly got down to contract drafting and lawyers, so we focused on spending time together in order to understand each other more deeply. Unlike the other potential partners I had flagged, we had no business history with these guys, so we were slightly wary. Mr. and Mrs. Koo invited us to their home. It was a funny place with a small living room where a giant TV and fish tank took up most of one wall. The original manufacturer's protective plastic was still wrapped around their black leather couch and chairs. Mei asked to use the bathroom, and when she returned, she relayed with a whisper in my ear, "They have one of those 'hole in the ground' toilets," similar to the ones I had experienced in Sichuan Province developing the

magnesium business. *This is a bad sign,* I mused. *What kind of people buy a $200,000 Mercedes (including tax) but won't spring for a proper toilet?*

A couple of days later, they took us to their favorite local seafood place and insisted that we eat the jumbo prawns. I tucked in, devouring at least three, which were smothered in a delectable chili sauce. I felt that some of the prawns were a little soft, though. After I returned to my hotel, full and tired, and started getting ready for bed, a sharp pain hit me in my side. Within another half an hour I had a high fever and lay sweating on the bathroom floor next to the toilet, interchanging between sitting and kneeling. A doctor was summoned to give me an emergency injection. It was at this moment that I finalized a theory that had been developing in my brain over the years regarding eating in the developing world. "When in doubt, SPIT IT OUT!"

Oddly, having eaten the same thing, Mei didn't get sick, though her tummy grumbled a little. I always teased her that her stomach is made of stainless steel. As I lay on the floor in a fetal position, I considered that the wrenching pain in my gut may be more than just food poisoning—perhaps an omen.

Despite the fact that the deal negotiations were continuing, I sensed reluctance on the part of Mr. and Mrs. Koo and was developing doubts myself. Though we'd made fast progress thus far, my hunch that we would run into problems was soon confirmed. They began renegotiating issues that had already been settled, causing delays not to mention frustration on my part. It almost seemed they had no intention of getting the contract done. They became more and more curious about how, precisely, one could make money in the stainless business and how our technology worked. After another week of going back and forth over details, I walked in to Mr. Koo's office and said point-blank, "Either we agree and sign a deal today or it's over."

He replied, thinking we were fully on the hook, "We've been thinking a lot about it, Stephen, and feel that Hartwell is not bringing as much to the table as we first thought. In order to close the deal, we need to have a 60 percent share."

Shocked, and using every effort to stifle my anger, I responded, "I'm sorry, Mr. Koo. This is totally unacceptable and very late for this kind of major change. Anyway, we'll consider your offer and get back to you. Give us a few days."

I recognized the importance of controlling my anger in negotiations. *I might have to face this guy in the market someday. Better not create a*

fierce enemy, I thought. But that was it. No more discussions. We walked.

Beaten but not broken, we returned home to Hong Kong to try to cut a deal on our home turf. We talked to two companies about a joint venture and yet again experienced a frustrating process. The first was Mr. Cheung of Sung Yee Hong, the company we had bought our first container of scrap from back in 1994. We had a solid relationship with him that was full of trust and mutual respect. *This should be easy,* I thought. *We'll make a quick deal and then I can focus on other markets.* However, Mr. Cheung's son, our regular contact, explained very openly that there was no point in discussing a deal as it was just not in their family DNA. The father would never go for it even if his son would. I was frustrated by Cheung Senior's backward attitude, and had a newfound appreciation for my own father's encouragement and business acumen.

The other company was Wing Kee Metals and the father-and-son team of Lau and Lau. Lau Senior had founded Wing Kee, built it into a respected enterprise, and eventually handed over the reins to his eldest son as per Chinese tradition. Lau Junior was a real character. He was always dirty, and his smudged glasses settled at an angle on his chubby face; a half-smoked cigarette perpetually dangled from the corner of his mouth. He had a bouffant hairdo like Kim Jong Il, the "Dear Leader" of North Korea, and when he smiled he closed his eyes in a tight squint. As for his abilities, to say that he was unprofessional would be way too kind. Yet I still believed that with our ideas and superior market knowledge and their experienced workforce, we could be highly competitive and I could keep moving. But even though I could have accepted them, it didn't matter in the end. Lau Junior may have been running the operations, but Lau Senior was still calling the important shots, and it was politely explained that Lau Senior would never allow a joint venture, same as Sung Yee Hong. The older generation would not accept a new partnership.

Just like Thailand and Malaysia, we were coming up dry and growing frustrated. Next we tried our luck in Singapore and the Philippines, but ended up with the same result. Everyone was eager to understand our strategy and learn about our technology, but these Chinese family businesses seemed to have no interest in adopting an American son. I was beginning to realize that we were perhaps seen as a threat to internal family stability, or even a challenge to the compli-

cated issues of succession and sibling rivalries. In my mind, all rational people would make business decisions based on the best growth opportunities, not antiquated custom. I felt my strategy was clear and the synergy obvious, but time and time again I ran into a brick wall.

I was really frustrated by their inability to partner with us, but I also saw it as a sign of weakness. I firmly believed that they would not have the ability to branch out regionally, as their focus seemed to be entirely on maintaining absolute control. *Based on the way they do business, if they want more locations, they'll need more relatives,* I smirked. Unfortunately this greater wisdom did not get us any closer to satisfying POSCO's requirements.

⌁∞⌁

It was now late November, six months after getting restarted with POSCO, and management was putting enormous pressure on us to open our recycling operations. Mr. Song called: "Mr. Greer, we have received an offer of a thousand tons from a dealer in Singapore. They say they are planning to open a yard in Malaysia and expand." Obviously POSCO had options if we didn't get our yards open soon.

In the formal nature of Korean culture, this was more or less a death threat.

"Mr. Song, this offer is total bull. Nobody in Singapore can do a thousand tons every month. If they can do it this month, it's because they've stockpiled it over several months, and that makes them a speculator. If the markets are going up, they will hold back material from you," I retorted, planting as many seeds of doubt as I could.

I quickly wrote a follow-up fax, explaining the weaknesses of our competitors and informing POSCO that we were in the process of negotiating joint ventures across the region. Mr. Song promptly replied, "Great. Mr. Kwon and I want to arrange to visit your partners together with you."

Shit, I thought. *They're not gonna let this one go.* I did my best to explain that it was a very sensitive time as negotiations were in the final stage, but to no avail. POSCO insisted that if we wanted future support, a visit from its executives was necessary. I was terrified that the firm's intention was to cut us out of the program. That may well have been the backup plan, but we had no choice. We invited POSCO to survey the Hong Kong market.

We arranged a whistle-stop tour, and I mean whistle-stop. We didn't leave time to pee, and there would of course be no discussions that included our potential partners. I also went all-out to make a good impression for our most important guests. I told Lilly, Triple Li, to rent a stretch Mercedes limo to accommodate everyone comfortably. I knew exactly what I wanted—just like the limo at the Grand Hyatt. Lilly came back to me and explained, "The car service only has one, but it's in light blue."

That sounded strange but we were running out of time and I was told it was my only option, so I confirmed it. The next week, I waited in the lobby of our building together with Mei and the POSCO executives, everyone dressed in dark suits. The limo slowly pulled up, and my eyes nearly popped out of my head. It was a stretch Mercedes limo all right—from 1980! Bright red, we piled into the vintage Merc. Everyone looked at the others awkwardly as the car sagged under our weight, but nobody made a comment as we trundled along, our spines absorbing every bump. I could've killed Lilly.

I had strategically planned to waste as much time as possible, and so had organized a 10 AM start "to avoid traffic." After a brief stop at Wing Kee's operations I informed our guests that we needed to press on to keep on schedule. Mr. Kwon was not pleased to find out that the next stop was a Chinese restaurant where a ten-course banquet had been pre-ordered.

"Your hospitality is appreciated, Mr. Greer, but we came here to survey the market and gauge your progress, not gain five kilos," he complained, looking despondent.

"We have plenty of time, Mr. Kwon, and the food here is quite famous. We don't want you to go hungry," I replied.

"Tomorrow sandwiches will be fine. This is not a luxury holiday," he lectured. He was well on to my ploy of distracting them from the purpose of their visit.

My other trick was bringing them to scrap yards with which we had no intention of partnering and where nobody could speak any English. We wandered around the dust-filled yards as the workers gawked at their foreign visitors who were struggling to find any meaning from their tour.

"Look, they even handle lead battery scrap," I noted encouragingly.

"We don't buy lead, Mr. Greer," Mr. Kwon intoned.

Happy about it or not, the schedule was fixed and I would not be deterred. *I kept my side of the bargain. You've had your tour. And I've bought us some time,* I thought. We sent them back to Korea with bags of Chinese goodies and deep bows. We'd gotten the Koreans off our backs for now, but we knew they'd be back.

Though obviously feeling the heat from POSCO, I also understood that having our own operations wasn't just important to them, but important to us as well. *We don't want to be just a cheap insurance company for POSCO like we were for Nickelmet,* I thought.

c◈◎э

Christmas was nearing and tension was building. Mei and I decided that the best way to face our struggle was to run away to Hawaii and recharge over the holiday. We checked into the magnificent Lodge at Koele, on the island of Lanai, for a ten-day golf extravaganza. We played at least eighteen holes a day and on one day managed forty-two. Chasing that little white ball around the course, the hours blended together. Whack, whack, whack. I sliced a five-iron into the trees.

"Damn it, Mei. If we're gonna build this business it's going to be from the ground up. We need to forget about shortcuts! Wars aren't won by the air force. It's boots on the ground and if we're not prepared for a ground war, then we shouldn't go to war," I exploded, paraphrasing General Schwarzkopf during the leadup to the first Gulf War. Granted, comparing the scrap metal business to war in the Middle East may have been a bit of a stretch, but I was fired up and sick of being jerked around by potential JV partners. Mei looked at me puzzled, slowly grasping my analogy.

"Okay, Steve. I'm with you. Just do it!" she belted out enthusiastically, quoting Nike and competing with me for corny clichés.

"Anyway, whatever you do will work out in the end," she continued with a supportive smile. "I don't just say that because of your lucky, thick palms. I saw your baby picture from the hospital. There is something even more auspicious about you."

I was an adorable little bugger, but never mind. In the picture, I was lying on my back looking eagerly at the camera with my right hand held up, fingers curled in, and my left arm across my belly.

"You looked just like a money cat!" she exclaimed with an affectionate giggle.

Money cats are those porcelain cats that you see in every store-front in Hong Kong or Chinese restaurants in America. The cat faces the door and with his paw is directing the money to come inside. As far as Mei was concerned, her partner had all the critical raw materials for success.

Mei is right. This is our destiny. We're not going to sit around waiting for people to accept us, I threatened Wing Kee and Sun Tak in my thoughts. *Someday soon we'll enter your markets and when we do, you're going to wish we were partners!* My competitive juices were boiling.

12

A LITTLE CLOAK AND DAGGER

Ready for the fight of our lives, Mei and I began the long march of setting up our own operations. Though the Asian economic crisis was a disaster for some, it offered up an abundance of empty warehouses for lease at distressed rent, used equipment at fire sales, and plentiful labor looking for work. I gauged that we would be able to open a recycling yard for about half of what it would have cost pre-crisis. Funding was also not an issue. Our trading profits were stable and HSBC was solidly behind us, though it insisted on Mei's and my personal guarantee. To a non-entrepreneur the personal guarantee may not sound like a big deal, but we slept every night with that on our minds. If anything catastrophic happened, the bank would wipe out Hartwell Pacific and then mercilessly come after the two of us. Though we had plenty of anxiety, I believed this was our moment.

We faced a critical challenge, however: converting a brokerage company into a metal recycling or physical collection business. We had originally started by purchasing scrap from the existing recycling com-

panies in the region and selling their metal to POSCO, but by opening our own operations in Southeast Asia we were in effect competing with those suppliers. Clearly this would not please them. The key
to our success would be to keep Hartwell Pacific's ownership of its
subsidiaries a secret until we could get a critical market share that
would satisfy POSCO's minimum purchase requirements. If our brokerage suppliers cut us off, we would be unable to fulfill our commitments to POSCO, and the fragile structure we had created would
crumble.

We decided to keep our secret by giving all of our subsidiaries
different names and hiding our ownership behind nominee shareholders—basically accounting firms. Once we were able to stop buying from our original suppliers in favor of our own subsidiaries, and
with POSCO's exclusive support, we would be poised to rapidly grow
our market share. The strategy was to hold the secret together as long
as possible until we could unveil a formidable competitor.

Mei and I began analyzing all of the countries and markets in
which we had suppliers to find the best fit. By now, we were very
familiar with all of the Southeast Asian markets, and in our opinion the
Philippines was the low-hanging fruit. In Manila, they refer to metal
recycling companies or scrap yards as junk shops, and, in my mind,
they were exactly that. As traders, we were never able to find a reliable
supplier. The companies operated in dark, dust-filled warehouses that
were full of flies and smelled more like garbage dumps than metal
recycling yards. Metals of different types were haphazardly mixed
together. I don't know how they did their inventory; I imagined that
they didn't. Our competitors seemed like a bunch of clowns, so we
decided that the Philippines would be the first place we'd open an
operation. We'd call this one GCG Recycling after my father's ini-
tials—George Collins Greer.

It was now time to deploy Narita—the sharp Filipina girl with
the penchant for highbrow literature. I approached her and she
responded very positively.

"Sounds great, Steve!"

Narita was always upbeat, but I am not sure she had given it
much thought. It was the first week of January, and she now wondered
when I was planning to do this.

"Now!" I said with determined enthusiasm.

"When now?" she demanded with a shocked look on her face.

"Now, now. Let's go next week and start looking for a site!" I exclaimed.

She cried, not the reaction I was looking for. They were not tears of happiness or sadness, but tears of fear. This would be a big step for her. She wondered aloud if she could handle it.

"Steve! I have no experience with this."

"Don't worry, Narita. We'll do it together. We have full confidence in you," Mei and I assured her.

After much encouragement and hand-holding, Narita finally agreed, and she left the next week to set up the company. She first needed to find a one-acre warehouse with good road access and decent security. Wanting to make sure we got a good start, I came over and toured Manila with her to help make the final decisions and to get a deeper feel for the market. This was a tiresome exercise. Manila's traffic is, in my opinion, the worst in Asia. The most we could manage was three meetings in a day if we were lucky. It was absolutely mind numbing, so I was eager to sign a lease and get back to Hong Kong. Narita was used to the inefficiencies, but they drove me nuts. I also struggled with the food. One lunch we pulled into a restaurant, and as we parked the car the door to the kitchen burst open. Three guys carried out a giant snake, I believe a python, that was wriggling desperately over their shoulders. They tossed it, *thwack,* on the parking lot pavement, and the guy who'd been managing the tail produced a baseball bat. He then bludgeoned the stunned snake to death in front of us. Once it was dead, the three "chefs" picked it up and heaved it back into the kitchen.

"Nobody can say the food isn't fresh," I quipped to Narita.

After making some key decisions about the setup of our operation, I returned to Hong Kong and let Narita do her thing. She was organized, and the team she put together—an accountant, a person in charge of operations, and about ten laborers—was hardworking and loyal. Once up and running, we quickly gained market share from our competitors.

Though in my view her competitors were a bunch of jokers, it doesn't mean we didn't have problems or that anything was easy. Most of the trouble we encountered was government interference. Manila is a minefield of corrupt officials and convoluted policies, and we were forever being shaken down by some low-level bureaucrat. Whether it was the fire department, licensing bureaus, the police, or the electric

company, roadblocks were always being thrown up. Luckily Narita was adept at maneuvering around them. When encountered, many foreign companies pull out the flag of their home country and loudly declare, "We are foreign investors; this is unacceptable." Big mistake. The locals translate that to mean, "We are rich people from another country who have lots of extra cash to give away!" After all, if you're being hassled it's because you must have done something wrong, even if it was a minor infraction.

Narita would take the local approach, saying something like, "We are a Filipino business that employs locals and we're still struggling. If you squeeze us, we'll have to close down and all those people will lose their jobs. This is not a Christian way to behave." The Philippines is a Catholic-dominated society, a legacy of the Spanish colonial era.

"Please, Ronnie," she would continue, getting on a first-name basis with her assailant. "Let me buy you lunch. If our company is going to survive this difficult economic time we need your support. Pick on the rich ones." Nine times out of ten she'd squeak by and the problem would be brushed aside.

Narita is very charming and persuasive. As the business grew, she always maintained close ties with the community, sponsoring local charities, entertaining the police, remembering birthdays, Christmases, and so forth. In the developing world, you have to have lots of low-level friends in the government. High-level ones can come in handy as well, but it's the junior ones who can make problems go away before they become major issues.

In addition to the government, the other problem in the Philippines is security. Manila is a famously rough town where violent crime is a serious issue. Unlike most other cities in Asia, in Manila, no doubt due to a legacy of US colonization and policies, everyone has guns. It's a part of the culture. When Narita took me to the cockfights, a favorite gambling activity in the Philippines, I was shocked to see that there was a metal detector at the entrance with a large hand-painted sign beside it stating, CHECK YOUR GUNS! To the right was a line of people and, much like a coat-check, they were handing over their weaponry in exchange for a receipt. The guns were then put in small cubbyholes behind the counter. I could imagine the potential for violence as angry punters who'd just lost their wages betting on chickens reclaimed their loaded pistols and headed out into the smog. Take

poverty, tropical heat, pollution, maddening traffic, and a little Latin passion, then throw guns into the mix, and you have a dangerous cock-tail. We took heavy precautions to protect our local and visiting employees: armed guards at the gate, a full-time driver who also car-ried a pistol; even sweet old Narita packed heat. But despite all our precautions, we were robbed on multiple occasions. One of our office staff was shot, luckily in the hand, while picking up some cash at the bank, and we had a truckload of copper worth almost $100,000 hijacked on its way to the port. Fortunately, we had insurance. Thankfully, despite all the hurdles to overcome, my confidence was well placed and we were profitable in our second month. I now viewed a scrap yard as a small financial printing press. *Though each one may not make big money, all we need is a lot of 'em,* I thought.

⋘❦⋙

Next stop, Hong Kong. As we searched for an appropriate piece of property for our operation, which is a serious challenge in land-starved Hong Kong, we were approached by one of the potential joint venture partners we had spoken to earlier. Lau Junior, the guy with the dirty glasses and bouffant hairdo, wondered if we still wanted to do a JV. With Hartwell's success in the Philippines, the thought of going back to a joint venture with people like the Laus was unappetizing. Plus, we had heard in the market that Wing Kee was having some financial problems due to its highly speculative aluminum and copper businesses. With some trepidation, we decided we would give it a try, but only on our terms. We insisted upon a 70–30 Hartwell–Wing Kee split and that the company be a new and separate operating facility focusing exclusively on stainless steel. We would, however, keep Hartwell's name out of the picture by naming the company Lo Kee Metals, a nod to Peter Sellers. In this partnership, we would get skilled workers, an experienced operations manager, and an active supplier list—and still own the vast majority of the enterprise.

In the ensuing months, however, we realized that all of our ini-tial assumptions about Lau Junior's incompetence were true. He was an inflexible and shortsighted business manager. New ideas were con-sidered a waste of time, and any extra benefit for the workers, such as uniforms and safety boots, were believed a waste of money. Lau was resistant to any change and modernization. The other problem was

that he was personally repulsive. After Triple Li made a trip to Manila together with him to visit Narita's operations and observe firsthand how a successful business was run, pretty Lilly came to me with one gentle request.

"Please don't make me travel with Mr. Lau again."

She explained that on the flight, the attendants had handed out hot white towels so everyone could freshen up. Lau Junior proceeded to bathe himself, including wiping out his armpits, and then threw the soiled towel on the armrest. The Cathay Pacific flight attendant gingerly retracted it with her tongs, staring at Lilly in horror. I've never again wiped my face with the hand towels after hearing that story.

Luckily, nobody would be submitted to that again. A few months into our joint venture, Mr. Lau got himself into further financial trouble speculating on copper, and we were able to buy his share of the venture at a fraction of its worth, making Lo Kee a 100 percent subsidiary. Of course, he started up again with his father across town within months, but we still came out ahead. Most importantly, all of the seasoned staff that had been seconded to the joint venture recognized that we were better employers and stuck with us. It's amazing what new uniforms and a daily pre-work meeting can do to raise spirits. Even though we didn't have much in common with the workers and none of them could speak English, we were able to win their hearts and minds through respect, personal attention, and a keen interest in their safety. Hartwell continued to grow.

After we got our team organized, I was able to get involved firsthand in the commercial expansion of the Hong Kong business, and we moved quickly from red figures into the black. In the process I found an opportunity to buy all of the stainless from the demolition of the old Kai Tak Airport, the same airport I had arrived at five years earlier. Kai Tak had recently been replaced by the new award-winning, Norman Foster–designed Chek Lap Kok Airport on Lantau Island. I toured Kai Tak's empty baggage claim halls to see what type of scrap might be available. The baggage conveyors were made of stainless as well as the baggage carts and containers, so there was plenty. It was a strange feeling wandering around, seeing and hearing the ghosts of the past. I could picture vividly that early morning in 1993 when I had stood there to collect my bag, wondering what the future would hold. I swallowed hard, taking in the thought that I had now been in Hong Kong over five years.

After soaking in the moment, I exited the dark, empty hall for the bright sunshine outside. Unable to resist, I drove my BMW flat-out on the runway, making a couple of exhilarating laps, all windows down, while taking in the spectacular city skyline and maxing out the speedometer. Finally heading toward the exit, much to the relief of the panicked security officers, I took one last long look at the old terminal before rocketing onto the expressway. Hong Kong had changed so much, and so had I.

⌒✍⌒

With Manila and Hong Kong under our belts, momentum was building. Our next targets were the bigger markets of Thailand and Malaysia. But, as the cliché goes, "Business is about people." First we needed someone to run those companies.

Nick Peterson, my Caine Road roommate in Hong Kong, had left his job as a trade representative for the state of Virginia and was now running the Malaysian office for Spencer Fuller, a large American defense contractor. At that time, there wasn't much going on in terms of defense transactions between America and Malaysia, as it was 1998 and Prime Minister Mahathir Mohamad had famously blamed America and the "Wall Street Jews" for the Asian economic crisis. He would not be awarding any beefy military contracts to Americans.

Nick's work was very highbrow: dinner with generals, lunch with the ambassador. However, it was more a continuation of his trade mission role and really lacking in any business content. He was always saying he wanted to get some real experience. When Spencer Fuller decided to close the Malaysian office, Nick started to think about other options. I mentioned that our industry wasn't sexy and didn't require designer suits, but it was hands-on work and I could offer him a deal if he was interested. He let me know that he was, but needed some time to think it over. I turned my attention toward trying to find a GM for Thailand.

I had another friend named Bill whom I'd met in Hong Kong when I first arrived in 1993. He had moved on to Vietnam to cash in on the impending economic boom that was to accompany the lifting of the US trade embargo. That boom took another ten years to evolve, but Bill was a creative and charismatic character who had found a way to survive off a web of small businesses, much the way Hartwell had

started. Anyway, I admired people who were living the same hand-to-mouth entrepreneur's existence.

Living in Ho Chi Minh City, Bill was near Bangkok and knew it well. If I was to continue our global expansion, I wasn't going to have time to get bogged down in Thailand. The fast-track idea was to cut him in on the deal.

Bill was busy. He would boom in a deep New York accent, "Steeeeve, I'm busier than a one-legged man in an ass-kicking contest!" But being so busy and stressed caused him to have a weak sense of punctuality and organization. He was perpetually missing flights, losing his passport, having his laptop stolen, or getting caught in the middle of a bar brawl. Alas, Bill had also been a Golden Gloves boxer. He always had hilarious stories about his trials and tribulations, like the time he crashed into a baby water buffalo on his motorcycle and was chased by an angry mob through the streets of Saigon, but I admit I was getting a bit concerned about getting caught up in these calamities. As we were coming close to agreeing on a deal, I asked him to meet me in Bangkok and booked a conference room in a good hotel to create a professional and serious environment. I arrived at 10 AM, the designated time, and waited for about ten minutes. My phone rang. It was Bill.

"Duuuude! I'm stuck in 'Nam. I'm comin' on the evening flight. Can we make the meeting tomorrow?"

That was the final signal for me; I decided against creating a partnership. It was awkward, but I handled it as smoothly as possible. This is the challenge when you involve friendships. Bill was too busy to handle our project at the time, and it would have led to a falling-out had things gone poorly. We remained good friends.

So who was going to run Thailand? I was having a cappuccino at a coffee shop along Sukhumvit Road, the main artery that runs through Bangkok, when it hit me. *Steel mills buy scrap metal. The guys who work at steel mills as scrap metal buyers must know where to find it. The guys who buy scrap at Thai steel mills are probably not paid that well. Maybe I can get one of those guys to join me.* So I got out the English version of the Bangkok yellow pages and looked under *steel.* I figured, *The biggest advertisement must be the biggest steel company.* I found a company named Sahavariya. *Never heard of it.* I called the main number, and a very friendly receptionist transferred me to the department in charge of

scrap. A gentleman answered the phone in broken English: "My name Prapast. How I can help you?"

I introduced myself and explained that I was interested in buying and exporting stainless steel scrap metal from Thailand and perhaps setting up a business in Bangkok to do so.

"I would like very much to meet you, Mr. Prapast, and discuss the local market," I expressed professionally.

He said he'd be happy to meet, but his office was far away and might be inconvenient for me to find. He could come to my hotel but would need a couple of hours to get there. This was amazing. He did-n't even know who I was, just some random *felang*—the Thai word for "foreigner"—but was still willing to meet me. I suppose he sensed an opportunity.

Prapast, a neatly dressed and well-groomed man in his forties, showed up at the hotel lobby. He was formal but gracious, and very generously explained the market, even offering to drive me all over Bangkok the next day to survey it. I took him up on his offer and we soon found ourselves working our way through the famously dense traffic, using all the back-alley shortcuts, chatting away all the while in broken English.

I didn't know Prapast from Adam, but we shared a positive ener-gy and for some reason he just seemed like a straightforward guy. Though we had simple conversations, I was able to divine that Prapast was actually quite intelligent. In fact, I found out later that he had a law degree. He didn't drink alcohol, spoke gently about his family, and was quite a devout Buddhist—very stable. I was learning quickly that just because someone doesn't speak your language well does not make him less competent. The genetic distribution of smarts does not have borders.

I discussed the plan, and Prapast was very enthusiastic about our prospects. After spending just two days together, I had a gut feeling that I had my man. I think he also recognized the opportunity of being the boss of a new start-up and, most importantly, believed in his own abil-ity. Prapast was eager to make his move and soon signed up as our new GM for Thailand.

The employment agreement was negotiated and settled, but he had one curveball.

"Hartwell is new in Thailand. I need to be paid six months in advance," he insisted.

Hmm. This goes against my instinct, I thought. I was worried about trusting him and concerned that he did not trust me. I discussed it with Mei. No big company would do this, and many people would treat the request as a great cause for concern, but we decided to go ahead. *Trust first,* I thought. *If he honors our trust, we've found our new GM. It's an amount of money we can afford to lose, and anyway if he is that dishonest we'll be lucky he's gone before he developed any greater authority or responsibility.* I shared an American cliché with Mei: "Give 'em enough rope to hang themselves, but not enough rope to hang you!"

"I'm sure it's not just about the money; he's looking for a sign of commitment," Mei added. "It's also about respect. If you show respect and have patience with his cultural differences, you'll win loyalty. You'll find this very valuable as a foreigner."

I totally agreed.

Prapast and I quickly found a site, hashed out a lease, pulled the trigger on some used equipment, and started the hiring process. Sticking with our covert strategy, we named the company TMR— Thai Metal Recycling—once again concealing the Hartwell name and shareholders.

I was extremely proud of our operations—bricks and mortar, people—a real business. I wanted to show my family what "Stever the good businessman" was building, so I asked my father, "the chairman," to come over from Pittsburgh for a grand Asian tour.

Dad, Prapast, and I set off to visit our newly minted Bangkok operations, Prapast and I jabbering away as usual. When we finally got out of the car and entered the vast, empty warehouse, with used fork-lifts and cranes randomly parked around it, Dad remarked with a snicker, "I couldn't understand a word you guys were saying."

"Ah," I explained. "That's because I'm fluent in Tenglish, or Thai English. I'm also fluent in Chinglish. The only people I can't under-stand are Scots, and we're Scottish!"

I had become a chameleon, unconsciously slipping into different accents, even adopting local mannerisms. I looked over at my father; he was smiling ear-to-ear.

Dad and I continued our Asian tour, spending a weekend at Angkor Wat in Cambodia before venturing on to Manila, Kuala

Lumpur, and Singapore, staying at the finest hotels and dining in gourmet restaurants. It gave me great pride to host my father. He didn't have to open his wallet once, including the business-class plane tickets. I guess I was paying him back for the mileage ticket he had given me to come to Hong Kong. I remember walking side by side with him on the treadmill in the gym at the Raffles Hotel in Singapore, the pieces of jade strung around our necks, bouncing off our chests. We'd come a long way together, and I was sad to see him return to Pennsylvania.

⌒⟨✕⟩⌒

After careful consideration or perhaps careless abandon, my old roommate Nick signed up to be in charge of Malaysia. He would be more of a partner than employee, though, accepting at-cost pay, including housing and expenses, and a share in any profits generated in Malaysia. Nick joined NAC—Nickel Alloy Collection, aka Hartwell Malaysia—with a high level of energy and contagious enthusiasm.

We found a nice little yard near the old Subang Airport—just a half-covered acre of land with a small, one-story site office. The landlord, Mr. Lim, was a very traditional Chinese guy with a mole on his chin, long hairs growing out of it reaching down a good six inches. I am told that hairy moles are lucky in some Chinese cultures—the longer the hairs, the luckier. This guy was a veritable leprechaun. He stared at me intently, pulling on his mole hairs, looking for a sign of weakness. Mr. Lim was a real stereotype of the bad guy in one of the old kung fu movies, and it was all I could do to keep a straight face. The negotiations went back and forth until I shut them down.

"Mr. Lim, I prefer your site but I have another option across town. If we can't sign today I have no choice but to take it. We can't mess around any longer. You have our offer and it's our bottom line. No more negotiations," I bluffed, knowing he likely didn't have many options in this bad market.

He slowly tilted his head to one side, stretching his neck muscles, twisting his mole hairs between his thumb and two fingers.

"I need to talk to my partners. I get back to you tomorrow," he explained.

"No way," I insisted. "If you want to talk to your partners, call them now. This is the end of the road."

He cautiously considered what I was saying then excused himself and made what I believe was a fake phone call, returning a couple of minutes later and looking at me seriously. He then broke into a smile and said, "You get too good deal. But okay. Not include anything. You take as is."

We both signed the lease, pleased with the outcome. *Always use time lines in negotiations,* I reminded myself.

We quickly set up the yard and recruited a team of about twenty people. We surveyed the landscape of potential suppliers, and with our superior pricing were able to promptly penetrate the market and establish a base share. Nick worked very hard and was even willing to don worker's clothes and boots and throw metal around the yard with his own hands when equipment broke down. Malaysia looked promising.

⚬◦⦇◦⚬

Back in Thailand, things were pumping along. However, we had a lot of work to do, and Bangkok had much stiffer competition than Hong Kong and Manila. Prapast was a shrewd operator, though, and the business quickly got off the ground. He was bold, a little too bold. He hired a guy on a motorcycle to sit outside one of our main competitors' operations, handing out flyers to the truck drivers who were delivering scrap. The flyers introduced our company as an alternative buyer with better prices. A clever idea, perhaps, but our motorcycle guy returned one day with a message for Prapast: "Be careful what you're doing. Bullets are cheap in Bangkok! You'd better quiet down."

We took this threat seriously, understanding well the chaotic and potentially dangerous business environment in Bangkok. With our experience in Manila, we were not naive about the realities of large cities in the developing world. In fact, I was warned early on that the price of a contract killing was no more than a few hundred dollars, and that if I stepped on the wrong toes this could be my fate. This was no idle consideration. That year, an Australian auditor for a major multinational accounting firm was murdered while auditing a large Thai company. He had uncovered some irregularities at this public enterprise and insisted on disclosing them. Someone had a differing opinion, and it was lights-out for the auditor, shot dead by a man riding pillion on a motorcycle.

Scrap metal is an industry dominated by local companies in Southeast Asia. Our entry into the market put direct pressure on their margins, if not threatened their very existence. Nobody likes to see a newcomer enter the market to "share their rice"—particularly if they are already facing difficulties related to the Asian economic crisis. Let's just say we would not be popular. Mei was very concerned about my safety and encouraged me to make my visits as short as possible.

I informed Nick of our dilemma, and he sprang into action with an absolutely brilliant idea. At the time a lot of dirty Russian money was flooding out of the former Soviet bloc, and one place where it was being laundered was in Bangkok. The word on the street was that many houses of sin were financed by Russian "black" money. Nick decided to spread a rumor that our business was a laundering front for the Russian mafia, who were famously ruthless, and put the fear of God into even the most ornery Bangkok thug. To ram the message home, Nick had business cards made up using the name Vladimir Rimsky. *Rimsky* was chosen after the great Russian composer. He would introduce himself to everyone as Vlad. Who can resist a good rumor? It spread like wildfire. People would ask us if it was true and we'd just vigorously deny it, asking, "Who told you that?!"—exactly what we thought would be expected of a Russian mafioso. We were never hassled by anyone going forward.

Perhaps our ruse was too convincing. Prapast and I were sitting in the waiting room of one of our big suppliers when the door opened and in strode Mr. Chumsak, a short and tubby man with a wild smile on his face. He shook my hand vigorously and then started singing gleefully in Russian, his arms pumping away to accentuate the notes. Prapast turned to me and whispered that Chumsak had been part of the Thai communist insurgency back in the early 1960s and had even trained in Russia. It was a little awkward not to have any idea what he was going on about, but I just smiled and shook his hand. Prapast explained with a giggle, "He think you Lussian" ("Russian" in Tenglish).

Our suppliers couldn't have cared less if we were Russian mafia as long as we had the best price, comparable service, and plenty of cash.

We now had four yards open in Southeast Asia, with all but Malaysia spinning profits. Our brokerage business with third parties was doing particularly well—in fact, together with the Grand Metal reusable business, it was generating a six-figure net income. This gave us great comfort and confidence, so we decided to break out of our tiny flat on Bridges Street and find a decent place to live a more adult life. I came back from a trip to Korea one evening and Mei brought me to see an apartment on Conduit Road, a relatively quiet street at the top of the Mid-levels. She enthused, "How do you like it?"

It was a decent-sized apartment with a balcony overlooking the harbor, much better than our current one, but I wasn't that impressed. After walking in the front door, I immediately said, "Mei, it has low ceilings and a narrow living room. I don't know what you're so excited about."

Tears welled up in her eyes and her face reddened. I immediately realized I had stepped over a line.

"I looked at fifteen flats, and all I was thinking about was finding a place where you'd be happy," she whined. "And you walk in here and dismiss it without even looking around."

I felt terrible that I had been so insensitive. This was an apartment that for her would have been a childhood dream, unlikely to be attained. Sometimes, after pouring out all my energy and emotion on customers and employees, I had nothing left for the ones I loved. It's not fair but it happens. Mei's sadness now turned to anger.

"You'd better learn to like it!" she yelled. "I've already signed the lease!" With that she stormed out, leaving me standing alone feeling like a jackass.

We moved in shortly thereafter. I grew to like, not love, our new home and felt it was a step in the right direction anyway. Its best feature was an Olympic-sized swimming pool that almost nobody used, which became my sanctuary during the hot summers. It was also the sanctuary for many of my friends, who signed in as Stephen Greer. That is one nice thing about *gweilos,* or foreign devils, as they call us in Cantonese: We all look alike.

Due to our expanding head count, we were quickly outgrowing our Hong Kong headquarters and began looking for more space. The economy was in terrible shape, and many property owners were in negative equity situations. We found out that an office on the thirty-seventh floor of our building was in default on its mortgage. It was

Heading to Hong Kong—putting on a brave face. (February 1993)

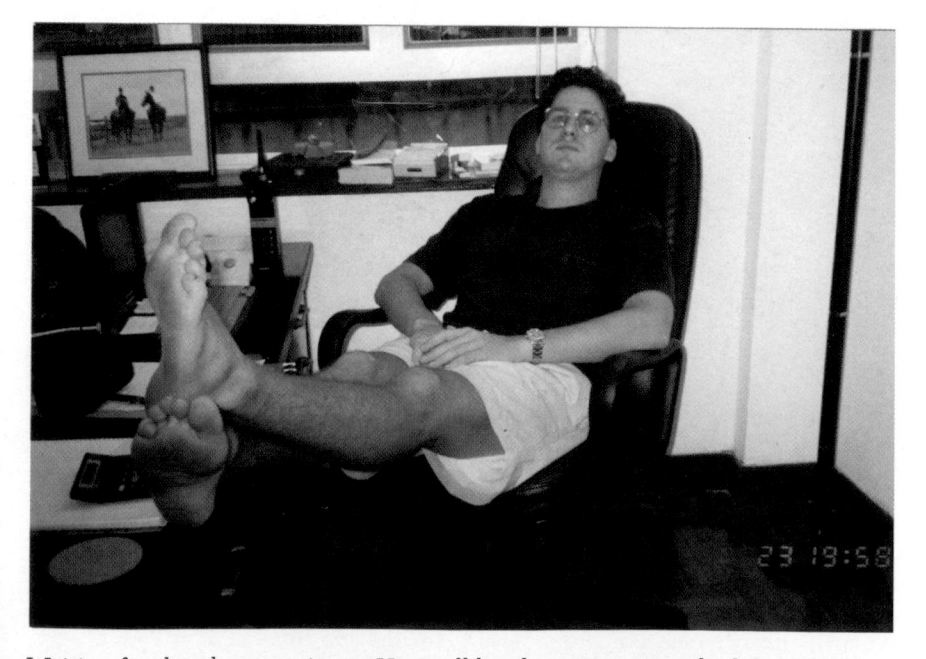

Waiting for the phone to ring at Hartwell headquarters. It rarely did. (1994)

Merry Christmas: little hands at work. Visiting the "gift item" factory in Fujian, China, after the Canton Fair. (1994)

You will marry a man from far . . . away. Mei and a fortune-teller at Venice Beach in LA during a scrap buying mission. (1995)

With Mei—buried in scrap. (1995)

Dad bearing witness to our first shipment. (1995)

My morning commute. Not
Park Avenue! (1995)

Beautiful magnesium ingots. (1995)

Preparing to meet the mayor in Henan—no gray hair yet. (1995)

The spoils of war, Kuwait. Burned-out remnants of the first Gulf War. (1995)

"Stephen of Arabia" with Mr. Al-Wadi. (1995)

Getting a taste of the good life in my new office at Nickelmet's Asian headquarters. (1996)

The 1997 handover party—Hong Kong was now part of communist China.

The chairman (Dad) visits the Thai company. (1998)

The opening of Grand Metal—a grand affair. (1998)

And with that, we were in business. (1998)

Mei yukking it up with the workers. (1998)

Getting our hands dirty in Mexico—putting my university degree to work. (1999)

Mei as a child in China during the Cultural Revolution, dutifully wearing her Chairman Mao pin.

With Matt after he saved our lives in Indonesia. (2000)

A little R&R off the coast of Mexico. (2001)

A beautiful day in Pennsylvania. (2001)

Young Entrepreneur of the Year. (2001)

Learning to appreciate Thai culture with Prapast on my left and the chief of the local police on my right. (2002)

With the team in Manila—starting to look professional. (2002)

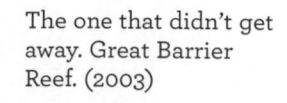

The one that didn't get away. Great Barrier Reef. (2003)

Signing away the company with Charlie. (2005)

Soaking in the moment after closing, unsure how I felt. (2005)

Celebrating the deal with Mei, Prapast, and Narita on the top of the Sydney Harbor Bridge. (2005)

twenty-two hundred square feet, roughly triple the size of our current office, with knee-to-ceiling windows stretching sixty feet along the waterfront. It had a postcard view of the harbor and the mountains beyond. Of course, we knew such a purchase would increase our burden with HSBC, but after calculating that the interest was less than the rent we jumped at it. *A gift from the heavens!* We now owned a piece of the rock that I'd landed on six years earlier, naive and full of dreams, and that Mei had arrived on twenty-one years earlier, full of anxiety about the future. This was the first piece of real estate either of us had ever owned and it felt great.

13

A QUEST FOR GLOBAL DOMINATION

ith the success of Hong Kong, Thailand, Malaysia, and the Philippines under our belt, I perused the world of expansion opportunities. I recalled the childhood board game Risk, a dice game that is played out on a Cold War–era map. The objective is to vanquish your enemy's armies and secure global dominance while leaving enough resources to defend your territories. Holed up most evenings in our office, a lone light in a dark building, I studied a coffee-stained map of the world and a well-worn encyclopedia sprawled out across our conference table. Rather than attacking the metal recycling majors head-on, I sought to conquer the markets where the competition was not well represented. China, Mexico, South America, Africa, Kazakhstan and other parts of Eurasia, even certain parts of the United States—there was no limit to my ambition, no location too remote. If enough rolls of the dice went my way, Hartwell had a fighting chance of becoming a global player.

My approach was not random, though. I had certain criteria for my chosen targets. For one, the scrap market should not be a black-

market economy. We understood from our experience with Nickelmet in Taiwan, where the industry standard was tax evasion and money laundering, that it would be next to impossible for us to operate a legitimate metal recycling business in such an environment. China, a market we drooled over, was now being ruled out for this very reason. The next criterion was to find markets that were synergistic with our Asian operations. The current and forecast trade flow of exports should be to Asia so that incremental tons collected would be aggregated with our current sales program, giving us more marketing muscle. More tons under our control would give us higher sales prices and thus better margins in each of our markets. Finally, I focused on countries or regions that had no domestic demand for stainless steel scrap by a stainless consumer or mill. I could deal with competing with other local exporters, but didn't want to fight with a steel mill, a highly capitalized corporation that gobbles massive amounts of scrap in its industrialized furnaces.

After careful analysis, I decided the order of development would be the southeastern United States and Mexico, then the rest of Latin America, and finally South and sub-Saharan Africa. The US Southeast was chosen because of its geography and lack of major competition. There was also more scrap in America than even the large stainless steel mills could use, resulting in an annual export to Asia of over three hundred thousand tons. The surplus scrap was naturally exported from the areas farthest from the Pittsburgh steel mills. Of these regions, the West Coast, Gulf Coast, and the Southeast, only the Southeast was still relatively uncovered by a major competitor. The choices were Charlotte, Charleston, Savannah, or Jacksonville. I settled on either North or South Carolina, as they were more centrally located, and Atlanta had a significant competitor challenging us in Georgia and north Florida.

Mexico also fulfilled all of our investment criteria, and offered an extra competitive advantage. The plentiful Mexican scrap was currently being trucked north across the border to Houston before being processed and then reshipped out to Asia via the Panama Canal. If we were to set up a yard in Guadalajara, the second largest city in Mexico and close to the West Coast port of Manzanillo, we could buy the scrap locally, process it using Mexican wages, and export it directly to Korea. No trucking to Houston, no US customs clearance, no Houston labor costs, and no Panama Canal fees. *No-brainer!* I also viewed Mexico as

an eventual stepping-stone to the rest of Latin America, a market thus far not covered by the leading global players and where almost all the countries were stainless scrap exporters. Sub-Saharan Africa had similar characteristics to both Latin America and Southeast Asia, but opening yards there could wait for the moment.

My vision was coming together. The problem was that Mei, now in charge of Grand Metal as well as general finance, shipping, and admin, was "up to her eyeballs in alligators" and getting worn out.

"Steve, are you sure you want to do this now? The business is big enough!"

"Of course I'm sure. We've got to strike while the iron is hot and stake out our territory. POSCO is searching the world every day for stainless steel scrap; if we don't take this opportunity to establish operations in these markets, someone else will," I explained.

POSCO actually loved our strategy. I was proposing to mop up all of the stainless steel scrap in the world that was not being handled by professional recycling companies and deliver it directly to Korea. Because I would not face competition from global majors such as Nickelmet, I'd be able to provide the scrap at a discount while negotiating a healthy margin for Hartwell. It was a classic win–win.

"Why don't you just trade from those regions? Why do we have to open yards?" Mei pressed.

"Come on. You know the life of a trader is very vulnerable. We need infrastructure to secure a sustainable, long-term business," I argued, knowing that she understood this important point. Realizing she'd lost the business battle, she tried a personal approach.

"I barely see you as it is. I'm under a lot of pressure to set up finance and admin systems. It's not easy being over here working alone. I thought we were going to be together."

I felt for Mei, but at this moment I was singularly focused on Hartwell's expansion.

"Mei, I'm coming back as soon as I get these operations set up. In the meantime, I'll expand Nick's role to both Thailand and Malaysia; that will reduce your burden. The Philippines and Hong Kong yards are on autopilot anyway."

That should give Mei some peace and Nick will be pleased with the expanded opportunity, I thought. Malaysia wasn't making any money thus far, and I knew he was beginning to have doubts as to whether joining us had been worth it.

In my mind, I was well on my way to building a global empire. As much as I loved and trusted Mei, I just couldn't let her concerns hold me back. I was determined to plant our flag in as many locations as possible. *There's no way we can fail,* I told myself. I felt invincible.

I now became laser-focused on getting yards in the United States and Mexico opened as soon as possible. I got out the yellow pages for Guadalajara and Charlotte and started cold-calling. The calls weren't working well in Mexico, as I don't speak Spanish, so I came up with a novel idea. *Taxi drivers know their way around cities and are often very gregarious and bilingual people. Why don't I tap into that?* So I flew to Guadalajara and hired a taxi on a flat daily rate. I asked the driver to take me to all the scrap yards in town, offering a $10 tip for each company that met my approval. The driver made a couple hundred bucks and I surveyed the whole market. He even helped me translate at no extra charge.

In Charlotte I hit pay dirt pretty quickly. I happened into a portly gentleman named Mel Edelman. He was a leading stainless steel guy in the Carolinas and at one point had been a major player in the United States until he was allegedly defrauded and more or less wiped out. Mel was crawling back up the mountain when I encountered him.

As I had done in Asia, I tested the waters through trading and negotiated a deal to buy about twenty-five container loads from Mel during my first visit. He explained during the negotiation in a smooth southern drawl, "I'm happy to do business with y'all but need you to understand that you'll have to be competitive on price, and in the current market I need six hundred bucks a tuunn."

He'd just made the biggest mistake in trading. At all costs, you want the other guy to shout his price first. I paused, giving a few moments for consideration, took out a calculator, pretended to do some math with a furrowed brow, and finally responded with a touch of twang and a smile, "Mel, I think you know six hundred bucks is on the high side. We need to help each other out here. I wanna get some business started, so don't try to make a killin' on our first deal." I then paused for effect and finished, "The very best I kin do is pay ya $580. Now don't squeeze me anymore. This is long-term business we're talkin' about. Let's not haggle."

Secretly, I was doing an Irish jig in my brain, as the "high price" of $600 that Mel demanded was already $50 lower than my current sales price. Mel acquiesced; we were in business.

By negotiating down to $580, I was now making $70 a ton as a broker, a cool thirty-five grand. *Damn, I should have asked for more.*

It's important to understand the mentality of a trader and the necessity of haggling. Had I simply accepted his initial offer, he would have been embarrassed for proposing too low a price. By haggling, I made more money, of course, but of equal long-term importance I had given him face by making him feel that he'd achieved a good price. Buyer's or seller's remorse is a powerful emotion. *Give in too quickly and they'll feel bad about it every time and will try to get you back on the next deal. I know I do when it happens to me.* This was going to be a barnburner. If I could make seventy bucks a ton as a broker, and Mel was making another hundred or more in order to cover overhead and make a sensible profit, Hartwell was going to clean up down in Dixie.

Though I'd given up on JVs in Asia, I thought perhaps I could pull it off in the United States. *If a JV works out, I can keep moving with Latin America and Africa,* I reasoned. I was always looking around the next corner and searching for shortcuts to accelerate growth.

After checking out his background and verifying his story, I put on the table the idea of a joint venture. It was warmly received. Mel said all the right things and agreed that we could create a profitable and synergetic business. We got right into planning mode, and after several trips to Charlotte, the big picture was done. Still, the devil is in the details. Everything kept being renegotiated until one day I realized that unfortunately this was never going to work. Mel wasn't looking for a partnership; he was looking for a guarantee. Perhaps this was due to his previous debacle. Once again, it became clear to me that we needed to take control of our destiny and go it alone if we were going to create a valuable enterprise. We'd done it before in Asia, and the Southeast was going to be even easier—it was in my old backyard.

I informed Mel that Hartwell had decided to pass on the JV opportunity, but hoped we could continue to trade. Not yet certain where we would set up without Mel, I threw my efforts back into Mexico.

Guadalajara was the place. All I needed now was a Mexican general manager, and I believed I knew just the right guy—Sergio Ramirez Sanchez, the thirty-year-old head of scrap sales at the steel mill where I had bought our reusable. We'd worked closely together on this business and even though I had entertained the heck out of

him, he had always refused to give me any information about my competitors. I believed he had integrity. Sergio's other merit was that he worked for a stainless steel distributor, and thus knew who bought stainless in Mexico and where to find the scrap.

I knew from our tequila nights that Sergio didn't like his boss, to put it mildly, so I decided to test his character one suitably inebriated evening.

"Sergio, why haven't you ever sought to gain personal benefit from our business relationship?" I posed, hinting at the possibility.

"Well, Stephen, this kind of thing is very common in Mexico and even at our company, but I live my life by a higher code," he concluded, proudly pointing an index finger toward the heavens.

"I respect you, Sergio," I concluded, raising a glass in his honor.

Bingo! I thought: *an honest general manager.* I told Sergio my plans for Guadalajara and shared my taxi-driver market knowledge with him. He thought it was brilliant and didn't hesitate to say he was on board. The opportunity to step out from the shadows and run a business is very tempting, and I was able to offer him just that.

We now had our GM and soon incorporated as Inox Reciclables de Mexico—Stainless Recycling of Mexico. The incorporation certificate was flamboyant and grand with gold seals and red ribbons—definitely one to be hung on the wall.

Sergio next found us a warehouse, acquired equipment, and hired a team. We were very optimistic about having such an experienced general manager. *None of our other GMs had any stainless steel or scrap experience, and they all figured the business out,* I thought. *This is one of the few guys we've been able to find and hire with relevant work experience.* Sergio was raring to go. His energy manifested itself in a stutter that, combined with his accent, strained communication at times, but what he had to say generally made sense or seemed logical. The investment dollars, however, were getting higher. Everything was expensive in Mexico—much more so than we had anticipated. I started to consider that Sergio could be making money on the yard setup. Prices for individual items, such as a used forklift, didn't make sense, not to mention he bought almost everything from the same equipment dealer. Though concerned, I was in a hurry and wasn't going to let a few cost overruns slow us down. I also didn't want to challenge him or doubt his integrity so early on. Regardless, I had to get back to the United States and work on the Southeast strategy. On the way to the airport,

I shared with a friendly and talkative taxi driver: "You know, I love Guadalajara and think our company has a great opportunity here, but I feel my general manager might be ripping us off."

Silent for a moment, he then looked up, catching my eye in the rearview mirror before returning his gaze to the road ahead: "My friend, we have a saying in Mexico . . . if a man has hands, he takes. I wouldn't be surprised." That seemed a bit cynical, but I was still concerned.

⚬✀⚬

Throughout Mexico's early setup stage I had been quietly exploring the market in the US Southeast, and I was now ready for my return to the region. I didn't want to go head-to-head with Mel in Charlotte, so decided to open up in Darlington, South Carolina. Darlington was strategic because it was just down the street from NUCOR, one of America's largest steel companies, but not a producer of stainless steel. We felt we could easily get to know NUCOR's suppliers of iron scrap, and approach them to add stainless steel scrap to their trucks to deliver to us. The other strategic point was that trucking costs from Darlington to the port of Charleston were fairly low, and the availability of vessels heading to Asia was plentiful. Since most ships going from America to Asia are empty, freight is cheap. It currently cost less than $1,000 to ship a container from our yard all the way to Korea. The reverse trip would have cost three to four times that. Curiously, Nickelmet, the biggest player in the American market, once had an operation in Darlington, but closed it when it found it was uncompetitive in shipping to Pittsburgh. We were thus able to hire some experienced people who had been employed by that operation in the past. The fact that Nickelmet couldn't make it work might have been a warning sign, but with POSCO's desire to have market share in the region and our low-cost competitiveness, we believed we would prevail.

In short order we signed a lease, and Hartwell Atlantic LLC was born. The Darlington Holiday Inn Express would be my new pied-à-terre in the Deep South. To say that Darlington was a boring town would be an understatement. Its main cultural landmark was its prime location as the halfway point between New York and Miami on I-95. Thus, the lobby of the Holiday Inn Express was always overrun by

droves of tourists, their children, and their pets. I'd imagined the Deep South having weeping willows, plantations, southern gentlemen, and beautiful blond belles just like in *Gone with the Wind*. For the most part, what I discovered in the towns where we were operating were motels, strip malls, and chain restaurants. I wasn't hanging around in charming Charleston and Savannah or chilling at the beach in Hilton Head. Reality wasn't living up to the romance.

Anyway, I was focused on the business. We were able to hire a trader with stainless steel scrap experience who was a very nice guy but did admit in his interview that he "wasn't so good at math." *Whatever, a trader who is bad with figures; at least he has customer relationships.* We were also able to hire a very solid and reliable accountant, Janice, who turned out to be the most valuable employee at Hartwell Atlantic. She really held the business together over time. With a critical mix established, a buyer and a straight-shooting bean counter, I now decided that I needed to recruit someone with the leadership ability to grow Hartwell Atlantic into a regional player. I wanted multiple operations in towns like Savannah and Jacksonville. This person had better also be numerate to help keep an eye on my main trader.

I'd met an Australian in Hong Kong, Rod Smithers, who was an equity analyst for a London investment firm with an educational background in accounting. Rod had expressed interest in joining up with me, had some knowledge of exchange-traded commodity markets, and was bored to tears cranking out research reports. I also believed the thought of traveling around the world on an entrepreneurial adventure sounded pretty good to him. Wanderlust is a very common characteristic of Australians.

Rod signed up and left for South Carolina. He found a reasonably priced house with three bedrooms, so we could stay there as well. On my first visit I drove through a small forest, across a stream, and down a winding dirt road that led to our Civil War–era farmhouse. It was a neat old white-paneled place, with a large backyard that abutted the stream—very pleasant during the day, but at night the floorboards creaked and the wind whistled up and down the old chimney, rattling the windows. Janice explained that "Crazy Rod" had rented the local haunted house. I'm not too proud to admit that I spent the rest of my South Carolina nights at the Holiday Inn Express. None of our other employees would stay there, either, and Rod's girlfriend was none too impressed when she came to visit.

We had now opened seven facilities in seven countries over a period of eighteen months. With total capital expenditure crossing $1 million, my adrenaline was pumping. So was Mei's. One evening in the Darlington scrap yard, after everyone had gone home, I stayed behind surveying the equipment. A hot wind kicked up clouds of dust into swirling cyclones that raced among piles of inventory filtering the sun's setting rays. *The operation looks good,* I thought. I called Mei to give her an update. She listened silently for a few moments as I rattled on about our progress, until she'd had enough.

"Steve! Do you have any idea how much cash we are going to need if all of these facilities hit your volume targets?" Mei shouted into the phone.

I was irritated by her tone and snapped back, "Of course I do! Don't worry about it; the banks will cover everything. We have no long-term debt. It's just inventory finance, and HSBC understands our business."

Mei snorted. "You're always so damn confident that everything will go our way. Even if the banks do give us the money we need, we are totally out of control. Malaysia is a month behind on its accounts, Mexico has yet to give us one clean accounting book, and I'm spending half my time in China arguing with Madame Yuen!"

"Look, Mei, we'll clean up the accounting. That's not what's important. The margin is there. We know the yards' purchase volume and roughly know their overheads. They will make lots of money. You'll see."

"Well, I'm not seeing the cash flow!" Mei shouted stubbornly.

"Well, when I'm done, you're going to have so much cash you're not gonna be able to count it! I'm working my ass off over here. I call you just to share a little good news, and you shove all this down my throat!" I retorted.

"You think I'm just sitting here doing nothing? You think you're the only one working hard? Everyone in the office thinks you're crazy. We can't keep up with your ridiculous pace," Mei fired back.

"That's why you're in charge of accounting, and I'm in charge of the vision. I'm the boss in this company, I set the pace, and now's probably a good time to let you know that I'm going to South Africa next week to crack open that market!" I was now deliberately pushing her buttons.

Mei exploded, "You can do whatever you want, but I'm controlling the cash and you're not getting a dime!" *Click.* She hung up.

Yeah right, I thought. *I'm the boss and I can do whatever I want. She's just lucky enough to be going along for the ride.*

In my mind, I had a vision and an organizational structure that I was building, and once all the pieces were in place, the glue would dry and Hartwell Pacific would be one of the top five players in the world. This wasn't a fool's dream. If we could execute the plan, I knew we would be in that position. Also, whereas the others were at one another's throats fighting for market share and profits in Europe or in major US cities, we were in regions that they had not yet entered. The market size in our regions would not justify two players, so one dominant company would serve as a meaningful barrier to entry. *We have the potential for oligopoly, or even monopoly, profits,* I imagined.

⟨❈⟩

I was now doing the "Hartwell commute": Hong Kong–Los Angeles–Guadalajara–Atlanta–Darlington–Atlanta–Chicago–Hong Kong. Throw in Thailand, Malaysia, the Philippines, China, Korea, and now South Africa, and I was on the road at least 75 percent of the time and logging well over two hundred thousand miles a year. I'd wake up in hotel rooms and it would take me a few moments to figure out what country I was in. I slept with a notepad next to my bed and would scribble solutions in the dark to problems that I'd dealt with in my sleep. Showers were rushed affairs as I nervously tried to get all the soap off so I could get out and get going. I remember making a New Year's resolution that year to sleep less. *The fantastic thing about having business on both sides of the globe is that we have an opportunity to make money and expand twenty-four hours a day,* I thought. At thirty years old, I felt like I was running out of time. It didn't occur to me that this pace would most likely put me in an early grave.

Thriving on a transfusion of adrenaline, coffee, alcohol, and cigarettes, I was able to push myself beyond my natural limits and on to South Africa. We needed to get started with at least a trading relationship there in preparation for our future move into that market. It would also add needed trading income to plug any holes in our recycling operations and help pay overheads. Though Mei and I eagerly awaited a reasonable paycheck, scaling up wasn't just about greed. The more income sources we could create, the better management we could hire, the better equipment we could buy, and the better we

could run our company. This was a good argument for opening more businesses, but of course multiple simultaneous failures would lead to almost certain bankruptcy. *As long as everything doesn't go wrong at the same time, we will survive.*

⌒⌯⌒

I made a reservation at the famous Westcliff Hotel in Johannesburg and got the concierge's help copying the *scrap* section from the yellow pages. I then got on the horn and called every listing. Using my normal cold-calling routine, I found the leading stainless steel recycler in Johannesburg. The company is called Metalmet. I was proud to find out that its president had heard of me and Hartwell Pacific. People around the world were talking about us. *We must be making progress!*

I booked a ticket on South African Airlines' nonstop flight from New York's JFK to JoBerg—the longest flight over water in the world.

I boarded the plane, exhausted as usual, and took my upper-deck seat in business class. A heavyset gentleman worked his way into the seat across the aisle as I worked on a beer. When we pushed back from the gate, the big guy started having a heart attack. He signaled for help, and the flight attendant made an urgent announcement looking for a doctor. The plane came to a jolting halt and returned to the gate, where paramedics boarded and an ambulance was brought alongside. They stabilized him in his seat with nitro, then heaved him off the plane on a gurney—not an easy task considering the steep and narrow stairs from the upper deck. I was pretty shaken up. I had looked at the guy's face as they pulled him out of his chair and wondered if that might be my fate someday.

After a few concerned minutes we were informed that the gentleman was okay and on his way to the hospital. The plane pushed back once again from the terminal, and as we crossed the Atlantic from Brazil over to Africa, a dark thought came to mind: *That was one lucky guy. If he'd had his heart attack out here I'm afraid he wouldn't have made it.* What happens when people die on planes? Do they just throw a blanket over the corpse's head and keep serving breakfast?

I arrived in Johannesburg in the morning, and was greeted at the airport by Anthony Stewart, one of the MDs of Metalmet, a very cheery and affable English South African with shaggy blond hair.

"You can check in to your hotel later. My partners are waiting for us; let's get right on to the operation," he suggested.

I was hurting from the flight, longing for a shower and a nap, but pressed on. We started with a tour of Metalmet's facility, which was impressive. The security was over the top. Johannesburg is a famously crime-ridden city, and I understand why they would have such security. What was odd, though, was that the facility had electric fences inside the perimeter as well; it didn't seem very safe. I guess the company wanted to keep people from getting close to the fence and throwing metal over, or it was meant to be a further barrier for anyone trying to get in.

We went inside the office and met the other two main principals. We got on well and negotiated a nice piece of business, giving Hartwell a $25,000 profit. Not bad for a first meeting. That gave me a momentary boost of energy. As we talked, a loud whistling alarm went off. I was a bit startled.

"What's that?" I asked.

Anthony nonchalantly commented with a chuckle, "Oh, one of the workers probably bumped into the electric fence."

Ah, I guess safety doesn't have the same priority in these parts, I thought to myself sarcastically. It was time for lunch. They didn't mention where we were going, but just noted that I'd like it. We pulled up to the restaurant and I immediately recognized that it was probably not famous for its cuisine; it was a strip club. I was numb to these things by now, as this is also a very common lunchtime activity in the Deep South and Mexico. So there I sat, midday on a Wednesday, eating my surprisingly good cheeseburger as the girls went through their routines. The music was loud so we couldn't really talk, which was fine by me as I was out of my mind with jet lag. The beers flowed. These guys were the fastest drinkers I'd ever seen, and they were very much encouraging me to keep up. There were lots of jokes and snickering: "Welcome to South Africa! I hope you're enjoying your safari." My head was starting to feel heavy when the scene suddenly turned nasty. There was a stunning black African woman doing a dance. Three very big white guys came in, sat down on stools right by the stage, and started yelling insults at her. They used the word *kaffir,* which I recognized is a very derogatory term. She kept dancing. Next, one of them threw a beer on the girl. She rushed back off the stage. I was angry as hell.

"Why doesn't management throw assholes like that out?" I complained.

Anthony replied in a warning voice, "Those are Afrikaans farm boys. You don't mess with them. Look at their ankles."

Each had one of the biggest pistols I'd ever seen strapped to his leg. What had started as a mildly entertaining diversion to my manic life had turned ugly. It was time to get the hell out of Dodge.

We left the dark strip club and as the door swung open, the bright midday sun hit me right in the eyes. Everyone was a bit wobbly. I was totally drained. *Great. This is over. Get me to my hotel so I can pass out.* But I was not that fortunate. One of the guys piped up, "Let's do one more pub—a cleansing ale!"

It was about three o'clock on a workday. I guess everyone was taking the afternoon off. I desperately wanted to leave but had just made twenty-five grand off these guys and there was the promise of regular monthly business. *Suck it up,* I thought.

The next place was a normal bar, but my new suppliers were practically chugging. Beer after beer was passed my way. The cheering was constant and my head was pounding. By the time evening rolled around I had no idea how many I'd had. I'd lost count at ten, and there were plenty more. The room started spinning. *This has gone a bit too far,* I thought. I excused myself and staggered toward the bathroom, barely making it to the stall before vomiting. I splashed cold water on my face, rinsed out my mouth, and returned to the table, where I was handed a fresh beer. *Okay, last one.* Finally, mercifully, it was time to go home. I scarfed down a sandwich of some sort and demanded that Anthony drive me back to the Westcliff. I was out of the shower and in bed within five minutes, asleep before turning out the light.

I awoke early in the morning to prepare for my nine o'clock flight to Hong Kong. Hung over, jet-lagged, exhausted, I stared into the bathroom mirror and was shocked by my appearance. Deep dark circles ringed my eyes, and my overgrown hair was flecked with gray. *Maybe Mei's right. Perhaps we are moving too fast.* I leaned in close, trying to find the young kid who'd arrived in Hong Kong in 1993, but couldn't.

14

TYPHOON SEASON

Already worn down by my over-commitment to global expansion, I now suffered a great loss. My grandfather, whose encouragement and truisms had guided me throughout my life, passed away at the age of ninety-six.

I jetted home from Hong Kong for the funeral service. I was nervous but could not stop thinking about other things. Mexico, Malaysia, POSCO, people, systems, the nickel market—it all hammered my brain, not allowing me the peace I needed to mourn properly. Reality couldn't set in. I had no experience with death. This was just another problem, a family issue that was serious more than sad.

Once inside the funeral home, I was led by my father toward an empty reception area, and then walked alone up to a table framed by large white bouquets. Photos of Granddad's life, memorabilia, and a wooden jar holding his ashes were spread out on the table in front of me. I just couldn't connect with that jar, couldn't understand that it could possibly contain my granddad, but then I glanced to the left. Among the memorabilia was a wooden cane that I'd given him when

I was a teenager. It had a carved handle in the form of the head of a bulldog, and he'd gotten a kick out of it, using it every day. I picked it up. Sensing him, I smelled it, trying to find a memory, and then broke down. My grief rushed out in an uncontrollable flow, but when it dried out, the healing process began. I was beginning to mourn my granddad and had released a mountain of tension. An entrepreneur's world can be a lonely one, and my family and close friends had served as critical pillars of support for handling the strain that my life had acquired. I had just lost one of them.

On the flight back to Hong Kong after a few warm days with my extended family, I looked out the window at the soft white cloud formations. I could feel Granddad's presence. I still get that sensation many years hence. For late-afternoon, north–south flights I book a window seat to watch the sunset. He almost always comes to mind. My grandfather is alive with me.

I've mentioned that Hartwell would survive as long as everything didn't go wrong at once. This principle was about to be sorely tested.

⌒◈⌒

I threw myself back into the business. Granddad would have wanted that. "Get back to work. And don't forget to turn out the lights!" he'd have said.

The business had been running well and making a decent profit, but we were having frequent customs problems in China with Grand Metal and the cost of solving them was skyrocketing. Mei explained the situation to me: "Steve, I don't trust Madame Yuen. Our cargo is stuck in customs regardless of what she asks us to pay—$10,000 here, $25,000 there. These unexpected expenses are adding up!"

More cargo continued to arrive, but it was the same story. This went on for a couple more months, until customs was satisfied with their cut, and then finally our containers started being released. We jumped into action, processing the material and preparing it for sale. Throughout all of these delays and headaches, though, it turned out we had one nice piece of luck. The nickel and stainless markets were jumping up big-time, meaning that our inventory had actually appreciated in value while it languished in the customs warehouse. Delays had in fact been making us a lot of money. We realized we'd gotten lucky and that the market had risen, but those questionable

one-off costs and delays would have killed us had the market been falling.

Seeing all this cash flying around and fat margins, Madame Yuen was absolutely squealing with delight and now pushing us to buy more. Unfortunately, she was getting greedier and greedier, finding any way to increase benefits that were paid to her while arguing endlessly against paying our workers well or spending money on anything if the funds did not first slip through her fingers. The situation came to a head when one day, our accountant phoned Mei and explained that Madame Yuen had just sold some of our material on her own without our approval or written consent, a move explicitly forbidden by our JV agreement. Mei went to China immediately and confronted her. Madame Yuen argued, "It was a good price compared with the last sales you guys made. I could do a better job managing the business myself!"

"Of course your sale looks good against historical prices. That's because the market is rising. I'm in the middle of negotiating with other customers at much higher prices. I guess I have to drop those deals now!" Mei fired back.

Madame Yuen was either the indirect beneficiary of the transaction or completely stupid, but either way, she was outside her authority. Mei realized Hartwell was no longer in control of the situation and feared Madame Yuen's greed would be unlimited. She owned the warehouse, and all the employees were scared because they knew about her father's background, so she had the power. We also recalled that it was her friend the judge who'd helped us get our licenses, which were normally very difficult to get. Even though we had contracts and agreements, we would not have found much support in the local legal system. *You don't have rights in China. You either have the power to do something or you don't,* we began to realize. It was at this moment that we understood that round-round Madame Yuen held us by the short and curlies.

Mei, still smarting from our clashes over my manic expansion plans, had a clear idea of what she felt we should do: Get the hell out of China. I totally agreed.

We had a strategy session about how to play our cards. Without being able to rely on the paperwork, we were forced to live by our wits and play off Madame Yuen's greed. A scheme was hatched; we knew there was no way of getting out of the joint venture and keeping our equipment, but we could at least grab our cash. Mei explained

to Madame Yuen that we had the opportunity to purchase more material and needed all the cash in the business to finance it. She took the
bait and helped us get it out of China, which at that time had very
strict currency controls. She no doubt took a nice cut on the foreign
exchange transaction, but didn't realize that we were the ones who
were playing her. There actually wasn't an order for more steel and
there would never be another.

We left Madame Yuen with her share of the profits and all of the
equipment, and walked away with the rest. Madame Yuen's reign was
over. Good-bye, Grand Metal—only about nine months from beginning to end. Thanks for the memories.

I had learned a valuable lesson. In the developing world, if you're
not in control of a joint venture physically, your position and value will
rapidly weaken. Better to keep partners as uninvolved as possible. And
if you must have active partners, the best way to keep them honest is
not contracts but the belief that they will make more money with you
than without you. Other than our lucky trading windfall, our foray
into China had been a bust.

✂

The Chinese have a saying in Mandarin: *Yi bo wei ping, yi bo you
qi*. Just as one wave subsides, the next one builds.

We had handled the first with deft aplomb.

✂

In the midst of dealing with the disappointment of being messed
around in China, problems started popping up in Malaysia. We could
feel the current pulling at our ankles, back to the sea.

Our company in Kuala Lumpur was doing more and more volume, and the profit margin was okay. The problem we had was that the
inventory kept growing on the books, but our people kept telling us
that the yard was almost empty—trouble. Our profits would not be
reaching our pockets, as our inventory had been leaking out the door.
We searched for every possible security breach, from people climbing
over the fence to people digging under it, but couldn't find the answer.

Convinced that the scrap wasn't walking out by itself, Nick and
I slept at the KL yard armed with golf clubs, waiting for the night

raiders to come. We sat in the operations manager's office, dozing in and out of sleep, peering into the yard through a small window. Night bugs danced wildly at the edges of the soft light from the security lamps where it disappeared into the darkness, and crickets yawned on as we strained to listen for any movements. The question that we hadn't considered was: *What will we do if we are outnumbered or outarmed and the police don't show up?* This was obviously a dangerous plan, if not plain stupid, but we were furious and determined to catch these bastards.

Nick cracked a couple of Heinekens and handed me one.

"This is great. We gonna spend every night at the scrap yard?" he quipped.

"I suppose we can alternate," I chimed in, breaking into a tired laugh.

Nick joined in, taking a deep swig from his can. We reminisced about our lives in Asia, the twists and turns that ended up with the two of us sitting in a scrap yard in Malaysia at two o'clock in the morning. I recalled the time we met, and what serious twenty-four-year-olds we had both been. The night droned on.

We awoke with stiff necks to the sound of the local roosters and the sunrise coming through the blindless windows. We toured the yard—nothing missing.

We beefed up security, hiring an extra night watchman. But like the wily mouse that always eats the cheese and never gets caught, our Malaysian bandits had the same tenacity. Even though we watched the paperwork carefully and surveyed the perimeter daily, inventory kept leaking out.

Next, we installed surveillance cameras. After discovering more missing inventory, we reviewed the tapes. Eureka, we found the perpetrators. A medium-sized man wearing a balaclava and holding a long stick walked into view of one of the cameras. He came closer, looking straight at us. I almost sensed a smile as he swung the stick and the camera went dead.

I stormed into the conference room where Nick and our finance manager, Annie, were discussing something.

"So much for $5,000 worth of surveillance equipment!" I complained bitterly. "And where were the f---ing security guards?"

Nick called the night watchmen into the conference room to hear their explanations.

"We not see or hear nothing" was the lead guy's reply.

"Wrong answer. You're both fired!" I exploded, knowing that there was no way they hadn't seen or heard anything. Had he explained that he had been threatened and tried to be of some assistance to us, I would have felt and acted differently.

Perhaps cameras serve as a deterrent in some ways, but they are obviously no match for a balaclava, a bamboo pole, and a well-placed threat or bribe to the security guards.

But how had they been getting into the yard without leaving a trace? And how did they get the scrap over the eight-foot-high, heavy metal fence? The answer was too simple to imagine. We had put up our fence with bolts, and at night one guy would simply climb over, unbolt a panel, together with his friends help themselves to our metal, and then put the fence back together. We learned the hard way to permanently weld all the bolts shut.

In the meantime, although we couldn't find the major perpetrator, we caught a small thief, a worker stealing from our warehouse. External theft was frustrating, but fraud or an "inside job" is the hardest thing to face in business. For an entrepreneur, nothing could be a more personal affront.

Nick informed me about the situation and, because I was in town, asked me to be in the meeting when we fired the worker. I knew him personally and had always been cordial, polite, and respectful, as I was with all our employees. We'd treated him well and even promoted him to an assistant manager position. I entered the conference room where the worker and Nick were waiting.

"Rahim, how are you?" I started, trying to connect.

"Fine, sir," he replied sheepishly, not looking up.

Niceties over, I confronted him with the evidence. Rahim couldn't deny it. I asked point-blank: "Why did you do this to me? Did I deserve to be treated like this?"

I was incensed that he would not reward our support and respect with loyalty.

He paused for a second, shrugged, and without looking up replied, "No, you didn't deserve that. You've been good to me. But I needed the money. I'm sorry." Then silence.

In that moment, my frustration and rage quickly changed into understanding, and then dismay. There was really nothing I could say

to that. He did need the money. He was poor and desperate. Would I have given him money if he'd asked me for it? Probably not, knowing that this would create a waterfall of requests from my laborers, who all needed money. I was upset and angry, even hurt, but did not call the police. I didn't want to exact revenge, though perhaps I should have set an example by having him publicly arrested. I didn't see how putting a poor village peasant behind bars would solve my problems, assuming the Malaysian police would have done anything in the first place.

I called all the office employees and the operations manager into the main reception area. Once assembled, I started to pace, emotion and theory flowing out in the form of an impromptu speech.

"We all know about the problems we're having with missing inventory. We have a good business model, but I can tell you we won't survive if we can't hold on to our inventory," I started, my confidence building. I searched the room for acknowledgment of what I had just said before continuing my monologue. "We can blame Rahim, and surely he's a bad apple, but I can also take a share of the responsibility. We left our wallet on the ground! If you leave your wallet on the ground, you can't blame the person who picks it up; you should blame yourself!" I punched out, continuing to pace back and forth. "I figure that out of every ten people, three are angels, beyond reproach, and six are solidly good people who, if treated fairly and with respect, will operate honorably. Unfortunately, one in ten is unscrupulous and, no matter what we do on our side, will seek to maximize his own benefit with no regard for us. These are good odds, but the key here is avoiding the bad 10 percent at all costs. Of course, I'm certain you are all angels," I added, lightening the heavy moment. "But as our ranks grow, we can't depend on having only angels, so we need a system that protects the company against this reality. As we build it, please understand why it exists and help me keep our wallet in a safe place."

I finished to total silence, but was confident that my message had been clear and well received. I did not expect thundering applause. As I always did after such meetings, I then went around the room and shook everyone's hand, catching his or her eye and making a personal connection. I would repeat this lecture with every one of our management teams. The response was very positive. Slowly, professional systems and controls started forming.

It appeared to be typhoon season. Just as we had absorbed the force of the last wave, I could see the crest of the next one forming. I received a call from Mr. Ko, our agent in Korea.

"You'd better get up here. POSCO has three containers of manganese steel sitting in their yard, worth about 25 percent of the value of stainless."

I took the red-eye from Kuala Lumpur, arriving in Seoul the next morning with little sleep. I had my staff in Hong Kong trace the container numbers. Sure enough, they matched shipments made from our own operation in Guadalajara.

Arriving at the plant in the southern city of Pohang, I was humiliated as the head of purchasing, Mr. Kwon, and the gray-haired plant general manager, Mr. Kang, escorted us to inspect Hartwell's substandard shipment. *What the hell is this?* I thought upon viewing the rusting pile of metal.

"I am terribly sorry, General Manager Kang. Our people are well trained, and this material came from our own yard. This must be a case of internal fraud," I explained with my head bowed, eyes pinned to the ground.

Mr. Kang cast a doubtful eye in my direction and lectured: "This quality is totally unacceptable! If it happens again, you are out! We don't do this kind of business. It is precisely why Purchasing General Manager Kwon is supposed to restrict suppliers to only the most reputable."

He then turned and walked away without shaking our hands, leaving the three of us bowing out of sync and stammering apologies in our own languages.

Mr. Ko explained on the way back to the hotel that although the general manager seemed very hostile, he was secretly supportive of finding a reasonable solution and understood our situation; he just couldn't voice it publicly.

"This is the Korean way, Mr. Greer. He remains a friend of Hartwell. This is not a catastrophic problem from the mill's perspective. No need for explanation, just sincere apology."

Completely dejected, I got on the phone with Nick.

"Can you get over to Mexico and find out what's going on? I'm in Korea and we are clearly getting worked over."

Thus far, Nick had the most fraud and security experience, and I had a dozen other matters to deal with in Asia. Not to mention, had I

told Mei I was heading back to North America, I feared she would have called it quits. We barely ever saw each other anymore, and that strain was building. I felt lucky to have Nick around. He could at least figure out what was going on, and then I could come over and help find a long-term solution.

Nick was a brilliant sleuth. He hired a private investigator to tail Sergio and found some software to check his e-mails. As it turned out, my early fears about Sergio Ramirez Sanchez were confirmed. Together with a supplier, he'd been cheating us, buying manganese steel as stainless and keeping the difference. The scam was simple, but idiotic. He'd book the shoddy inventory at our company as stainless and then ship it to Korea. He must have hoped POSCO wouldn't notice, and that he could continue his scam indefinitely, but POSCO was not stupid and it didn't take long to catch the rat. We showed Sergio the door, and Nick held the reins until we could figure out what to do next. Sergio was furious.

"You will regret this!" he threatened.

Amazing! I thought. *Caught red-handed, fired but not prosecuted, and he's angry?* In fact, he sued us for wrongful termination, and the labor council required us to pay him an attractive settlement. Could someone explain this logic?

Sergio was now gone, but our problems with fraud continued. I hired a fifty-year-old guy named Humberto Escuerda to take over the purchasing part of Sergio's job but not to be GM. He had lived in America in the 1960s and spoke perfect English. He also had experience in scrap metal and in stainless steel but was unemployed and basically begged me for a chance. He'd promised me the world in a deep, lazy voice.

"Stephen, if you hire me, I can deliver the whole market. I know everyone. It'll be easy. I've always just needed someone like you with the resources and know-how to support me."

He was a very jovial guy, with a pot belly and a mouth full of neglected teeth that were deeply stained from decades of smoking. He'd break easily into a leg-slapping belly laugh that would leave his jowls wiggling. I used to chuckle when he'd pull in to work in his beat-up 1980s Oldsmobile station wagon, whose odometer had long since stopped counting. He'd turn the key off at the ignition, and the old car would rumble and sputter for a minute or so before giving up, sighing in its parking space. I enjoyed his company, but his life was

another Mexican tragedy of being screwed over by this guy and that guy. His son had problems and I tried to offer advice to a strained father. I was used to all these stories.

Humberto had been working for us for a few months when I visited the company on one of my global tours. Andrea, our accountant, explained: "Everyone in the market knows Humberto is getting kickbacks and running some business through a middleman."

We gathered some evidence and caught him in a lie.

"Stephen, I barely know that guy. I rarely ever talk to him," he responded emotionally.

"Then why does your mobile phone record show fifteen calls to him in the last week?" I shouted, ending the debate. "You'd better come clean if you want me to consider giving you a second chance."

Of course, I had no intention of doing so. He started to cry softly and then totally broke down, covering his face with his hands, the fat on his body trembling with the deep sobs. Unable to watch a man twenty years my senior in such a condition, I put my arm on his back.

"What's up, Humberto?" I asked with concern.

He explained morosely, "I'm sorry, but I desperately needed money because my wife"—a nice lady whom I'd met on a couple of occasions—"has cancer and needs surgery or she'll die."

Humberto really broke down when he spoke that last word. He further explained that if she wanted to get the surgery for free from the government, she would have to wait in line, wasting critical time, and they wouldn't give her the best treatment available.

"How much are we talking about?" I asked.

"One hundred thousand pesos," he replied, at the time around $10,000.

I thought about it for a moment and even wondered if this was a con. But his tears were not faked and I considered that I would steal if I had to in order to save Mei's life, though I certainly would have tried the high road first. I came up with an idea that I hoped would solve the problem. I felt bad for him and his wife. I also needed an experienced trader and with Sergio out, we had a short bench and were desperate for scrap. I was very concerned at this time about how we were going to handle the purchasing.

"All right, Humberto. I'll pay for the surgery personally and you pay me back over the next two years deducting from your paycheck. But I pay the doctor and hospital directly by check," I offered. He

hugged and thanked me. "And you better walk a very straight line at work," I added.

"I will. I will. I never meant to break your trust. I was desperate. I'm sorry, Stephen," he ended.

I confirmed that his wife truly needed the surgery. I was now experiencing firsthand the kind of good money could do. I was proud to be able to help. Mei and I agreed that in the midst of all this bad news, at least we had done something admirable. *Good things come to good people,* or so we hoped. Humberto's wife had the surgery and survived, and he continued to work for us.

However, about six months later a supplier came forward and explained that Humberto was ripping us off again. He was demanding kickbacks from them and they were tired of it. We looked into it, and several employees confirmed separately that this was the case. Furious, I confronted Humberto.

"I saved your wife's life. How could you do this?" I pressed, trying to gain an understanding.

He wept, apologizing and explaining that he needed the money for his son. The bullshit flowed along with his tears until I'd had enough.

"You're out! Forget about the money for your wife. That was charity to her and I'll never regret saving a life, but we're done."

Remarkably, he begged for another chance.

"Steve, believe me—"

"No chance, Humberto. You're out," I interrupted, this time pointing toward the door.

I watched his slumped, six-foot frame shuffle out to his dust-painted station wagon and then disappear through the gates. This is my last image of him.

This one really hit me personally and made me think deeply about a story I was once told about a scorpion and a turtle:

A scorpion and a turtle are standing by the edge of a river, the turtle preparing to cross. The scorpion, also wanting to cross the river, asks the turtle if he might hitch a ride on his back, as scorpions can't swim. The turtle responds slowly, in a deep turtle voice: "You are a scorpion. You will sting me and I will drown."

The scorpion, ever the smooth salesman, counters quickly: "I'm not stupid. If I sting you, we'll both drown."

This makes sense to the turtle and, being kindhearted, he allows the scorpion onto his back and heads out across the river. Halfway across, with a violent thrust of his tail, the scorpion stings the turtle in the back of the head. The turtle cries out in pain: "You fool. Now we'll both drown! Why would you do this?"

The scorpion ponders the conundrum and then calmly and politely replies: "I am very sorry. But you see, I can't help it. It's my nature."

15

DON'T DO BUSINESS WITH FRIENDS UNLESS YOU ARE PREPARED TO LOSE THEM

In the face of relentless challenges, we decided to divide our problems and conquer them one at a time. Mexico was up first. Though the overall situation was not catastrophic, Mexico was taking a lot of senior management's time and energy, and had yet to show any bottom-line profits. However, in our minds, the natural market margins remained very healthy and the potential huge, so we decided to stick it out.

After dealing with Sergio, Nick had returned to Asia, where his financial interests were, and Mei and I continued running around the globe lighting fires under people's butts in some places and putting fires out in others. We clearly recognized that Mexico needed full-time supervision by a senior management person. Shorthanded, we decided to move Rod, the Australian, down from the United States to take control of the business. Hopefully, he could have a positive impact.

I let Rod settle in for a few months, and then went to review progress. Unfortunately, things had not improved and in some ways had even digressed. As I toured the yard I smelled marijuana. One of the workers was swinging playfully from a rope that had been fastened to a broken-down crane. He actually waved to me with a big smile on his face. As far as I could tell this was the most unproductive bunch of people I'd ever seen. They weren't just smoking on the job, which was forbidden at our Asian operations, they were doing drugs! This was nothing like what I'd experienced in Asia, where our workers were diligent and though often burdened by poverty were generally clean living. Things in Guadalajara were clearly out of control, and there was still little to no management oversight.

It was time to make some major changes. First, our accountant advised us to change payday from Friday to Saturday, as the workers would all go out and get drunk on Friday night and barely half of them would show up for work the next day. *Why didn't I know about all of this? Rod is gonna have to go and we're going to have to get an ass kicker of a general manager in here.* Terminating Rod's employment was hard for me at the time. I liked him a lot but had no choice.

With Rod now out, Nick, Mei, and I moved to Guadalajara ourselves to get things under control and to make a big push at reviving our Latin American fortunes. We found a company in a state of total chaos, and the accounts were a mess. In the end, we had to replace the entire local management team. I then visited almost every one of our suppliers, boasting about my vision for the new Inox Reciclables de Mexico and its plan for market leadership, but we would now have to deliver on that promise. It was hands-on work, seven days a week, at least twelve hours a day, but there was a great deal of camaraderie. We were early to rise and in the yard by 7:30 AM. Barely taking a break for lunch, the three of us would line up on stools at the neighborhood taco stand and stuff down tacos before heading back to work. My personal record was eight. The *carnitas* ones were delectable. Nick could be found marching around in blue jeans, cowboy boots, and a baseball hat clinging to a bullhorn, directing the movement of tangled piles of metal. I also threw myself into the mix. I remember asking a worker, "How long will it take to move that pile of scrap that's causing the bottleneck?"

It was a relatively small pile. He took a careful look, swaying side-to-side, trying to make a fair estimation.

"One and a half days" was his reply.

I argued passionately, "It can't take more than half a day, maximum!"

"Loco!" was his response, making circles at his temple with his index finger.

I put on overalls and gloves and grabbed three workers. We cleared the pile in about four hours, but I learned an important lesson on worker safety that day: Don't wear fancy loafers when working in a scrap yard. I dropped a piece of steel and broke my toe. Nevertheless, it was important to get our hands dirty and start leading by example.

Most evenings after the majority of the employees had left, Nick and I would knock back a beer and smoke butts waiting for Mei and the girls in the accounting department to finish up around 9 PM, after which the three of us and a well-deserving employee or two would roll into our favorite steak house for some prime beef and a bottle of red.

No matter how frustrated or exhausted we got, we were always able to make light of our Mexican predicament. Nick had been to a bullfight one time and, reflecting on our struggles, relayed a story.

"The picadors were stabbing this defenseless bull, blood leaking from its wounds, as the crowd leapt cheering to its feet. Next the matador lined up the exhausted and wobbling animal for the kill. Unbowed, the brave bull made a last valiant yet fruitless charge, only to meet the matador's sword with the nape of his neck. It was at this moment that I realized: We're the f---ing bull!"

The year 2000 was fast approaching—the new millennium. Mei and I had paid a deposit for a trip to Zimbabwe to attend a black-tie New Year's party at the famed Victoria Falls Hotel with some close friends from Hong Kong. This was to be followed by a canoeing safari down the Zambezi River; an opportunity of a lifetime and a millennium party for the record books. Nick had a romantic trip to Thailand all lined up with his girlfriend. None of these grand plans would come to fruition. The three of us ended up working in the scrap yard in Guadalajara until just past 10 PM on New Year's Eve. We planned to celebrate at midnight at one of our favorite restaurants. Unfortunately, we did not have time to back to the hotel to change, as the streets were clogged with traffic. We arrived at the door covered in dust, and headed to the bathroom to wash up before being seated. The maître d' then escorted us to a small table in the very back of the restaurant. People glared at us disapprovingly. They were dressed to the nines and we

were in dirty jeans and khakis, Nick in his signature cowboy boots. We ordered a bottle of champagne and the mariachi band played on as we toasted the end of the twentieth century. This was not as romantic as Victoria Falls, but I knew that someday it would be a very fond memory—a battle memory.

⌒◇◇◯◯◦

Having survived the overblown Y2K global meltdown, we set out to find a GM for our Mexican business. There was a young man named Miguel Calderon who was a maintenance contractor for our industrial equipment. He was a big, nice-looking guy with a well-trimmed mustache and goatee, his hair carefully spiked with copious amounts of gel. He was always smartly dressed in pressed slacks and black leather shoes. Miguel worked for his father, a very kind and gentle man who had started his life as an abandoned child in Mexico City. The story was that his father had lived on the streets selling Chiclets, small packets of chewing gum, and ultimately was given a job as a floor sweeper by an executive of the Ford Motor Company. Señor Calderon worked his way up the ladder, ultimately taking charge of a production line. He became an expert in hydraulics and finally started his own business in Guadalajara distributing and maintaining them for Vickers, the well-regarded British company. It was not a big business, but I deeply admired the gusto and determination it must have taken to overcome his hardships. I try to remember that story every time I walk by a street urchin selling trinkets or cleaning car windows in a poor city. Most of us should admit to being members of the lucky sperm club.

I got on well with Miguel. He was a genius who could design equipment on the back of a napkin, as well as build it himself. He never needed a calculator for anything. At the same time he was very charming and affable.

Miguel seemed to understand business well and took a great interest in our company. He told me exactly what we needed to do to turn things around, and I agreed with his ideas.

"Esteban, you need to kick some ass around here. The inmates have taken over the asylum," he joked. "You need systems and rules. I'd fire 75 percent of the people working here. You need better equipment and a totally different layout!" he continued seriously. I needed this. I needed that.

"Okay, Miguel. I totally agree, and you're exactly the guy we need to do it!"

I proposed that he join us as our GM for Mexico. We both knew that this would be a much better opportunity for him than staying in the family business. I thought so highly of Miguel that I imagined he could be head of Latin America and even help us on a global basis once we got Mexico spinning cash. The only obstacle was that his father needed his help with the family business.

"I want to join you, Stephen, but my father is against it and very worried about what will happen to the business if I leave," he explained.

"Tell your father that if he ever needs help we'll be very supportive, but this is too good an opportunity for you to pass up. It is, Miguel," I emphasized convincingly.

Miguel went away promising to see what he could do and thanking me for my confidence in him.

"I know I can do it, Stephen. It would take me six months to get this place going, and the market potential is big. I know lots of places around the country to get scrap, even Guatemala. Mucho dinero to be made," he said, rubbing his thumb and forefingers together with a big smile.

After much discussion, Miguel received his father's blessing and became our third GM for Mexico. The first step was to clean house. When we finished, there were very few of the original thirty people around. Miguel instituted the basics, which had been neglected. Better uniforms and safety gear were issued. No more smoking on the job. You could no longer bring guns to work. Obvious, right? We actually had to use a metal detector to check workers for weapons coming in and out to make sure they didn't have scrap metal squirreled away in their bags. Organization structures, security systems, performance reviews, and maintenance schedules were instituted. A strict "three strikes and you're out" rule was put in place. Sergio and Rod's legacy was chaos, and in just a couple of months we were a professional and organized team.

With our new management in place, we were now super-bullish on Mexico. It had the best gross margins in the group and the largest market potential. I decided to get focused back on Asia and let Miguel work some magic in Guadalajara.

Nick was in Malaysia holding the reins, but as far as I could see we weren't really getting anywhere. In fact, the Malaysian situation had worsened while Nick was in Mexico. The true test of management is not how things are going when a manager is around, but how things are going when he isn't. Nick was very smart, full of ideas, and loved the big picture, but in my opinion he wasn't systematic and organized. He was a maverick genius who would oversleep and miss a flight because he had been up all night reading ancient history. Though he was working hard and was very dedicated, as he had demonstrated by spending the millennium with us in the scrap yard instead of with his girlfriend in Thailand, Nick had no clear idea about his monthly overheads and never did his expense reports on time. Every couple of months he'd hand in a huge pile of credit card receipts to the accounting department without any backup information. When we expanded his role to include Thailand, the first thing he'd done was lease a house in Bangkok and purchase two dogs as pets. They were Thai ridgebacks, a fairly aggressive breed. Prapast used to ask me why the company should pay the dogs' veterinary bills, which were higher than some of his staff's salaries. With Nick traveling all the time, the dogs were neglected by the housekeeper, and eventually had to be put down after attacking a neighborhood child. Nick just wasn't practical. He would be great in a crisis and then drift when the mundane job of day-to-day management reared its ugly head.

Mei and I returned to Malaysia to help push our agenda forward there. One night in our room at the Kuala Lumpur Hyatt, one of my many homes around the world, my frustration got the better of me. I called Nick to arrange a meeting time for dinner, left a message on his answering machine, and promptly hung up. Exhausted and in a foul mood, I then went on a tirade, venting to Mei, "This guy couldn't manage his way out of a paper bag in the rain! Partnering with him was a huge mistake! He is so totally disorganized!" *BEEEEP.*

The phone had not completely hung up and Nick's answering machine had recorded everything. Mei and I racked our brains to think of a way to delete his messages. As we were brainstorming, my phone rang. It was Nick.

"Did you just call and leave a message on my answering machine?"

"Yes. What time are we having dinner?" I responded without expression, wondering if he had heard the last part of my message.

"Seven thirty is fine but there was a weird message on my machine, like somebody talking in the background." His voice had an unusual edge to it.

Feeling a sudden surge of confidence, I decided to be bold and lie like hell.

"Hmmm, funny, I have no idea."

It was never spoken of again. But a day or two later while the three of us were on a long drive down to southern Malaysia near Singapore, Nick spoke up and said that he wanted to renegotiate our deal. He felt he was having a global impact, fairly citing his efforts in Mexico, but noted that his incentives were based on only two of our businesses, which were not yet delivering meaningful profits. Both sides were uncomfortable about the lack of profitability in Malaysia and Thailand. Mei and I took some time to think about it. We valued Nick's friendship, companionship, and the heavy lifting he'd done thus far, but recognized he wasn't good at day-to-day management. However, Mei and I felt that we could create a more global, strategic position that could play to his strengths. We came up with what we believed was a fair proposal, and offered it to him.

"Nick, I've got an idea I think you'll like. We want to bring both your focus and incentives into play on a global scale. I'm CEO, Mei is CFO, and you could be our global COO. Forget the old profit share deal, continue to have your costs covered by the business, and we'll give you 10 percent of the whole company outright."

Nick thought for a moment, and responded, "Steve, we're on the same page, but I think 30 percent is a more reasonable split. Aren't we all basically equals?"

Not in my mind. And not in Mei's, either. We felt the business was worth a decent amount of money, and that while we had invested a hell of a lot of cash, Nick hadn't invested anything other than sweat. All the sales were based on my relationships with POSCO and finance provided on the back of Mei's and my guarantees. Not to mention, Hartwell Pacific had started in 1993 and he had joined at the beginning of 1999. It was clear that the expectations gap between us was vast. I explained gently: "I can't see how we can come together on this."

"I trust that it's not your intention to screw me, but I feel my number is also fair and reasonable and anyway, you hold all the cards," he sighed, casting his eyes toward the floor.

"Nick, it may look that way from your perspective, but my intentions are very sincere. I would feel terrible if you thought we would try to take advantage after so many years of friendship," I countered, trying to handle this sensitive situation as smoothly as possible.

"Perhaps it is best if we just shake hands, settle up somehow, and move on," Nick concluded.

I totally agreed at this point, and sensed that perhaps he actually wanted an exit more than the 30 percent. Together we discussed a way to buy him out of his Thai and Malaysia profit share, which was at that time worth nothing based on historical performance, but hopefully would hold some value in the future. We came up with a figure that Nick was happy with, and then we all shook hands and talked amicably about old times.

Nick headed off to Bali, taking a sabbatical and learning how to surf. He kept in sporadic contact for a while, but the friendship was not the same and eventually he moved to America and we fell out of touch. Don't do business with friends unless you are prepared to lose them. We weren't prepared and are sad that we lost a very good one. Mei and I pressed forward.

It's so difficult looking back. It's easy to say people failed us or someone failed, but the reality is that when things went wrong it was everyone's fault, including mine. I'm sure I could have given Nick more support, spending more time with him in Malaysia. They say success has a thousand fathers, but failure is an orphan. I was one of a few fathers of our failures, but I can live with that. You can never be a long-term success in my opinion if you don't learn to take responsibility for your mistakes.

Anyway, now was not the time to be sentimental. Problems loomed in Malaysia and it was time to get down to solving them. Hopefully, this time the solutions would stick.

16

FIXING MALAYSIA

ith Nick no longer in the picture, Mei and I threw ourselves wholeheartedly into fixing Malaysia. The first thing we found was that we were still having problems with missing inventory. Rumors persisted that our operations manager Anthony was involved, perhaps with the support of the local *kampong* gangs, which take their name from the Malay word for "poor village."

I remembered hiring him. He was a bright and energetic Indian guy, around forty years old, and had a clear mind as to what needed to be done. He turned out to be a very hardworking, hands-on manager, and I appreciated the energy he brought to the place. Unfortunately, there was a fair amount of circumstantial evidence to support the theory that he was ripping us off—*A little too smart perhaps.* Either way, at the end of the day Anthony was in charge of the warehouse and things were going missing, so I figured he was at least indirectly responsible. I had also been told that he was a real hothead and that nobody liked to work with him. We decided to sever Anthony and prepared a fair settlement that went beyond our minimum legal requirement.

I called him in for a meeting in Nick's old office. I sat behind the large executive desk and he took one of the black leather chairs in front of it, bouncing his leg and staring at me intently with a nervous smile. His long skinny frame was taut, as if bracing for a blow.

"Hi, Anthony. Thanks for coming in," I started. "As you know, we've had a significant problem with missing inventory, and that is causing us great concern. In light of this, and due to the fact that you were in charge of inventory, I'm afraid I have no choice but to terminate your employment and make a fresh start with a new manager."

Anthony just stared at me, the smile gone. His leg began bouncing faster now, causing his whole body to tremble. I continued, filling the awkward silence.

"Look, Anthony, I know you're a hardworking guy, but the fact of the matter is that you were in charge of the warehouse and a lot of inventory has gone missing."

"I didn't take anything! You have no evidence of that!" he exploded, interrupting me.

"Anthony, Anthony. I'm not saying you stole it," I emphasized. "I'm saying we've lost confidence in your ability to run operations. We have thought long and hard and come to the painful conclusion that we have to make a change, and our decision is final. We will treat you very fairly." I then handed him a white envelope containing his severance letter and a generous check.

"If you sack me, you'll regret it!" he warned. His face twisted into a scowl as he folded the envelope and shoved it into his blue jeans without looking at the contents.

"Perhaps we will, Anthony. These are the difficult management decisions we have to make," I explained sorrowfully.

Anthony shoved back his chair and stormed off. *Well, that's the end of that,* I thought. *He took the check.* However, I soon learned the matter was not yet settled; Anthony called that afternoon.

"Stephen, the company has violated some serious Malaysian laws and if you don't reinstate me, I'm going to turn you in to the government." I sensed a perverse pleasure in his voice.

I went ballistic. "What! Which laws? We're good citizens and if we've done anything wrong, I'd like to know what it is so it can be rectified," I finished cautiously, considering the possibility that he could be recording the call.

"You'll find out later if you don't clean things up with me," he threatened.

"Anthony, I have no idea what we've done wrong! I am already giving you more than is required. It's time for you to take responsibility for the problems we've had and move on," I lectured.

Meanwhile, my mind was racing. *If there was anything serious, Nick would have known about it and he would've let me know,* I thought. *Anthony's just bluffing.*

Still, I knew it was prudent to take his threat seriously. Not wanting to set a company precedent of paying blackmailers, I hired a globally famous private investigation firm to support me. Their solution was to dig up some dirt on Anthony that we could use as a counternegotiation. It didn't feel right, but by now I had lost my Midwest American, play-by-the-rules sensitivities. This kind of dirty fighting was not the way I had been raised but I suppose had become a survival instinct.

It turned out that Anthony was originally a Christian but had married a Muslim, and, in accordance with Malaysian sharia law, had converted to Islam. However, he had been very outspoken about his negative views of Islam and even still wore a crucifix around his neck, which, again according to sharia, is blasphemy. This seemed like a pretty minor issue, but the American investigative firm informed me that it could land him in jail or at least cause him to lose some government entitlements. I was told he would "fold like a cheap suit" when confronted with the allegations. I was still not comfortable with the nature of these negotiations but, pardon the pun, went on faith.

We set up a meeting in the breezy, palm-lined lobby of the Hyatt and picked a quiet corner where couches abutted large tropical plants. The ex-FBI agent working on our case taped a wire to my chest. He also put microphones and recording devices in the potted plants in hopes of catching Anthony trying to blackmail me again. Meanwhile, the burly agent sat nearby, reading the paper anonymously in case things got rough. Tourists and businesspeople milled about, oblivious to what was going down around them. Wetness spread across my armpits following the seam of my shirt as I sat trying to look relaxed while nursing a Coke and eyeing the lobby for Anthony. *This is crazy,* I thought. *We have every right to dismiss this guy and are treating him fairly and now I'm caught up in a scene from a bad B movie!* I caught sight of Anthony out of the corner of my eye, walking briskly across the lobby. I stood, gesturing for him to grab a seat next to the leafy plant.

After a brief pause, I started: "I'm sorry this has become so awkward, Anthony. I have always liked you personally."

We discussed matters as amicably as possible, outlining the problems in the company and rehashing my decision to let him go, but it was a feeble attempt at breaking the tension. After we'd exhausted all the small talk we could muster, Anthony made his demands.

"I want six months' pay for the stress and embarrassment you've caused me, and, in addition, I want to be reinstalled as the operations manager."

What a joke! I thought, allowing myself to smile at the absurdity. *How did he come up with this?*

"There is no way that is going to happen, Anthony."

I then recited the script we had rehearsed about the blasphemy allegations and the seriousness of sharia in Malaysia.

"Anthony, I am not the one who started this dirty fight, but I am prepared to finish it. I've hired an investigative firm to do a background check on you, and they came up with some pretty damaging allegations related to your practice of the Muslim faith. I think you know what I am referring to."

He grew red-faced as I spoke and, as soon as I finished, jumped to his feet and stormed off without a word.

As it turned out, Anthony was not bluffing about creating a sensation. One day, as we routinely went about cutting up scrap metal and loading containers, the Atomic Energy Licensing Board (AELB) arrived with two police squad cars and the local media. Wiry Anthony was out in front of the lynch mob, gesturing and yelling in Malay. The police had to physically remove him from the premises after I complained that he was trespassing.

Anthony's little secret was that a piece of radioactive metal from a hospital X-ray machine had been found in our yard. The previous operations manager had instructed the men to safely dispose of it by putting it into a barrel and then filling the barrel with concrete. Testing the barrel revealed no radioactive readings and they had left it in the warehouse, right where it was found by the AELB. Though not a criminal offense, as dumping it in a river would have been, we learned that our disposal method was against the rules and regulations and we would be subject to hefty fines. In short, this was going to be a major brouhaha.

I again went to our highly paid international investigative firm for advice. Its reply was that on an hourly fee basis, it could help me

negotiate with the Atomic Energy Licensing Board. *Great! I'll probably spend more on fees than fines.* I was looking for a little free help, considering they had completely misread the Anthony situation, but they made it clear that wasn't going to happen. I decided to forget about trying to nail Anthony for his religious inconsistencies and negotiate with the AELB myself by pleading ignorance and promising to educate our entire team on radioactive safety and policy.

It took us almost a year to deal with the AELB, during which I often raged to anyone who would listen, "The government bureaucracy in Malaysia has to be the worst in Southeast Asia!" My case with the AELB was being handled by what local businesspeople call a *haji*, or Muslim theocrat. Just getting an appointment to see him could take months, and even then it was ridiculously inefficient. Once I got the appointment, I would sit in the waiting room all day for a five-minute meeting in which little progress was made. I was always told to wait until further notice, as my case was still under consideration. *If there is no progress, why did you accept the meeting? You could have told me that on the phone! Don't you give a damn if my business, which employs locals and generates economic growth, survives or not?* Finally, matters got settled after we hired a local consulting company, recommended by the AELB officers themselves, to negotiate a settlement on our behalf. Consulting is a good business in Malaysia and is a large employer of privileged locals. In the end, it cost us a cool $50,000 to clean up the mess.

After such an expensive and emotionally draining debacle, we decided to move our operation out of that damn neighborhood and rebuild. Mei stayed for three months straight to help set up our new operation. We recruited almost an entire team of new people so we could have a fresh start, and on a sunny spring day we loaded up our remaining inventory and beat a retreat across town. Unfortunately, by the time we got everything organized, we figured out that a lot of valuable metal had left the old yard but never arrived at the new one. The rumor was that our externally contracted truckers, after realizing that we were not well organized on the receiving end, had made a pit stop at one of our competitors and lightened their load to the tune of $100,000. I had learned well along the way that calling the police in the developing world, particularly as a foreigner, is a complete waste of time unless you have incontrovertible evidence, which we didn't. Even if we had, it still probably would have been useless; people just bribe their way out of trouble. We were getting used to pain by now and

shrugged it off. Over the years, Mei and I had developed an ability to unemotionally address the past and analyze what went wrong, only allowing our emotions to come into play when focusing on the present and future. To use an American cliché while evoking the Chinese allegory of water symbolizing money: It was water under the bridge.

The year 2000 had been one for the record books in terms of learning. Mei and I used to joke that every time we took a hit, we got an MBA. This had been a very expensive education. My grandfather always said, "The best school is the school of hard knocks and its colors are black and blue!" I wore the colors of that school.

❧

The pain of our total Malaysian education did have some positive impact. Mei and I were determined to make Kuala Lumpur our best-run company with the most effective systems and security. Our new slogan was: "Trust in systems. Systems will protect the company, and the company will provide for all of us."

I owed it to everyone to move in that direction, but in order to build these systems we needed to understand our vulnerabilities. How could we be ripped off? We held a brainstorming seminar in Bangkok with around twenty employees, representing all departments and including our top ten managers throughout the region. We started by going around the room, each person sharing ways they thought the company could be cheated.

Narita spoke first, eagerly raising her hand. "Suppliers can leave one tire off the edge of a scale while weighing out. In this scenario they weigh in heavy and weigh out extra light."

Tommy, our Malaysian operations manager, chimed in: "The truck driver can stay in the car when weighing in, and get out of the truck when weighing out. The driver is now literally worth his weight in metal."

Prapast next came up with the key point of the day: "Internal conspiracy between suppliers and employees is the greatest threat and perhaps the most difficult to defend against. Protecting against this will require a real team effort."

Having identified potential and actual threats, we moved on to creating systems and structures to solve these problems. I was surprised to find that not only were management's proposed solutions quite good, they were more stringent than I would have instinctively creat-

ed. Now, instead of a team bridling under new restrictions and controls, I had a team that was creating and leading them. Some examples of these new systems were:

- Weight bridges would now be monitored from the office using CCTV cameras. Further, we created the position of weight bridge controller, which would be filled by someone from the accounting department and not the operations department—usually a young woman with thick glasses.
- The night watchman would be locked outside and forced to do regular patrols around the perimeter, punching strategically placed time clocks every thirty minutes. Even if criminals came to bribe or threaten him, he wouldn't have access. Brilliant!
- We created stringent systems of checks and balances. Anything related to matters of material value required multiple approvals. Any internal fraud must therefore be a multiperson conspiracy, and that demands a criminal mind more than simple opportunistic greed. Don't leave your wallet on the ground!
- No single person should have a key to the operations. Management would be divided into three teams and at least two keys, one from any of the two, would be needed to open the gates. This double-lock system became the cornerstone of our warehouse security.

Ah yes, bureaucracy. Once a freewheeling entrepreneur, I now fully embraced the meaning of that word. *Bureaucracy is better than bankruptcy.*

Overall, the meeting was a landmark success. Beyond finding solutions to security threats, we had just conducted our first regional management meeting, and it had been effective not only due to the fact that all the key people were assembled, but also because we involved a diverse group in a problem-solving committee. It had occurred to me that if we were going to survive we needed everyone's help, and the only way to truly get it was to treat people as peers, not underlings, and to be patient listeners. Shy people were goaded into participation to get their insights and so no one would be able to say he or she hadn't been involved. All ideas were posted on a wipe board and discussed and debated by the team. My role was to manage the debate, decide when to end it, and draw up the summation. By involving everyone in decision making, we created a culture of ownership

and passion for the company. I discovered that a consensus has more legs than an edict. We also learned to celebrate the identification of weaknesses or mistakes as an opportunity to improve rather than to find someone to blame.

Hot off the success of our meeting, and in need of consistent management systems throughout the group, we held another regional meeting, this time in Kuala Lumpur, and flew in all our country GMs. We decided now to make KL stand as a model for our other current and future operations.

Again in a democratic fashion, which involved some moments of heated debate and resistance, we decided to flatten our organization structure and fit it into a system of checks and balances rather than relying too much on centralized authority. "Shared authority is a shared burden," I argued. I also explained that if we created a system together and it wasn't working, or management was unhappy and had a credible alternative, we could sit together and change it. "Nothing is permanent. We control our destiny," I promised. "We need to have a flexible bureaucracy."

In the end, we created three divisions: commercial, operations, and finance. The GM or country manager would be in charge of commercial and operations reporting to me, but would not be in charge of finance. Finance would report directly to the CFO, at the time Mei in Hong Kong. In that way, the head of finance couldn't say, "I knew about the fraud or problem but didn't report it because I feared retribution from the all-powerful general manager." Finance people became vital for creating a professional business culture without kings or queens—powerful individuals who autocratically control all decisions. It created a balance much the way Mei and I worked—power-sharing business partners.

The system of checks and balances we created in turn covered all the critical areas of operating a metal recycling business while focusing on protecting our assets, in particular our cash and inventory. To name just a couple of examples:

• It would now take three people to write a check. One person would control the checkbook and keep a log of all checks written. Then, one person from finance and one person from commercial would need to sign each one.

• All deliveries would need to be approved by the operations manager or person in charge at the time of delivery. Same procedure for any material going out.

Mei and I also led by example, following all the systems ourselves. I insisted on the trunk of my car being very publicly searched
whenever I left one of our facilities. We'd argue or debate publicly,
which was at times difficult. *How could she undermine my authority?* I
thought at first. In fact, it didn't undermine my authority but rather
served as a shining example of how business leaders need to share
power and be open to criticism and debate. *Everyone is always watching
the CEO,* I thought. *Your behavior is critical; "Do as I say, not as I do" won't
work.*

These important regulations were strictly enforced and required
group consensus to change, but we gave our managers a high level of
autonomy on other matters. This could be frustrating, as at times we
had differing views of a modern corporation, but their ideas were usually low-cost, effective, and suited to local cultures, so I let my desire
for control take a backseat. As my grandfather once told me at the
steeplechase track, "The best breed of horse is the one that gets you
over the fence!" In one particular instance, Prapast wanted to paint our
cranes a light purple color. I thought this was crazy and very effemi-
nate. *Why don't we paint flowers on 'em while we're at it?* But purple is a
national color in Thailand, and his feng shui master had told him it
would bring the company luck. *Purple cranes it is then.* I stayed focused
on the critical issues.

Now that we had created what we believed would be a winning
management structure and philosophy, it was time to implement it.
This would require our employees, many of whom had been with the
company from the beginning, to change or evolve with us. It didn't
always work. In Malaysia we had an accounting manager, a Chinese
woman named Annie. In the face of a management vacuum caused by
involving Nick in Thailand and Mexico, she had promoted herself to
Queen of Malaysia. She had simply been the alpha female in the pack
and had asserted her authority over her peers through force of personality as well as intellect, or at least street smarts. It may sound good
to have a capable employee who wants to lead, but once you lose control of the person, it's hard to get it back. Annie had recognized, not
unreasonably, that we depended fully on her as the most reliable local
during our early crisis times. However, she felt that this gave her freedom
and power beyond reproach. Employees came to us in tears complaining
about her overreaching; she'd yell at laborers who were taking a break,
for instance, rather than discussing her concerns with the operations

manager. We tried to balance the power, but she just kept threatening to resign. If we disagreed with her she'd burst into tears and wail, "If you guys don't trust me, then I'll resign and get out of your way! Sniffle, sniffle, sniffle." She was extremely political and didn't have a nice word to say about anyone except herself. We tried as a team to convince her to change and buy into our management philosophy, but failed. In the end, after many attempts to keep her, we gave Annie the boot, accepting one of her faux resignations. She was shocked. Although Annie couldn't change, I have the highest respect for the way many of our early-stage senior managers let go of their absolute control and evolved into professional executives.

With Annie out, the critical issue we now faced was a lack of a GM in Malaysia. Rather than recruiting one, running the risk of new management failure or creating another king or queen environment, Mei and I temporarily grabbed the reins and set about rebuilding the team from the ground up. Now semi-based in Kuala Lumpur, we would collect even more frequent flier miles.

With all these efforts, we were on our way to becoming a well-run corporation rather than an entrepreneurial venture. I wished I had thought of some of these simple things earlier, but that's the problem with a low-cost start-up. We had viewed investment in security as an expensive luxury and systems as cumbersome bureaucracy. We had put our faith in individuals rather than teams, and it had cost us dearly. Live and learn. The amount of money stolen over the years due to poor security and weak control systems was more than $1 million. If your employees are resisting logical systems that protect the company and are telling you that you need to go on trust, alarm bells should be ringing loudly.

17

HARTWELL PACIFIC'S INDONESIAN VACATION

Malaysia is geographically a very long country, stretching 468 miles from Singapore in the south to Thailand in the north. The market is fragmented into three main cities and ports, Johor Bahru in the south, Kuala Lumpur in the center, and Penang in the north, so it's impossible to competitively consolidate the scrap into one city. Thus, in order to gain meaningful national market share, we really needed to operate in each of these regions and export from it directly. Johor Bahru, or JB, was a smaller market, but less competitive or crowded than Penang. We thought a dominant position in a small market was better than fighting for a smaller share of a medium-sized market like Penang—same volume, better margins. We therefore decided that JB was strategic enough to pursue and happened to find a scrap yard that was closing down but still had some life left on its lease. We were able to buy its assets on the cheap, and soon we were in business.

Opening in JB seemed to be the right decision, but it meant that we would have to run a fairly tight ship. Our volume would be small,

so there would be no room for major errors. What we really needed during this critical first stage was a trustworthy individual. We had the systems; we just needed to avoid fraud and did not have any spare employees to send there from another operation. *Perhaps one of Mei's relatives could be a short-term fix until we got to know our new employees. She has a huge extended family,* I thought. This went against my instinct about family businesses, but it seemed like the perfect Band-Aid, so long as we had a plan that all parties were aware of to unwind the situation and move to a professional corporate structure over time. Sometimes trust trumps everything, certainly in the earliest stage.

I asked Mei, "Do you have any family members who can handle JB until we can get a proper management team in? Perhaps a cousin?"

Mei smiled and responded quickly, "My mom! Her husband is Malaysian-Chinese!" Mei's mom and her stepfather were living a simple but pleasant life in the Kowloon district of Hong Kong. It is very obvious where Mei got her street smarts: Her mother is a real firecracker. Though only five-foot-two, she had been a competitive swimmer who represented Fujian Province in national competition. She is a determined person who never backs down from a good argument but always keeps her cool. I've never seen her raise her voice, but I've also never seen her give in. Even the Cultural Revolution, which tore apart her family in a sad divorce and broke so many people's personalities and sense of humanity, could not suppress this strong-willed woman. After surviving that, the Malaysian bureaucracy would be child's play. As is the case in most underdeveloped countries, even those with talent never get a chance to show their potential. This would be her chance. Though the thought of Mei's mom working for us felt funny for me, I was on board for whatever would work.

We asked her if she and her husband would like to spend an expenses-paid year or two in Malaysia and put a little retirement money away while keeping an eye on our new business in JB. They would of course be well looked after. She was pleased to take part in our adventure and to have a change of environment for a while and enthusiastically signed on. I sensed she had a little something to prove.

Mei's mom, referred to as "Madame" by the staff, had that place running like clockwork in no time. She had no background in business but with basic street smarts and a focus on details, she built a nice profitable company. Every penny was accounted for, and not a kilo of inventory went missing. Tight inventory controls go hand in hand

with a successful recycling operation; it's as simple as putting the right things in the right piles. It's amazing how many people screw it up. I just needed our facilities to supply a quality product, on time, while reasonably controlling overhead costs and avoiding fraud. Mei's mom delivered. I loved visiting JB. The company had a beautiful chili garden and fishpond for feng shui. They took in a stray dog, named him Fook Zai, Lucky Boy, and he became our security guard. Fook Zai was a prolific lover, a real Don Juan of the *kampong,* and over time we had at least ten guard dogs/pets. I always left feeling comfortable that JB was in good hands. Malaysia, now under control, would not be having any negative hits going forward.

⌒⨯⌒

Exhausted, Mei and I decided to reward ourselves with an exotic holiday in Indonesia, the birthplace of Mei's mother and father.

Mei's father came from a large household in Bali, where he was one of ten children. His family was quite well off, and each child had his or her own maid—clearly a good gig. Nonetheless, he had left his family home in his twenties with his three younger siblings to move to Fujian Province, hoping to regain his national identity and help Chairman Mao "save China." It was with great pride that many members of the Chinese Diaspora in Southeast Asia went back to the homeland from which their ancestors, escaping war and famine, had fled during the 1920s. They remained fiercely patriotic. In Mei's family's mind, they were not Indonesians. Even though they were successful immigrants, they were Chinese and second-class citizens in a foreign country. At that time it was illegal to even learn Chinese characters in Indonesia. The government feared the Chinese rather than embraced them.

Unfortunately, in 1958, upon Mei's father's arrival in Xiamen, the capital city of Fujian, he and his siblings were liberated of the gold that their father had given them as their future inheritance. They were asked to donate it to the country to show their love, and not long after were sent to the countryside. Instead of a heroes' welcome, they were put to work in fields for reeducation. After Mei was born and the unfortunate divorce, she and her father bribed their way to Hong Kong to rebuild their lives. Some might be scarred by such harsh childhood experiences, but Mei is proud of her heritage. Overcoming

these challenges has made her who she is today: a strong, independent-minded woman who is not easily intimidated.

Mei had not been back to Bali in several years, so we thought we would meet some of her family and then head off to Indowana, part of a famous luxury resort chain. Indowana is very remote. You fly in a small propeller plane to Sumba, which is three islands east of Bali and about a third of the way to Papua New Guinea. You then board a speedboat owned by the resort for a one-hour cruise to a private island. The island has only one resort, and the resort comprises but twelve tents lining a beautiful lagoon. You can snorkel right off the beach and be swimming with giant turtles and black-tipped reef sharks—very wild. Mei and I were both experienced divers but hadn't done it for quite a while. Each day we kept hearing about a remote dive site called Raya Reef, where there are lots of sharks and large pelagic fish like manta rays. The only negative was a very strong current, so it was only recommended for advanced divers.

I really wanted to go but Mei was hesitant. She was afraid of the strong current. The manager of the sporting activities, Billy, was a hefty Australian with a red face, faded tattoos, and well-worn skin, a tribute to his years at sea with the merchant marine. He assured her that she would have no problems, and for extra comfort he would be her dive-buddy. "No worries, mate!" he said with a grin. Mei relaxed and agreed to go.

The next day we strolled out along the jetty and boarded the boat. It was a large sportfishing yacht as the site was quite far away, and we had to get out to the reef on the open ocean. We shared the ride with another couple, and quickly made friends. I was wearing a cap that sported the insignia of Falling Pebble, a club in Pennsylvania that my parents frequent, and upon boarding the other guest walked up to me and asked if I was a member. After I replied yes, he told me that his grandfather had founded the club—small world. His name was Matt, and he introduced his new bride, Tamara, explaining that they were now living in London and that he was helping his wife with her business. Tamara was a successful entrepreneur with a luxury shoe brand that was really taking off called Jimmy Choo shoes. *Interesting,* I thought. *You never know whom you'll meet on a scuba diving trip.*

We shared entrepreneur war stories a bit and then got on to discussing the local scuba diving. An hour later, we pulled up to the dive site and surveyed the scene. There were a couple of small, uninhabited

islands dotted around, but other than that that it was just open ocean. During our briefing we were told to grab hold of a rope that would be attached to the anchor line. Next, we had to jump in and grip our masks tightly so they wouldn't be swept off our faces. The boat and rope were taut against the anchor due to the surprisingly strong current. After descending about fifteen meters, we would be able to swim freely, and then could slowly drift back to the boat at the end of the dive.

"Is everyone ready? Gear check. Buddy check. Let's go," Billy barked. As soon as I hit the water and felt the full force of the current, I began to panic a little. *Wow. This is a new experience,* I thought. My breathing quickened, and I worried about Mei—*her legs are not as strong as mine.* But I looked back and saw that Billy was in the water with her, and that she was safely situated between the anchor line and him. I relaxed slightly, but still continued to breathe more heavily than normal.

When we got to the bottom, I checked my air. I'd used up half due to the heavy exertion. I looked over at Mei and saw her ruefully checking her gauge as well, so this was going to be a short dive. I stuck with Mei and Billy, while our boat buddies Tamara and Matt went in a different direction with another guide. We kicked hard, working our way along the reef but enjoying the beauty of the ocean floor.

We came upon a group of sharks swimming in the same direction. They were whaler sharks, slightly bigger than the typical reef sharks with longer, wispy tails, and we were very close. Sharks are beautiful creatures and I'd been in the water with them many times before, but never in such close proximity. Suddenly one peeled off from the others and doubled back aggressively. It arched its fin and appeared to look straight at me. I had been told before that this is a warning sign and I stiffened, my heart racing beneath my wet suit, but it then turned and disappeared ahead. *Better keep your distance,* I thought.

When we got down to our minimum air level, I signaled Billy. It had been a short dive, as I'd expected. Mei, Billy, and I surfaced about twenty or thirty feet downcurrent from the boat in open ocean away from the anchor line, as we unfortunately hadn't been near it when we ran low on air. Looking around, we realized that nobody was on deck to greet us. I thought, *We're early. They probably aren't expecting us yet.* Billy kept yelling the names of the boat boys, but evidently his voice

was disappearing into the wind as the current began to move us swiftly away from the boat. I wasn't panicked. *They always see you and then just motor around and pick you up.* However, I noticed that Billy was quite nervous. He now had his flipper off and was waving it in the air. He shouted, "Damn it, you stupid shits. See us! See us!"

Billy was an experienced diver and should have been carrying a mirror to reflect the sun or an inflatable orange "sausage" as tools to help the crew find us. However, for whatever reason, he had nothing. We had nothing.

Soon we were well away from the boat, and I could tell we were moving very rapidly.

Billy looked at me and said, "See that island over there?" It was a beautiful green outcrop with a sandy tip about one kilometer downcurrent and another kilometer crosscurrent. "We're going to swim for it," he continued.

What the hell? I thought to myself.

Not wanting to panic Mei, I forced a modicum of calm and replied, "That's awfully far. Won't the boat just come and get us?"

Billy's response was chilling. "You don't understand. This is a matter of life and death. Get on your backs and start kicking! Where are all the f---ing fishing boats?" he exclaimed. "Usually they're everywhere!"

The swells picked up, and our boat soon became a speck on the horizon. We could see it moving, but understood that it was circling. *Don't the idiots know we're in a heavy current? How could we be in the same place?* I thought.

I held on to Mei's inflatable vest by the collar and relayed the plan. She said nothing. We lay on our backs and started kicking. Strangely, I was very calm. The sun was warm and soothing and the water lapped gently over my chest. I saw Mei look down into the depths, where the light disappeared into absolute darkness, and couldn't help but think of the shark that had doubled back on me during the dive.

"Don't look down, Mei. Arch your back and just keep kicking," I said.

"But I'm tired," she replied. "And that island is very far. There's no way we'll make it."

"Just relax then; I'll kick for both of us."

I squinted and looked to the sky. Kick. Kick. Kick. From time to time I would look over my right shoulder, the downcurrent side,

and keep my bearing on the island. It didn't look that much closer but I could see the low, dark green underbrush clinging to the soft sand, the light reflecting white off it. *Don't panic,* I thought. Kick. Kick. Kick.

Suddenly the water got lighter. I looked down, where I could see a reef and sand. *We must be getting close,* I thought with a surge of relief. But to my horror, I couldn't see the island when I glanced over my right shoulder. *Is my mind playing tricks on me?* I spun quickly to my left and looked over my other shoulder. The sandy spit of the island jutted out into the blue ocean about five hundred meters crosscurrent. We'd missed it. The shallows below had just been an underwater reef reflecting light back up to the surface.

I looked over to Billy. I was still clinging to the back of Mei's vest. "We missed it. What now?" I asked.

He was pale as a ghost and muttering something to himself.

"Next stop Sulawesi, mate," he said in a thick Australian accent.

"Where's that?" I said.

"About a thousand kilometers due north. You can stop kicking. It's out of our hands," he ended solemnly.

The problem was not the amount of time we'd spent in the water thus far. It was the current, which was pulling relentlessly like a dark force, inexorably drawing us out into the open ocean to meet our fate.

My heart sank. I pulled Mei closer and tried to be as positive as possible.

"We missed the island. But don't worry, the boat will come get us soon."

She simply smiled. I thought to myself angrily, *This is my fault! She didn't even want to go.* I considered the parallel between this situation and much of the business adventure on which I'd dragged Mei. *You've got all these dreams and ambitions. Have you considered the negative consequences your grand plans could have on others?* I lectured myself.

The swells grew deeper, rising to about four or five feet in height. Up to the peak and down to the trough. Up to the peak. Down to the trough. At the peak of the waves, I looked longingly out to the horizon in search of a boat, but instead found nothing but the sky above and darkness below—no land or boats in sight. The sun was beginning to drop, creating a beautiful shimmering effect on the water's surface, but the natural beauty had sinister consequences. Due to the dancing reflections, we would not be spotted from the air. If they didn't find us

soon, they probably never would. *Billy will be the first to go as he's not wearing a wet suit. That is, of course, unless we're taken by sharks before hypothermia sets in.* I morbidly imagined all the possibilities.

I looked to the sky and thought of my family, my friends, and most importantly Mei. I considered life and what I had felt, either consciously or subconsciously, were matters of importance—money, prestige, popularity, possessions. All that shit was out the window. The only thing that mattered was a boat heading our way. *If we're saved, I'll remember all this,* I thought. I prayed for a chance to get life right. I wanted to ask Mei to marry me right then and there, but I was afraid that if we survived she'd think I'd asked her at a moment of weakness. There would be a time for that, but it wasn't now. I also worried about making her emotional. I held her at a slight distance, my mask beginning to steam up. She was so calm and quiet. *What inner strength.* Or maybe she didn't understand the seriousness of our predicament. It's eerie. As humans we think of ourselves as strong animals that struggle violently to survive. But sometimes, when you face death or the possibility of death that is beyond your control, a peaceful calm comes over you and you just accept your fate. I have seen the same thing with wild animals in Africa. There is a moment before death when the prey loses hope and, though it is aware that it is being eaten alive, it stops struggling. It's as if it suddenly says to itself, *Okay, let's get this over with.*

⚬◈⚬

On the boat, a different scene was transpiring. Matt and Tamara had surfaced on the anchor line about ten minutes after we had. They relaxed on board while the boat boys circled the reef looking for us. After about half an hour it struck Matt that there was no way we could still be down there. "They must have surfaced," he said. The boat boys and the other relatively inexperienced guide were starting to panic.

Many years ago, when Matt was in his mid-twenties living in Florida, he had decided to get his captain's license. Thank God! He took the helm of the ship, up in the tuna tower, and sent the boat boys below. He then quickly called in a mayday alert to the hotel, and they told the local mining companies and airlines to put planes and choppers in the air. Next, he threw a buoy into the water and watched its direction, trying to time its movement. He estimated that we had been

in the water for about an hour and a half in roughly a five-knot current, part of the time underwater and part of the time on the surface. He would chart that course, and when he reached the planned distance he'd turn and head west in case his line was wrong.

A seemingly interminable hour had passed, and I'd almost forgotten about our "guide" when Billy shouted, "There's a boat!"

Sure enough, it was coming right at us. We took off our flippers and now, every time we reached the peak of the swells, we would wave them in the air. Ours were black but Mei's were pink, so we grabbed her flippers to wave them higher. The boat was getting closer and closer on a beeline, heading straight for us. I hadn't realized how big the swells were until I could see and hear the boat crashing up and down on them.

As it got closer, Matt cut the engines. I could see him hanging over the side, waving to us. What a beautiful sight. He yelled, "Swim for the boat!"

My legs were cramped and not responding well. I rolled over onto my front, still clinging to Mei, but we were just tossed around in the swells. Matt dove in headfirst and swam to us. I handed Mei over and he dragged her to the boat. I grabbed the ladder and Matt pulled me aboard, and then helped Billy. Matt was running the show, scurrying around while the boat boys stood frozen, a couple of them with tears running down their faces. We dropped our gear and flopped down on the couch. Matt handed me a beer and I saw that Tamara was smoking a Marlboro Light—my favorite.

"Can I have one of those, Tamara?" I asked.

I lit the cigarette, breathing deeply, letting the warm tobacco fill my lungs. Mei glanced at me disapprovingly. We'd made it.

We then heard the story behind our rescue and found out that Matt had not seen us until the boat was practically on top of us. As he gently put it, "You guys are lucky. Had I turned and headed away you'd have been gonzo by the time I doubled back. With the sun going down, you would've spent the night at sea." Not a thought I relished.

We got back to the resort, and only then did Mei and I realize we were both in shock. We lay down on the bed, and Mei finally broke down, sobbing in my arms.

After calming ourselves with some Johnny Walker, we headed for dinner and met Matt and Tamara at the bar. We emotionally expressed our gratitude and indebtedness, my hands still trembling a little. We

owed them our lives! It was surreal, sipping cocktails among the other diners; we had seamlessly rolled from death to life, terror to absolute normalcy. I reflected on the fact that our deaths would have mattered very little to 99.9 percent of the world. It made life seem rather trivial. Leaving the island, Mei and I promised each other and ourselves that we would keep life in perspective.

"The only thing that matters is a boat coming your way."

⌒⧓⌒

Getting back to Hong Kong, we started our busy lives again, both traveling to different cities and solving different problems. This time, however, I was determined to keep my priorities straight. A couple of months later, on one of the rare mornings when Mei and I were in the same city, I gingerly slipped a big diamond ring on her finger while she lay sleeping. She developed an annoyed expression but remained in her dreams. I then crawled back into bed with a bundle of eighty-eight roses, one for every month we'd known each other—rounded up to a lucky number, of course. I gently nudged her until she opened one eye slightly. Half asleep and disoriented, she took in the roses and fidgeted with her finger. As her eyes opened fully, I quietly asked her to marry me. She was totally surprised but with a wry smile responded, "Aren't you supposed to kneel down?" I suppose the tradition is to ask before you put the ring on the finger, but I felt mine was a better method of negotiation.

Many people propose in exotic locations, in fancy restaurants or hotels, but I had a reason for waiting until we had some quiet time at home. We were always in exotic locations, fancy restaurants, and hotels, chasing around the world in opposite directions. To me, home was a very symbolic place to get engaged. It was a warm moment in the midst of the chaos and treachery that surrounded our lives. We'd been through so much together and were somehow surviving. I knew life had a long road ahead, but I couldn't imagine having someone better on my side. I'd wondered from time to time along the way, during periods of cultural misunderstanding, whether the differences in our perspectives would make it difficult to be married, but I was wise enough to realize that those are just details; mutual respect matters above all. In fact, I feel the cultural differences and perspectives make our life together more interesting and add color

and spice for both of us. I also knew that there was no one I would meet in my life whom I would respect and trust as much as Mei. They say that most marriages end in divorce, and I predict that many more stay together out of a sense of loyalty, commitment, or even fear of being alone. However, a lucky few find their soul mates; Mei and I had found each other.

18

THANK YOU, MR. BENTLEY

Although life was full of happiness on the home front, Hartwell's Mexican operations were struggling once again. While focusing on kicking Asia into gear, we had left Miguel Calderon, the clever engineer, in charge in Mexico. He made many improvements and significantly developed our volume, but still seemed to have big problems turning inventory. We kept saying: "You have five hundred tons. Ship it! What are you waiting for?" The answer was always the same: "The machines is broken. The equipments is down. It will be fixed mañana."

Having learned that slow-turning inventory is usually associated with missing inventory, I immediately flew to Guadalajara to investigate. The first thing to do was to take stock of all our metal, kilo by kilo. This isn't easy in a scrap yard. It's not a matter of counting boxes or pallets; you need to load everything up onto industrial scales and weigh it. It was a major undertaking that Miguel felt was a complete waste of time.

"We'll know the weight when we ship it!" he exclaimed in frustration.

"Miguel, the problem is we're always taking in material and mixing it with the old inventory so there's no way to determine the starting point. We have to do the stock-take no matter how painful," I insisted.

What we found when we got to the bottom of the pile was bad news. We were missing about two hundred tons of material, valued at over $200,000. Miguel was furious.

"That *pinche* rat bastard Sergio. We'll get the police involved and put him in the jail! I have friends! I have connections! This guy is dead!" Miguel had a flair for the emotional.

As I digested Miguel's fiery tirade, I considered all the angles. There was of course no way to prove that Sergio was the culprit. It could just as easily have been Miguel or some other key employees. I had my doubts. *But this is a great opportunity for him. He wouldn't be so stupid as to blow it like this,* I thought. We'd made a big mistake by not doing an inventory check the day we kicked Sergio out, and I convinced myself that this was my fault. I wanted to believe in Miguel; he seemed so capable. Not to mention, I didn't have a backup. Miguel was also swearing to God, on his late mother's grave, on anything and everything, that he would never cheat the company.

"Stephen, I want to be your partner someday and I'm going to prove I'm worthy of that. Look me in the eyes. I will never lie to you!"

I knew that this was all a bit over the top but had nothing to gain by refuting his claim of loyalty. I would need to either support him or fire him.

"I know, Miguel. Don't worry. We have a great future together," I confirmed.

Okay. Let's move on; what other choice do I have? But let's get an accountant in here whom we can rely on 100 percent, I thought. Mei had a childhood friend from Hong Kong, Joanna, who had since immigrated with her parents to America and settled in Queens, the urban suburb of New York. Joanna had received her CPA but was bored working in a Manhattan accounting firm and had been living with her parents her whole life. This was a perfect ticket out of that trap, and she jumped at it. We now had the ideal formula—a charming local GM with an expertise in hydraulic equipment and an accountant we could trust, one to entertain the clients and keep the machines humming, the other with an eagle eye on the cash and inventory. I could smell it. This

was going to be our best business. Miguel and I would march south to Buenos Aires following the best margins in the industry, dining on Latin American delicacies accompanied by great Chilean wine, and fishing for marlin on weekends. I would someday soon build a beautiful Spanish-style hacienda and ride horses throughout my agave plantation, soaking in the warm Mexican sun—ah, the romance.

With the team in place, it was time to make a big push for commercial development. We plastered a giant map of Mexico on the wall of the conference room—Oaxaca, Veracruz, San Luis Potosi, Puebla, even Guatemala. Red pins were inserted demarking potential suppliers, white pins for large industrial sites, and yellow for competitors. This was my normal way of visualizing the market to help me understand the required logistics of servicing our potential suppliers or defending against our rivals. Miguel now insisted that we needed trucks to do the job: "Good trucks with loading cranes attached!" The distances were long, and we couldn't rely on used vehicles. "New trucks!" We would also need to upgrade our equipment. "New balers! Better cranes!" We needed "bobcats," a cool forklift-type piece of equipment with a grabber on the front. We needed to pour more concrete and upgrade the electricity to handle the targeted increases in volume. Learning from our experience in Malaysia that cheap security ends up being very expensive, I was supportive of any investment in this area—extra cameras (in out-of-reach locations), stronger reinforcement of our gates and doors. We also implemented the new management and security systems designed at our Bangkok and Kuala Lumpur leadership meetings. Miguel's most compelling point was that if we invested the right amount, we could do the necessary volume without bottlenecks and thus keep our inventory low and easily countable. I totally agreed.

I was nervous at first because we'd built every business so far on a shoestring, but trading was pretty profitable in Asia so we had the cash. *Why don't we do this one right? We have the people. God knows we have the market. Let's go for it!* I thought. Capital expenditure skyrocketed. Miguel's convincing personality combined with my desire to dominate the market and become a huge global player proved a dangerous cocktail, and soon we had over $500,000 in additional capex in Mexico. It was a beautiful operation on one hand, but after adding in accumulated losses and write-offs our commitment to this business that had never made a profit had blown past the million-dollar mark.

Though nervous about the level of investment, I remained excited about the pace of progress, and Miguel seemed really committed. *Things are coming together,* I thought.

I also enjoyed life in Mexico. I started working out in the gym and got my weight down—fighting fit, though I was still smoking over a pack a day. I preferred the arid Mexican climate to the sweltering humidity of Southeast Asia, and I loved the food and atmosphere. The French call it *joie de vivre.* The Mexicans have it in spades—at least the ones with money. I invited Mei to visit our operation and to join me for some marlin fishing in Cabo San Lucas. She was eager to catch up with her old friend Joanna and to check up on me, so she came right over. Upon arriving, she was duly impressed with the operation but very skeptical of the size of investment. Business aside, Mei enjoyed the trip and was delighted to discover that the Mexicans, like the Chinese, eat every part of the animal, including the innards. Her favorite was *cabrito*—baby goat stuffed with its own guts.

After catching up with Joanna and reviewing all the details of the finances, we headed off to Cabo in search of our first marlin and a romantic weekend away from work. Sportfishing is a vacation activity that we both enjoy. A wife that likes fishing—got to love it. It was a beautiful morning out on the Bay of Baja, and sure enough I got a big strike from a blue marlin. After a forty-five-minute fight, I wrangled it to the boat for a tag and release. We also caught a durade or mahimahi and had some fillets barbecued for us that night, as well as some sashimi (hamachi) from its flank as an appetizer. Life was sweet.

⌐◦◦◦◦◦

It was time for Mei to go back to Hong Kong; I would follow her shortly. But before I left, I sat down with Miguel and made him an offer that would hopefully align our interests and keep him on a straight path. I told him that if he could get the Mexican subsidiary to pay back its losses to date and the capex, I would give him 25 percent of the Mexican company outright and Hartwell would finance everything going forward, a deal that any businessperson would drool over. We would also put him on our global board. The high-school-educated son of an abandoned street child would become an equity holder, as well as a well-paid board member, of a multimillion-dollar international corporation. He had never left Mexico and would now see the

world. I truly felt this deal was lopsided in his favor, but I was willing to do anything to turn Mexico around and get our investment back. Miguel was thrilled.

"I won't let you down. Thank you for having confidence in me," he gushed.

We shook hands and toasted our future with a fine Chilean Cabernet, grilled sweetbreads, and giant steaks at my favorite Argentine grill.

I returned to Asia confident that we had secured Hartwell's future in Latin America. Though things were looking up, there was one dark cloud on the horizon. After gaining significant market share, we were starting to find fierce competition from recycling companies in Houston, in particular from Nickelmet's subsidiary in Galveston. We had cost advantages, but Nickelmet was not as willing to walk away from the Mexican market as we'd hoped and was now putting pressure on our once fat margins by bidding up the price of Mexican scrap. I was concerned, but maintained my belief that with our lower costs the Americans would not fight a losing war. *You can't stop evolution, and there is no reason for Mexican scrap to go to the United States just to be reexported to Asia. Logic will prevail,* I thought.

⌒✗◯◯⌒

Passing through South Carolina on the Hartwell commute, I chewed on a deep-fried onion loaf at the Outback Steakhouse in Darlington, South Carolina, our financial exposure weighing on my thoughts. Just then my mobile phone rang. It was my lawyer, Nigel Hambros, a partner at Litchfield's, a leading old-line Hong Kong firm.

"Steve, a venture capital fund based in London has contacted me looking for investments in Asia. I thought you might be interested," he offered encouragingly. I paused briefly, soaking in the possibility of some financial support.

"Ah . . . Yes we would!" I concluded, without much need for thought. We needed funds to back up difficulties in Mexico while things turned around there. The timing was perfect.

The interested investor was the $50 million KLM Asia Venture Fund. It had been mostly a tech fund, raised to take advantage of the dot-com boom, but tech was dead and they still had about $25 million left to invest. Hartwell had not tried to raise funds during the dot-

com era, but even if we had, without a "scrap.com" strategy nobody would've been interested. I just didn't believe the Internet offered anything special to the metal recycling business model and couldn't force myself to try to join the party. However, by 2000 the boom had busted and money began looking for a new home or strategy.

A meeting was set up with Peter Bentley, a tall and athletic Cambridge-educated Brit who had worked for the investment bank Merrill Lynch in Hong Kong. He now lived in London and was CEO of KLM. I met Peter in the lobby lounge of the Island Shangri-la Hotel. I had given him a detailed business plan and financial forecasts by e-mail, and he'd confirmed his interest. We sat down to make friendly conversation over tea. Peter opened, "So, Stephen, how much of Hartwell would you give me for a million dollars?" I nearly choked on my Earl Grey.

"Hmm. I'll have to think about that and get back to you," I responded coolly, shocked that we were already talking turkey.

"Please include your justifications and get back to me by the end of next week," he ended, looking at his watch.

And that was that—not at all how I imagined these things went. You had to work your ass off trading scrap metal to make a buck but could make a million over tea trading your equity. The light was now on bright in my brain. *You don't get rich trading crap or scrap. You get rich trading equity.*

Mei and I discussed this together, and I bounced the situation off my circle of close investment banker friends who introduced me to the world of EBITDA (earnings before interest, depreciation, and amortization) multiples and comparative valuations. I was taking a crash course in corporate finance. It's amazing how much and how quickly you can learn when your butt is on the line.

A number was reached for a valuation of the company, and charts and graphs were created to back it up: 10 percent for $1 million. We were able to come to that number by stripping out all the one-off "hits" to profitability such as inventory write-offs in Malaysia and Mexico, moving costs in Kuala Lumpur, and so on.

I argued, "You should be worried if we hadn't made mistakes yet. With every challenge we overcome, our company becomes stronger and our equity more valuable."

Peter agreed that these adverse expenses were one-off in nature, but to be honest, as a general facing the field of battle, I didn't think

the company was worth $10 million. If you were to add the hits back in and subtract them from our profits, we had about a break-even business. We did have an impressive geographic footprint and growth record, though, now operating in seven locations in six countries and employing around 150 people after just two years of business. But we only had about $1.5 million in assets. The value was based on forecast rather than historical earnings, and it was hard to say how those would pan out. If someone had offered less than this valuation for the whole company, I would have voted for taking it and walking away. The stress and anxiety of the business at this point were wearing me down; it seemed whenever something went right in one place, something went wrong in another, creating a seesaw effect with our cash that never left anything in our pockets. In my mind I believed the company had potential to grow, but I also inwardly worried that it had the potential to blow up. Though I was beginning to crack, Mei remained solid and urged caution.

"Steve, I'm skeptical of KLM. Peter's getting the deal of the century, considering how hard we've worked thus far."

I countered fiercely, trying to end the argument. "Mei, how hard we've worked doesn't matter to Peter. It only matters how much value we've created and the potential for earnings growth! If you haven't already noticed, we need the money. There's a giant sucking sound coming from the drain in Mexico."

"I'm more aware of our balance sheet than you. I'm in charge of finance, remember?" she reminded me. "Let's not give away the farm." Mei and I both compromised our emotions, and committed to negotiating a reasonable deal for a minority stake. Always analyze the extreme left and right, upside and downside, then you'll naturally find the middle. The middle is where good deals consistently get done.

Another meeting was scheduled for a month later when Peter would be back in Hong Kong, once again in the lobby of the Shangri-la. I thought it strange that as people sipped tea and cappuccinos around us, I was closing the biggest deal of my life. But we weren't closed yet; Peter had a surprise for me.

"We discussed Hartwell and don't think it's worth doing a million-dollar deal. It's only worth it if we can put more capital to work. We'll give you $2 million for 25 percent." *Poker face! Don't smile!* I thought inwardly. *Think about something else, baseball, whatever. Don't react!* I kept my cool and gave my standard answer.

"Hmmm. I'll have to think about it and get back to you."

I learned this from the Koreans. I would pitch a deal or a strategy to them with great emotion and cunning, putting all my cards on the table to make my best case, but they would just stare at me blankly and say, "We'll think about it and get back to you." Smart, very smart. A push for immediate commitment at this moment would have been a clear sign of weakness.

I came back to Peter a week later, even though I had discussed it with Mei and a short list of advisers and crafted my response within twenty-four hours.

"Twenty-five percent is in the ballpark but 22 percent is a much better number. Twenty-two in Chinese is very good, as 2 or *yee* in Cantonese sounds like 'easy' and is thus considered very auspicious. Double *yee* or 22 is 'double easy,'" I wrote.

Peter responded shortly thereafter, "22.8 percent is even better as 8, or *baht,* means 'rich,' and thus it will be double easy for us to get rich."

We were now just playing around—22.8 percent for $2 million. I only recommend negotiating in that way with someone who is an old China hand or Chinese. It's a good way of haggling for a bit more while keeping emotions light, as long as it is a concept that is culturally understood.

❧

The deal was done—at least until we started sorting through the hundred pages of documents. Peter had suggested his lawyers would draft the documents and each party would pay its own legal costs, which I accepted with a sigh of relief, as I wouldn't be paying the $100,000 bill for drafting.

His next concern was what I would be paid in salary. Not wanting to burden the company at this early stage or spook valuations, I replied: "$150,000 plus housing, which will bring total compensation to around $200,000 based on where I'm living."

Peter came back to me the next day and inquired, "I just want to be clear that this is $150,000 per year, not $150,000 per month."

I responded indignantly, "This is precisely why this deal is so good for you. You have straightforward partners who aren't too greedy!" Things were proceeding surprisingly smoothly.

It was November 2000 and we were pushing the document back and forth, arguing spiritedly with their lawyers over details. I have learned over time that lawyers are paid to be difficult; bad cop is precisely their role. Mei and I would not let go of any clause until we believed it was fair, and we took everything personally. After haggling with the lawyers, I had a list of business points that could only be settled between the principals. I had learned something about Peter during this short period: He could be strong on the telephone, and was a real tough guy by fax or e-mail, but was much softer in person. Peter wouldn't be coming to Hong Kong before our agreed deadline of December 31, so I decided to go to London to meet him face-to-face.

We agreed to meet at his firm's offices on Belgrave Square around 11 AM. KLM was located in a very impressive town house, with antique tapestries hanging delicately from the walls and Greek busts fixed on faux Ionian columns. I was ushered into a meeting room and seated at a meticulously polished antique table under a huge crystal chandelier. There was a quiet formality and elegance to the room that impressed me. Though it was Old World in some ways, video-conference screens hung on the walls and everything was wired with the most modern technology. This was also where they ran their billion-dollar hedge fund. Peter sauntered in.

"Howya doin', Steve," he started in an exaggerated American accent.

"Jolly good morning," I replied, doing my best Prince Charles.

We made the normal chitchat. "How was your flight? Did you fly BA or Cathay? Lovely weather we're having today." Even when things were tough, it was always cordial and there was always time for a little friendly small talk before getting down to work. Pleasantries behind us, we got to the issues at hand. I very painfully made a compromise or two, the ones I'd prepared in advance to make, and then we resolved most of the important points surprisingly quickly and easily.

Satisfied with the result, I now wanted a break. I believe that once you have what you need, hanging around is all downside; not to mention, I had caught Peter looking at his watch periodically.

"I don't know if you had anything planned, Peter, but I hope you don't mind if I meet an old friend for lunch," I requested.

His face melted into a sigh of relief.

"Absolutely, Steve. Enjoy. Why don't we meet back here around four?"

"Perfect," I concluded, standing to grab my bag.

In reality, I would be eating alone. I had a reservation at my favorite restaurant in London, Wilton's on Jermyn Street. My father had taken me there one time when we visited London together. I ordered the same thing from memory: half a dozen Colchester oysters, a Dover sole on the bone, and a crisp glass of Chablis. This is one of those places where it's best not to look at the bill, but the nostalgia made it well worthwhile.

After a pleasant but exhausting dinner that evening with Peter and his wife, I crashed for the night and headed back to Hong Kong in the morning, completing my forty-eight-hour round-trip jaunt. I awoke on the flight as we passed the Himalayas entering Chinese air-space. *If we get KLM on board, all our troubles will be behind us,* I thought wistfully. I know it sounds crazy, but I love these long flights—looking out the window for landmarks, taking time to contemplate life. I always thought of the world as an enormous place as a kid, but the more I travel, the more I realize how small it is.

As Christmas neared, Mei and I were pleased with the deal and generally satisfied with the contracts. Our advisers also informed us that the terms of the documents were "all very standard"—famous last words. The agreement was to be closed by the end of the year; Peter made it very clear that this was a drop-dead deadline.

Mei and I were home in Pennsylvania for the holidays nervously awaiting the conclusion of the agreement. It was after dinner on December 28 when we closed. Our trusted assistant Lilly, Triple Li, called to confirm that $2 million had been received by our bank, and faxed through our statement. There it was dangling in our account: a two, a comma, three zeros, a comma, and three more zeros. What a sight. What a Christmas.

19

THE SCHOOL OF HARD KNOCKS: ANOTHER MBA

While the negotiations with our investors had been playing out in London, we had run into a problem in South Carolina. Fortunately it wasn't fraud-related, but it was very serious nonetheless.

Hartwell Atlantic was more or less being managed by Janice, our accountant, and the combination of the company's competitive overhead and her leadership had allowed us to make some small profits. However, there had been a major and dramatic shift in the market, causing a structural economic change that appeared to be life threatening to our company.

Prices of stainless steel scrap in America had suddenly jumped up due to increased local demand and a shortage of supply. In the commodities business, we say that commodities flow where they want to go, not where we want them to go; traders simply jump into the stream and ride the rapids. In the months prior to opening South Carolina and throughout our first year, stainless steel scrap wanted to go from the East Coast of the United States to Asia. Korea would pay

more for it than Europe or Pittsburgh simply because it had a long-term shortage, whereas the United States had a long-term surplus. The Koreans needed it more. But herein lay the problem. Commodity markets always find their equilibrium due to the natural flow of business. When a price in one place is attractive, commodities move there to satisfy demand, but often create corresponding shortages in other places when too much is exported. Pittsburgh now had a shortage and was looking to the Southeast to fill it. Our competitors were aware that this happens from time to time and were set up to either export by ocean container or send railcars to Pittsburgh. The latter was their strength. We did not anticipate this shift in the market, so unfortunately did not have railcar access. We'd need to either invest a million dollars to build a rail spur, just to get close to an equal situation with our competitors, or sit on our hands and wait for the market to come back to us. We chose the latter and for six months we literally couldn't buy one ton of scrap. Our team was sitting there in an empty yard, nervously staring at one another, wondering what the future held. I flew to South Carolina to search for a solution but couldn't find one. It became clear to me that Pittsburgh's demand for southeastern scrap was strong and showed no signs of weakening anytime soon. We were going to have to make a critical decision whether or not to persevere.

After careful analysis, we decided to shut it down. We had made a macroeconomic error, and there was no solution. I knew the market would probably come around at some point but recognized the trade flow between Pittsburgh and Korea would be a regular seesaw, so we did something smart and wound up Hartwell Atlantic, taking around a $450,000 hit. All terminated employees were treated well. We even gave Janice the company car. I have always believed that employees should not be unreasonably punished for management's mistakes. We could afford to pay up so we did, and thus left South Carolina and our team with hugs, a few tears, and thankfully no animosity.

With the situation in America resolved, it was time to tell Peter that we had burned 25 percent of KLM's investment. We set up our first board meeting on a Monday at 10 AM. I couldn't sleep the night before. *He's going to take my head off,* I thought.

I waited anxiously in our conference room for Peter to turn up. He wasn't aware of the news I was to deliver and loped casually into the room with a warm smile. I nervously greeted him, "Morning, Peter. Can I get you some coffee?"

"Just a cup of a tea would be fine. Thanks, Steve."

Mei walked by, glancing through the conference room window.

"You deal with Peter, but if you need me, let me know," she had said.

After settling into my seat and handing him a set of board papers, I stammered a bit and then rolled into my game plan: Deliver the good news first and close quickly with the bad.

"Business is great in Asia. Look at the Philippines. Thailand and Hong Kong are also doing well and Malaysia is coming along. Third-party trading is very profitable, and Mexico has enormous potential. Latin America could roll out just like Southeast Asia has. There's only one dark spot: We need to shut down South Carolina," I finished, breathing in deeply, gauging Peter's reaction.

He sat quietly and flipped through the board pages without expression, then tapped them on the table and said in a distracted manner, "Right. Sounds good, Steve. I hate to do this in our first meeting but I need to cut it short. I have a lunch with Robert Kuok"—the billionaire owner of the Shangri-la Hotels. "If you need to talk about anything else, I can meet you for a drink tonight at the Shang. You mind if I take these papers with me?"

"Not at all," I replied, pleased to be avoiding his wrath.

"Gotta run, Steve, all the best," he said, slipping the papers into his briefcase and then standing to shake my hand.

After Peter got into the elevator, I returned to the conference room and sat alone in mild shock—*Almost a $500,000 write-off and not even a blink.* I'd originally hoped that Peter was going to be an active partner, but at this moment I was quite pleased to learn he wouldn't be.

⤜✼⤛

We took stock of the situation to date, and Mei and I both agreed that we were overextended time-wise. If we were really going to continue our drive for top-line growth and further develop infrastructure for our current operations, we would need some more senior management support. We decided to recruit a COO, a notion that Peter Bentley fully supported. He was always pressing me for a "hit by a bus" scenario. As in, "If you get hit by a bus, what happens to my investment?" Mei was furious. It's very bad *joss,* or luck, to talk that way in

Chinese culture. Death or bad outcomes are not a topic of discussion. You don't even joke about it. Though I appreciated her concern for me, I totally understood where Peter was coming from. So far we had a solid management team, but no obvious choice for a potential successor who could take over in a worst-case scenario, or at least offer more execution support for my global plans.

I harked back to Daryl Patton, the chicken-foot king. He was a solid ten or so years older than me and had the maturity and experience we were looking for. He was a seasoned executive for a large trading organization, spoke some Mandarin, had worked independently in Asia for many years, and had a straight-talking common sense that I appreciated. He was also available, having left the poultry trade. Daryl would be expensive, but not as expensive as someone who had run the show in Asia for a big branded company.

We had some discussions and he agreed to join for market pay plus an incentive plan that gave him significant upside. It was big money for me at the time, and he would be by far the highest-paid executive in the company, but we all agreed that this was what Hartwell needed. Daryl spent some time in Southeast Asia learning the business, but bringing him on board slowly was not an option. I hoped he was ready to help me with some heavy lifting in Mexico.

⁓⦅⦆⁓

Despite all our investments in Inox Reciclables de Mexico, slow-turning inventory continued to be a problem. Rumors were also coming back from Guadalajara that our Chinese accountant, Joanna, and our GM, Miguel, were having an affair. Miguel was married with two cute daughters, so the infidelity was a troubling issue beyond the obvious conflict of interest. Mei went to Mexico to discuss it with her old friend and got confirmation that this was the case and that she was "out of control" in love. We knew we had to make a change. Joanna knew it, too, so we started preparing to get her out of Mexico. The combination of business challenges and the emotional turmoil related to the affair left her delicate Chinese skin covered in heat rashes and her hair falling out in patches. She would easily break into tears when being asked even the most routine business questions. She was clearly having a nervous breakdown, but thankfully agreed to hang around for a few more weeks to smoothly hand over her work.

I sent Daryl to help prepare for a change of finance directors and to see if we could speed up the turnaround, which, despite the improvement of many other metrics, had yet to produce a bottom-line result. This was the problem or trap with our Mexican business. It sucked not only our financial capital, but also our human capital. All focus was now on Guadalajara, and our offensive strategy was turning to a defensive one.

Daryl was detail-oriented, analytical, and able to see not only that the business opportunity existed, but also that our challenge was human.

"Your problem is Miguel, Steve. He schedules meetings and never shows up, or says he's visiting customers in Mexico City only to be spotted in Guadalajara. I don't trust that guy for a second," he lectured.

"That's just not the Miguel I know. But anyway, keep a close eye on him, Daryl," I replied with concern.

I was aware Miguel didn't like having Daryl looking over his shoulder, but I had assured him it was just temporary and that anyway, "You caused it by fooling around with Joanna!"

He apologized for the indiscretion.

"Stephen, what do you want me to say? I am a man, not a saint. Let's get refocused on the business." I totally agreed with that.

In the meantime, we were still facing fierce competition from the companies in Galveston, namely Nickelmet, putting even further strain on our Mexican business. We had to stop throwing good money after bad, so I started to think of alternative plans. I figured we should approach Nickelmet and propose a joint venture. In my mind it was about getting out of a price war and also letting someone else handle the day-to-day management headaches in Mexico. I believed this was a natural win–win, as Nickelmet was also suffering from the price war.

I heard that Nickelmet's chairman, Max Heinecke, was in the Asia region, so I e-mailed him to set up a meeting and explain my idea. He replied that he was busy but could meet me for an hour if I flew to Taiwan.

It was April 2001 when I arrived in Taipei and checked into Max's hotel, the Sherwood. I met with him over tea in his suite to lay out my vision for a joint venture and broke into my elevator speech.

"We have a three-hundred-strong base of small suppliers all over Mexico, and Nickelmet currently can only buy from big dealers with export capability. Our fingers reach deeper into the market! We have

a perfect facility with great assets and a good solid team of accountants and workers. We are the only company in the market with a 'direct to mill' contract. What we need is daily management, and Nickelmet has plenty of Spanish-speaking people in Galveston who could do it easily. We could also end the Mexican price war with the stroke of a pen. Max, this is a no-brainer," I concluded.

He nodded slowly, his arms folded across his chest, "Stephen, we could never do a JV with you. It just would not be palatable for the board after your previous dustup with the company. But we'll buy you out," he said with an air of finality.

A bit taken aback, I paused for consideration and had a sip of tea. *That would be wonderful,* I thought, and then responded slowly, "I am open to this, but we'll need to seal a deal quickly if we are going to do it, and it needs to be highly confidential. I don't want my staff to know about this or they might fear losing their jobs, particularly our GM Miguel—it's a sensitive moment."

"Okay, Stephen. Let's work in that direction," Max agreed, accepting my outstretched hand with a perfunctory smile that let me know the meeting was over.

Within weeks we were in detailed negotiations with his minions, and a buyout was being drafted. I was confident that the deal would get done, so I signed an exclusivity agreement stating that I wouldn't approach any other potential bidders. The value of the assets now needed to be confirmed, the goodwill negotiated, and then board approval secured at HQ in Germany. I was shooting for a high valuation, as I knew that Nickelmet was losing money on Mexican scrap and this deal would make it immediately profitable. My target was $2 million. I ran this by Nickelmet's Gulf Coast president, and he replied coolly, "I can't imagine we'd pay anything over $1.4 million." It sounded like a number that had been discussed internally. *Fine. Hasta luego, Mexico!* I thought.

⌒✖⌒

Unfortunately these final months would not go smoothly. Daryl had been in Mexico for a while now, trying to keep everything stable as the merger approached. He called me one Sunday morning.

"Steve, I don't know how we can handle this guy Miguel. He rarely comes to the office and doesn't even return my phone calls."

I was very concerned and called Miguel.

"What's going on?" I demanded.

"Daryl is full of shit. He just wants to get rid of me and take over. He's jealous of our close relationship," Miguel replied, spitting fire.

Could it be a conspiracy? Or is it just paranoia? I wondered. Our first GM, Sergio, had been a disaster, we were in a price war with Nickelmet, and my GM who can't keep his willy in his pants is now being accused of negligence. *Can I get a break here?* I jumped on a plane.

I arrived in Guadalajara and met Daryl at the airport.

"Miguel is acting very strangely. I can't find him," he complained.

"What do you mean can't find him?" I said incredulously. *I've never heard of such a thing,* I thought, hoping Daryl was wrong.

"I'm sure he'll put on a song and dance for you, but I can tell you right now, this guy's a nonstarter," Daryl concluded.

The next morning I arrived at the office and waited for Miguel to show up. I waited and waited and then called his mobile phone several times, only getting his answering machine. I left message after message, like a spurned teenage lover, until his phone's memory was full. *What the hell's going on?* I complained bitterly to myself. I was livid and panicked. *If Nickelmet gets wind of this, it could seriously weaken our negotiating position, or even scare them off.*

Our senior accountant, Andrea, confirmed what Daryl had told me about Miguel's disappearing acts. She also explained that suppliers were calling and threatening her, saying we owed them money. Mei's old friend Joanna, who had not yet left, was very distant and uncomfortable about everything but assured, "I still trust Miguel. He has some issues but the business is making many improvements." We were doing more volume and the yard was certainly operating better, but this did not allay my fears.

Daryl begged to differ. "I think he has some serious personal issues. He turns up at the office randomly and paces around like a maniac."

I knew these were not good signs, but I was still in disbelief. I'd spent tons of time with him. He was a pretty heavy drinker, as were half the people I knew, but had never showed me any signs of going over the edge.

Deciding to check out the allegations that we owed people money, I flew to Mexico City to meet with one of our biggest sup-

pliers, Señor Cordoba. As I descended into the ever-present brown smog that is generated by its twenty million inhabitants and trapped by Mount Popo and the surrounding hills, I was beginning to wonder if this whole Mexican adventure would end in tears. I climbed into a green Volkswagen Bug taxi, a signature of Mexico City, and inched my way along in the dense traffic through the rough barrios, sucking on carbon monoxide and getting quite a head buzz.

I arrived at Señor Cordoba's facility and was ushered into his office. He was soft-spoken and cordial, and I believe he realistically understood that I was not the source of his problems, but rather the probable solution. He explained, "This Miguel guy is a very bad man. Everyone in the market knows he is cheating you. He spends all his time with the whores in the strip clubs, spending your money."

I understood that in Mexico just about everyone was working an angle but also that everyone bad-mouthed one another. "That *pinche* son-of-a-bitch, father of a whore" is a common description of a competitor or adversary. You learn to take these aggressive comments with a pinch of salt. Señor Cordoba was very convincing, though, and had calm eyes that did not divert from mine. I believed them to be truthful.

As I would eventually learn, the scam went like this. A supplier, such as Señor Cordoba, prepared a shipment and sent the truck to our facility in Guadalajara. The truck was unloaded, the inventory registered, and the payment made through electronic transfer by Joanna and Andrea. The problem was that the account number we were transferring money to was not Señor Cordoba's, but rather an account carelessly registered under Miguel's wife's maiden name. We traced it. The gig was up. This was obviously a suicidal conspiracy, as inevitably the supplier would come forward to get payment. This was not the thought process of a highly intelligent man like Miguel. It was a desperate grab for cash.

Not wanting to break with tradition and seeking to build bonds with our key employees, I arranged a dinner. I always believed in the old maxim "A family that eats together stays together."

Miguel hadn't turned up for three days and I wasn't expecting him at dinner, but about six o'clock he called Andrea to inform us that he would be coming. *Joanna must have reached him,* I thought. I saw Miguel enter the restaurant and rose to go meet him, but he bypassed the main dining room and instead headed straight to the bathroom.

The tension at the table was palpable as I left to follow him. He came out of a stall and walked up to me with his chest puffed out, glaring down his nose with an expression that said, *What are you looking at?* His eyes were shiny glass marbles, vacant of the person I knew. Miguel is an imposing figure at about six-foot-three and probably 220 pounds, so I suddenly felt unsafe.

"How could you do this?" was all I could muster before promptly making my exit for the comfort of the main dining room. He joined our table, sitting at the far end away from me, and ordered a double vodka tonic. Everyone chatted uncomfortably and ate the meal. We had a nice red wine as usual, but Miguel ordered vodkas one after another, eyeing me from across the table. I ignored him and entertained the team as if nothing was wrong. Daryl watched me nervously, trying to gauge the situation, partially pleased that I now understood where he had been coming from. After dinner, Miguel approached me.

"We need to talk," he slurred.

"Yes we do, but you're in no condition for that. Meet me tomorrow for lunch at the Intercontinental Hotel where we can talk about everything privately," I said. *And safely,* I thought. "I'm worried about you, my old friend," I added regretfully, leaving him standing at the front door of the restaurant.

In the morning I put an extra security guard at the yard and gave instructions that Miguel was not to be allowed in. Sure enough, he showed up and was turned away. I watched it unfold together with Andrea through the security cameras. He was furious, but no match for our beefy guards and their rottweiler. He scowled at the camera and stormed off, slamming his car door.

Around noon, I waited for Miguel at a table in the center of the Intercontinental dining room, nervous but eager to get this chapter behind me. Miguel marched purposefully across the lobby, his face taut with anger. He strode past the maître d' without acknowledging him and sat down staring at me menacingly, a trickle of sweat forming on his forehead.

"You know it's over, right?" I started.

"I did not do nothing! Anyway, you are selling the company!" he replied.

How does he know? I was shocked that our prospective deal had already leaked into the market, but waved my hand dismissively.

"It's too late for all that, Miguel, and there is the issue of funds that were transferred to your wife's account. Our lawyers have indicated that this is categorized as serious fraud and is a jailable offense."

He stood, pushing in his chair, and grunted, "You are the one going to Yale!" then turned and stomped out. As he crossed the lobby, he looked back once more, aiming his finger at me. A nervous smile came over my face. Making light of the way Mexicans pronounce *J*'s like *Y*'s, I thought to myself, *I always wanted to go to Yale but never had the grades to get in.*

Our accountant Andrea was concerned about her safety, so we arranged for a security guard to park outside her house at night and escort her to and from work. I stopped taking taxis and only used the hotel limousine, whose driver was made aware of the situation. I knew life is cheap in Mexico and figured Miguel's naturally hot blood was boiling.

We promptly sat down with our lawyers in their drab conference room to figure out how to get our money back. Frankly, the amount on which we had evidence, $50,000, was not material to the business situation, but we estimated that the real figure Miguel had gotten away with through various scams was probably much more. We had learned from Sergio that firing people in Mexico was very sensitive, but we thought we certainly had just cause for doing so in this case.

"Not so fast," our lawyers told us. "You should not have locked him out. This is against section 3175 of code 211, subsection 3 of the labor law." I stared back in disbelief.

"But this was a volatile and dangerous situation!" I responded, exasperated.

"Did you make a police report?"

"Well, no. Not yet. This all happened at lightning speed. This was yesterday for God's sake! This guy might be dangerous!" I retorted.

"You know, the laws in Mexico are different than in your country," one attorney responded calmly, trying to bring the temperature in the room down a notch.

I could tell this was going nowhere. The lawyer explained that on the one hand Miguel owed us money that he had stolen, and if he didn't pay us we could charge him with fraud and put him in "Yale." I chuckled to myself again. *Apparently of all the Ivy Leagues, Yale has the greatest representation in Mexico.* On the other hand, we owed him

$10,000 in lieu of a notice period. In other words, in Mexico you need to give criminals fair notice of termination.

"It's simple," the lawyer explained. "Miguel owes you $50,000 and you owe him $10,000."

"Got it," I confirmed, my elbows on the table, palms pressed together.

"We'll make a deal that you pay him ten, he pays you sixty, and we clean the slate."

"Check." *At least there's some cash coming our way,* I thought. "So we don't have to compensate him for the notice period, right?"

"Right, señor," the lawyer continued smoothly. "But you have to pay him the ten first, as this is required now since Miguel has already filed a labor complaint and we have not yet filed criminal charges. But don't worry, you'll get the money back right away."

"What?" My heart rate picked up a pace.

"In Mexico, once you file criminal charges it will be out of our hands because you cannot drop them. Criminal charges are not crimes against you, but crimes against society," the lawyer explained.

"This wasn't a crime against me?!" My heart was now pounding.

"Señor Greer, if we press criminal charges, we lose our bargaining chip and you won't get any money from Miguel. Then you'll have to make a separate civil suit and that could take years." The word *years* echoed in my brain. Now I lost my cool.

"Let me get this straight! This guy *steals* $50,000 from us, we fire him—"

"Incorrectly!" the lawyer interrupted.

"But we have to pay him $10,000 in order to get paid?" I finished.

"This is correct, señor. But I guarantee he will refund your money and pay back the $50,000 because a guy like Miguel won't spend one day in a Mexican jail. He knows that in Mexico getting into jail is easy but getting out, well, this is another thing," our counsel concluded.

On top of all our employment and fraud problems, we would soon find out that we had been chosen to be audited by the tax authorities—*More lawyers and accountants,* I thought. We would now have civil and criminal lawyers, as well as KPMG, on the payroll practically full-time. What a mess.

I was growing to understand that Mexico's antiquated legal system, which is constantly under repair, simply makes doing anything

productive extremely complicated. Even KPMG told us it struggles to keep up with the changes in the laws. There is also rampant corruption in the government at every level that plays with all the gray areas created by the complicated legal and tax system—the grayer the better. The professionals don't seem to understand the reason for all the regulations, only offering opaque explanations such as, "That's Mexico, my friend." I quote my wise grandfather yet again: "When the government gets involved, the crooks go to work!"

At the time I was absolutely convinced that the majority of people making any money in Mexico were government officials, lawyers, tax consultants, and a handful of billionaires. It felt like everything in Mexico was out to kill us. *Nick was right. We are the f---ing bull,* I thought. This was far different than in Hong Kong, where I felt everything was efficient and supportive of commerce. In the end, Miguel Calderon opted out of his scholarship to Yale, settling the $50,000 claim. I never heard from him again.

With Mexico finally getting cleaned up, I could focus on more important things. Mei and I were scheduled to get married June 9 and the deal with Nickelmet was set to close in July, August at the latest, so life was really coming together. I relaxed and went into wedding and honeymoon planning.

20

MR. AND MRS. GREER

Mei and I finally got married on a sunny weekend in Ligonier, Pennsylvania. After somehow surviving all our business calamities, not to mention the Sea of Flores off the coast of Indonesia, it was now time to formalize our commitment and take this partnership to another level. Most people would not consider wedding planning to be taking a breather, but it was great for me to get my mind off Hartwell Pacific. Over two hundred people, including Topher, Bernie, and Ian, whose couch I'd slept on when I arrived in Hong Kong, as well as many other important friends from the past, were there to celebrate. We had guests from twelve countries. Having been living a life on the road, dedicating 90 percent of my time to work, it felt great to be surrounded by so many good friends. I drank in the camaraderie, and it rejuvenated my spirit. It was a spectacular three-day bash with golf, fishing, and traditional Chinese ceremonies—a real East meets West affair.

Friday was set aside for Chinese ceremonies, while Saturday would be more Western. As per Hong Kong tradition, you don't take

a bride as much as negotiate for one, so Mei was kept safely in a bedroom, the door sealed with a red ribbon. To gain access, I, supported
by my friends, had to pass a series of tests about Mei's life, our relationship, and my devotion to her. Failure to answer a question correctly resulted in punishments, such as push-ups, fines, or shots of
Tabasco sauce. After I survived the gauntlet, Mei's bridesmaids negotiated with my groomsmen for her release. No matter what the price,
the amount could only consist of the number 9, or *gao* in Cantonese,
meaning "longevity." The bridesmaids shrewdly negotiated a price of
$999.99, and I finally got to see my bride. Mei was wearing a tradi-
tional red-and-gold Chinese cheongsam, a one-piece dress, buttoned
at the collar, with slits down both legs starting below the hips. She was
stunning. Mei's mother and father then arrived at the guesthouse, representing Mei's family's home, for the traditional tea ceremony. We had
to kneel down in front of them to offer tea, asking for their blessing
and showing respect. As we bowed our heads, Mei's father burst into
tears. Mei's parents had divorced when she was six and she had lived
together with her father ever since, but now, technically, she belonged
to the groom's family. I understood his sentiment and assured him in
broken Chinese that he could borrow her anytime he wanted, particularly on poker nights. That seemed to console him a bit. After honor-
ing her parents and receiving their blessing, we headed to my parents'
house, the home of Mei's new family. During this trip, the bride's feet
are not allowed to touch the ground—only a lowly bride would walk
to her future husband. My brother and friends got really into it and
built a sedan chair out of fence rails to transport Mei. We then knelt
in front of my parents and again offered tea to secure their blessing and
acceptance of my fiancée. Mom and Dad seemed vaguely disoriented
and confused, but played along as best they could.

Saturday was one of the most beautiful days Pennsylvania could
offer. Wearing black tie and a red-and-green embroidered silk vest in
a Tibetan motif, I stood at the altar and waited for Mei. Dressed beautifully in a long white gown, she stepped out of an antique carriage led
by two elegant black horses and strolled down a small hill along a
waterfall, her arm linked with her father's. I thought about everything
we'd been through together and hoped the future would only be better.
The ceremony was followed by a cocktail reception, which included a
traditional Chinese dragon dance and the detonation of firecrackers to
scare away evil spirits, and then we partied the night away. Nickelmet,

Miguel, POSCO, the nickel market, and all the rest of Hartwell's stresses were completely out of my mind, as was I. Note to the reader: Stay away from the vodka fountain.

One important milestone that passed during our wedding was that I quit smoking for a second and final time. As part of the fun, Mei made me publicly sign a contract committing to it. I quit cold turkey and haven't had a puff since. I can be disciplined when I want to be.

Sunday came and we were exhausted but ready for our honeymoon. A romantic at heart, I'd planned out a real humdinger. A black limousine ferried us from my parents' home for the three-hour drive down to Washington, DC. We checked into a suite at the Hay-Adams Hotel, and dinner was served in our room by the window as we watched the White House glowing under a glorious full moon across the street. The next day we toured the major monuments, a proper introduction to America for my beautiful Chinese bride. She stopped at the Korean War memorial, and I noticed tears rolling down her cheeks as she read the inscription: FREEDOM IS NOT FREE. Here was a girl who had escaped the Cultural Revolution with her father, keeping only what they could carry. She understood freedom far more than I did or ever will.

After a quick stop in Paris on our way to Morocco, we checked in to the plush Sahara resort in Marrakesh owned by the same company as the Indonesian resort where we'd nearly lost our lives. Remorseful about our near-death scuba diving experience, they'd offered us ten days free at any one of their properties worldwide, and I had chosen Marrakesh. It's a beautiful resort, and we were upgraded to the Presidential Suite. Our two-story house had a swimming pool that came into our living room, where there was a fire burning during the cool evenings. Every morning they cleared the rose petals that covered our candlelit pool. As far as I am concerned we are square, but Mei says I am too easily bought off. The highlight of the trip was when we ventured out into the Sahara Desert on camels with our private guide and camped under the stars by a raging bonfire. *Unbelievable.*

We had one last stop on our honeymoon. We were booked from Marrakesh to Frankfurt and then connecting on to Hong Kong with a six-hour layover. We couldn't check our bags through so we collected everything in Frankfurt. As we killed time waiting for check-in to open, Mei asked why we were flying back on a Friday. We didn't have

anything planned for the weekend. "I would have loved to have seen where you worked in Germany," she purred.

A pilgrimage to MacDermid where my career had started? Not a bad idea. We could visit nearby Baden Baden. An hour later we had our flights changed and were packing our things into a rented Mercedes convertible. We hit the A5 north–south autobahn at over a hundred miles an hour and accelerated from there. Mei didn't know what she was getting herself into. I didn't need a map. My feet and hands remembered all the turns in the road. We made very good time down to Bruchsal, and soon stood in front of the gates of the MacDermid factory. The company had moved but the site looked the same. It was at this moment, overcome by nostalgia, that I realized how much had transpired over the years. It was hard to digest. The last time I was here, I had been a boy entering his career, but now I was a weathered entrepreneur. I never took much notice of time; the days, weeks, months, and years just blended together. But at this moment I realized that although I was still young, more than a third of my life was over.

After a short but sweet weekend in Germany, it was now really time to get back to reality. When I arrived in Hong Kong, I found a nice wedding gift waiting. I had been nominated by my friend Mark Duff, an entrepreneur who started Hong Kong's first Internet brokerage company, for the DHL/*South China Morning Post*'s Young Entrepreneur of the Year Award. This is one of five awards given out each year to leading businesspeople in Hong Kong. Awards are chosen by a very elite group of business leaders, so it would be quite an honor if I won. I was pleased just to be nominated and under consideration.

It was now late June and I was nearing my thirty-third birthday. It had been a pleasurable month, but it was time to close the deal with Nickelmet and finally get the hell out of Mexico.

21

YOUNG ENTREPRENEUR OF THE YEAR

Flattered by the Young Entrepreneur nomination, I now needed to prove I was worthy. Time was flying by and we needed to nail down the deal with Nickelmet, but things seemed to be getting bogged down with lawyers. I was supposed to have received a Letter of Intent by the end of June, and it was now almost the end of July. I decided to fly to Pittsburgh and camp out at Nickelmet's US headquarters to get everything wrapped up efficiently. I figured this was a small deal and was just getting pushed to the bottom of someone's pile. *For a company with over a billion in revenue,* I thought, *$1.4 million is peanuts.* Their vice president of business development, Randy Smalls, assured me, "Steve, it's a done deal."

Max explained that board approval should be just a "rubber stamp," a formality, so I wasn't concerned. Their people were in Guadalajara going over our books and evaluating the assets. The accounts weren't such an issue as this was going to be a purchase of assets, not the company, and the goodwill payment, or difference

between the buy price and the asset value, was going to be based on noncompetes, supplier lists, and several other minutiae.

Randy now had a small surprise for me: "We've determined that the assets are worth only $425,000. Adding in the goodwill value of $500,000, we can't pay more than $925,000." I was pissed off. The original $1.4 million valuation was based on $900,000 in assets and $500,000 in goodwill. But now that Miguel had melted down, I just wanted out so I could focus on Asia. *Fine, $925,000. At least we can get half our money out of Mexico.*

"Let's get the documents done quickly," I said reluctantly and grumpily. Nickelmet prepared to take over the business. The plan was for them to be running it by the end of August. At least one reason the timing was important was because Nickelmet owed Taiwan some material on a contract and the market was going up, making this a negative position. They hoped as an added bonus to redirect our unsold Mexican inventory from the Koreans to Taiwan to help cover this contract. I told Randy, "As long as we receive market price, you can have it," trying to be supportive. I now felt it important to let POSCO know what I was doing so they wouldn't plan on receiving more scrap from us from Mexico. The company understood my situation and agreed that it made sense to put more effort into the Southeast Asian market.

The board meeting for our deal was scheduled for August 15, and Nickelmet now had two employees in Guadalajara almost full-time. With the presumption that the deal would be closing shortly, there was no reason to have Daryl stay in Mexico, so he returned to Hong Kong. Unfortunately, it soon became clear that Hartwell no longer required his services as we were scaling back our global expansion plans dramatically. As our most expensive executive, Daryl saw the writing on the wall and exited gracefully. I appreciated and respected the way he handled the situation. There were no hard feelings.

Back in Mexico, Randy assured me again that it was a done deal. He was also exasperated by how slowly things were going at headquarters. "I don't know what the big issue is. The board is so damn political!" he confided. I really felt that we were in the same boat, but I didn't realize at the time how different our boats were.

Time passed quickly and one day I received a curt e-mail from Max: "The decision is to be pushed to September. My fellow board members had questions and we didn't have satisfactory answers prepared."

I instantly fired back a short response of my own: "What questions?"

Barely two minutes passed before my inbox pinged again: "Mexican legal questions about incorporations, among other things."

Incensed, I bitterly typed, "But you guys have had lawyers advising you for two months. I thought you got all the answers to your questions?"

There was a long pause as I tensely waited for Max's reply. Finally, it arrived: "Don't worry. Good things come to those who wait. Our guys weren't well prepared and they screwed up the opportunity to get it signed off. Just wait a month."

Randy called shortly, and also expressed his exasperation.

"Look, Steve. We have to keep going. This will get done."

"But Randy, while you guys are dragging your feet, I'm financing this business and taking the operational risk of running it. Nickelmet is getting all the benefit and we're not even getting paid! Not to mention, Miguel has melted down because he knew he was going to get fired and I don't have a GM anymore," I pressed, knowing that the problem with Miguel wasn't entirely Nickelmet's fault.

"We'll work something out. We're all old friends. But if you want to be a big pain in the ass about it, Steve, we'll pull out this weekend and you can have the business back," he retorted.

"Have the business back? I've lost my GM, given up POSCO, and started shipping to your customer in Taiwan with whom I have no relationship. You've been my biggest competitor historically and now know all the strengths and weaknesses of our business. You've even reviewed our customer lists and historical performance. How can I take the business back?" I yelled at the top of my lungs into the phone.

"Well, you'll just have to wait for the September board meeting," Randy replied, ending the conversation.

Unfortunately, the board meeting was scheduled for September 13, 2001. I didn't know at the time, but business would be the farthest thing from all of our minds on September 13.

❧

Tuesday, September 11, 2001, I was having dinner with my top managers from around the region in Hong Kong following one of our now monthly "Group Exec" meetings. As we walked past the bar on

our way out of the restaurant, I noticed that there was a crowd of people staring at an overhead television. It was around 9 PM Hong Kong time, 9 AM New York time.

A plane had crashed into one of the World Trade Center towers. As I watched intently along with the growing group, a second plane crashed into Tower Two. In shock, I told my team that I needed to go home right away. I sat on my couch and watched footage of the Twin Towers collapsing and the Pentagon burning. United Airlines Flight 93, the one that did not reach its target, crashed in a Pennsylvania field only a thirty-minute drive from my parents' house. I knew right away that this meant war. Mei coaxed me to come to bed but I couldn't. For two days and many nights after that, I sat and slept on the couch flicking among CNN, the BBC, and CNBC, watching the preparations for invasion. I was in a total fog. I think being far away from home during such a crisis made it even more difficult. I wanted to be with my people, not in a foreign country. Few in Hong Kong could understand how I felt. Anger, sadness, anxiety, anger, sadness, anxiety, rolling over and over again in the night as I lived America's daytime hours, watching the events unfold. Though I missed home, there was an outpouring of sympathy from people from all over the world. I particularly remember entering Malaysia, where a young Muslim immigration officer wearing a navy blue head scarf took my passport. She looked up and caught my eye. "I am terribly sorry about what happened to your country," she said solemnly, returning my passport. There was complete solidarity around the world in support of America and Americans.

I was soon informed that due to the events of September 11, all acquisitions by the parent company of Nickelmet were on hold. I immediately notified Max that we needed to sit together and figure this out. I was facing liquidation in Mexico at this point if Nickelmet pulled the plug on the deal. Max would be traveling through Asia in late September and agreed to meet in our conference room in Hong Kong. The letter of intent had expired, and we needed a new agreement.

Max was led into our conference room. I was cordial, but had my laptop out on the table. This was not going to be a talk-and-walk meeting; we were going to sign something. Max suggested a "Tolling Agreement": Hartwell would still own the company, but Nickelmet would pull all the strings, making all the purchasing and sales decisions.

Key Nickelmet employees would gain unfettered access to Inox Reciclables de Mexico to make sure that we did what we were told and processed all material to Nickelmet's specification. In addition, all transactions would become much more complicated. Hartwell would buy material on Nickelmet's behalf using funds advanced from Nickelmet, then immediately sell the material back to Nickelmet at a price that reimbursed Hartwell for its overheads. In this way Hartwell Mexico would become a break-even business, but all profit would be left with Nickelmet in Galveston. Sounds simple, right? In consideration of this, Nickelmet would pay a $20,000-per-month tolling fee. This is less than it pays one of several senior executives in its US company. We would do this until the board approved the original deal, which Max imagined wouldn't be later than December. "Wait until things cool off a bit," he said. "This is the best I can do."

What a confusing mess. Basically Nickelmet would pay us $20,000 a month until it got the board approval and bought the business. I had faith that this would happen but was definitely growing concerned. It was now too late to approach other potential buyers or partners, and we would certainly have been approaching from a position of extreme weakness anyway. We typed up the agreement and signed it right then and there. What choice did I have? At least now I could concentrate on growing the business in Asia and get paid during the delay.

⌐⍅⍆⌐

While waiting for Nickelmet's decision on the Mexican acquisition, I made a tour of all our companies. They had come so far. Our Philippines market share had ballooned to about 60 percent, Hong Kong was over 50 percent, and Thailand and Malaysia were both running at around 40 percent. After fighting it out in the market for the past five years, we were now able to fulfill our contracts with POSCO entirely from our own operations. Our business was well under control and improving every month with regard to quality, efficiency, and competitiveness. These were some of our most important corporate goals, and in a sense we could say "mission accomplished."

I can't tell you how great it was to see my team. Triple Li, Prapast, Narita Sabino, Philip Wu, Carrie Woo, Helen Hon, Ruby, Ms. So, Mr. Wong and his team, Elaine Tan, Arul, Tommy Tan, Samran, Ms. Oh

Kornchanok, Mr. Goh, Alberto Ogalinola—the list goes on—were all solid, hardworking people, doing their jobs, making problems go away, and most importantly generating healthy profits. Note that these are all Asians, and it is an almost fifty–fifty split between men and women. Localizing management and having a good mix of men and women in the workforce had developed into an important management philosophy.

⌒◯◯◯∘

After my world tour, I was feeling very positive and confident that I was coming into my own as an executive. It was at this time that my transformation was recognized officially. I had won the DHL/*South China Morning Post*'s Young Entrepreneur of the Year Award.

Suddenly our story was headline news in Hong Kong. I was reading about myself in the very paper in which I had searched for apartments back on Haven Street eight years earlier. The newspapers in Pittsburgh got wind of the story, and a feature article appeared there with a large photo. My university alumni magazine also ran the story. I am not a showboat, but this did feel good.

There was a black-tie gala dinner in Hong Kong, and my parents flew over just for the occasion. At the end of the meal, the winner of each award's name was called. There were five. A flattering bio of each recipient was read out by the emcee, an anchorwoman for CNN. When my name was called, I walked awkwardly through the applauding crowd of about five hundred with a spotlight in my face, nervously trying to hold my smile as a throng of photographers flashed away. As I made it to the stage, I started to gain confidence from Hong Kong's overwhelming support for a young entrepreneur. Mei should have been up there with me, but luckily she's not the jealous type. I could see her beaming with pride. My mom was as ecstatic as Mei, also wearing a huge grin. It made me so happy to see that. I remembered how she'd cried when I got kicked out of boarding school. She had been terribly concerned about my future, and I hadn't given her any peace. If that period was a low point, this was definitely a high for my whole family. We celebrated at the Grand Hyatt with a champagne party along with many of my friends, sponsored by Dad. The next morning over breakfast, I proudly laid out the *South China*

Morning Post and read aloud the article on Hartwell Pacific. It was a great moment.

However, like all type A personalities, I succumbed to an emotional low as soon as the applause subsided. I grew very uneasy and started to question the meaning of the award. After all, we had just suffered major setbacks in South Carolina and Mexico; this was not a time for victory dances. I knew the award was a positive thing, but it made me even more afraid of failure. One of the panelists had actually joked, "Congratulations. The DHL/*SCMP* awards are a kiss of death. See you in a year." He was kidding, but with public praise does come the risk of public failure. I wanted to get the award out of my mind and move on.

22

GETTING
BACK ON
THE GROWTH
TRACK

With award ceremonies and family bonding behind us, we refocused on growing the business. But we were not eager to go gallivanting around the world opening new operations. The last thing we wanted to do was to get out of control again. Though concerned about stability, I believed that if we were to go public or offer a decent return to our venture capital investors, not to mention ourselves, we would need a good growth story. However, this would be difficult because we had roughly 50 percent market share in our core commodity, stainless steel, in the countries where we operated. Growing further would cause us to cannibalize our margins. We would need to bid up prices to gain share, overheating the market with our own demand or need.

The answer to our growth issues was clear. We would process other metals at our existing facilities. I started thinking: *What can we get from the same customers? What can be brought on the same trucks?* The two obvious metals were copper and aluminum. They were generated from similar sources as stainless steel, such as demolition, household waste,

or light industrial manufacturing like electronics. This would be strategic synergy, but there were challenges. Copper and aluminum are very competitive commodities, the favorite gambling tools for the local Chinese metal speculators . . . sorry, I mean recyclers. In fact, they are some of the most volatile metals in the world. If we wanted to play with them, we would have to have expert knowledge on all the different grades of scrap and their varying values. We would also need in-depth knowledge of the daily and even hourly price movements as well as medium-term trends. Further, copper is roughly six times more valuable than stainless steel, so fraud would now be an even greater concern. It had taken us eight years to become experts in nickel and stainless steel; I did not want to spend eight more years figuring out new product lines while making all the normal beginner's mistakes.

To shortcut the painful learning curve, we decided to bring in a strategic partner with expertise in copper and aluminum. This would give us the technical product and market knowledge we needed as well as raise some capital. If we did it right, we could jump-start our growth strategy and increase the probability of success. Unlike our previously targeted joint venture partners who clung to their equity for dear life, I had no issue with selling down mine in the name of growth or even just cashing out. My dream was not to pass a scrap metal business on to my kids. I had been a lifelong student of business, and in my mind there was a right time to exit every enterprise.

But how are we going to get a good valuation for Hartwell? I thought. Businesses are traditionally valued based on historical earnings and projected cash flows, but our historical profitability for the group had been badly diminished by our forays into the United States and Mexico. Our shaky past could hurt us, even though the future looked much better.

At this moment, I recalled a childhood memory. My teenage sweetheart's father had worked for Mellon Bank. During the savings-and-loan crisis in the 1980s, Mellon created two banks: the "good" bank and the "bad" bank. All of the nonperforming loans were stripped out of the good one and left in a holding entity. The good bank was thus a nice clean company that could look to the future with a high P/E or stock price. My girlfriend's father was in charge of the bad bank.

The Mellon Bank idea is perfect, I thought. *North America is our bad bank and Asia is our good bank.* All we had to do was strip out the prof-

it-and-loss statements and we had two separate companies—one quite profitable, one unprofitable. Take out any hits or losses related to the closure of America or problems in Mexico, and anything else that could be justified as one-off in nature, and we had the true historical earnings for the Asia region. With that we had a basis for forecasting the potential of the business. Value the good company, selling equity in it at an attractive multiple of earnings, and hold shares in the bad company looking for some asset recovery.

Peter Bentley liked my plan so much that he enthused, "You should have been a deal guy on Wall Street."

Master of the Universe, finally!

The search was on for a strategic or industry partner. We decided to offer shares in just one of our companies: the Philippines. Our operations there were nice and profitable, so we could get a high valuation. This would have two possible outcomes. In one scenario, the strategic partners might like the smaller deal, as it would be a way to get their feet wet in Asia without having to invest too much money. At the same time, we would gain the copper and aluminum know-how in the Philippines and then transfer it ourselves to the other countries. In the other scenario, the investors might become aggressive if they thought we were holding something good back. We could then do a larger-scale deal at the holding company level. Both were winners in my book. I wanted capital and I wanted help.

We contacted Andara Metals in Los Angeles, our first copper supplier back in 1994. They always drove a hard bargain as traders, but their quality and reliability allowed the company what people called the Andara premium. They held the gold standard for quality in our industry. Who better to teach us the business than our old friends?

The Alans, owners of Andara, were also a very wealthy family that had grown as rich from Los Angeles real estate as they had from metals. Money would not be an issue.

I flew to Los Angeles and pitched them in their boardroom. Robert Alan, great-grandson of the founder, was immediately interested and said: "Let's structure a deal. We've been in LA for a hundred years, and we need to make some moves."

Discussions went on for a couple of months until I was beckoned to the Alans' vacation home in Palm Springs. *It must be to wrap up the deal,* I thought. It was a real family affair. The night I got there I had dinner with about ten family members, including their wives. No

business was discussed. The next morning we met at the house for breakfast to talk about the deal, after which I would catch a flight to San Francisco, connecting on to Hong Kong.

I was led into the kitchen and offered a seat at the breakfast table. Kids were running around playing, getting ready for the day's activities, jumping on Daddy's lap. I was jet-lagged and trying to focus on the deal, and this was driving me crazy. It was cozy and personable, but not my style to negotiate major life decisions with kids running around interrupting our conversations, which went something like this:

"So, the Philippines is interesting to us. Harry, put on your coat and help your sister get ready. What were we saying?" After endless pleasantries—"Are you hungry? Have some cereal. Are you sure? How about a muffin?"—we finally got down to business.

Robert's cousin Howard piped up, "Robert and I are very interested, but some of our family members aren't sure we have it in our stomachs to develop a business in Asia. For one, none of us wants to fly to Manila for board meetings. So, we're going to talk among ourselves and get back to you. We don't want you to be discouraged and we want you to keep in touch. We remain interested."

I thanked him for his consideration and headed to the airport for my twenty-hour journey home. *What a colossal waste of time!* I would keep Andara Metals on the back burner, but pursue other options.

Next on my target list was a huge publicly listed company in Australia called Oz Recycling. I had loosely approached its CEO, John Apple, a year earlier about doing something together, but he had said the timing was bad and sent me packing. I had assumed he was referring to the Asian economic crisis but had found out later through the media that he was announcing his retirement. The new CEO, Damien Cotswald, had just now been appointed.

I cold-called Damien, dropping his predecessor's name, and got an appointment. It turned out to be his first as CEO; he hadn't even received his new business cards yet. I told him this was very auspicious. Damien was in his mid-forties, with a youthful spiky hairstyle and an energetic patter. Long worry lines were carved across his high forehead, however, showing that though he seemed easygoing, he had worked hard to get to his position. We hit it off pretty well, and I laid out Hartwell's history and plans. He called in his head of international, Muru Balamarugan, a very affable young guy, who grabbed a chair next to me.

"Oz Recycling is very interested, but we won't be doing any small deals," Damien noted. "We'd want at least 50 percent of the whole business, or nothing." There went the Philippines idea.

"I'm listening, but would much prefer a smaller warm-up deal," I countered, playing hard to get.

Never let them see you sweat. We were baiting a marlin, and it was a long way from the boat.

"Okay, let's figure out what a fifty–fifty joint venture would look like," Damien said. "Muru, you work with Steve and let me know once you've hashed out a term sheet." *He'd taken the hook!*

Muru got back to us with an outline for the deal. They wanted to buy 50 percent of the company outright, paying half now and half in two years if the business maintained its earnings and provided a 25 percent return on capital employed (ROCE), which they called "Rocky." If earnings dropped, the price would be ratcheted down to reflect a lower value. They also wanted to have options to buy out the rest of the business in five years based on a multiple of earnings formula for the average of the last three years of that period. This was becoming more a staged buyout than a long-term partnership.

We can play with this, I thought. After everything we had been through, the potential of walking away with millions sounded pretty darn good. We were also comfortable with the "earn out," or payment over time, because we believed Hartwell's earnings would grow and their target ROCE was reasonable, considering that our own ROCE was running at over 100 percent in Asia.

We put together a deal team: Mei and I versus their best and brightest, which appeared to include at least one representative from each department in their company. Negotiations proceeded over the next two to three months until we got stuck over a financial technicality. Deter Pickets, Oz's persnickety head of accounting, was fighting for an alternative definition of ROCE called ROCCE, return on control capital employed. Instead of being required to provide a 25 percent return on capital investment, Hartwell would have to show a 25 percent return on that capital plus any bank loans or other debt used to finance inventory. Who could have imagined that one *C* could mean so much? Everybody had their textbooks out, with Mei scribbling formulas furiously on a notepad, until I'd had enough.

"You can put the textbooks and calculators away! We need to give you an acceptable return on your investment and that's it; how we

go about financing our inventory is irrelevant as long as we don't ask you for more money! End of story!"

Not really. It turned into a real shit fight, and foul language was bantered around. I felt certain that these guys wanted to do a deal and that they wouldn't blow it over this whole "Rocky" problem. We all agreed to take a break and to keep planning the business side, leaving the details for later.

Though negotiations were tough and stressful, I did find a bright spot. Mei and I absolutely loved Sydney. I became a regular at the Observatory Hotel, which has without a doubt the best blueberry pancakes in the world. It also has a great indoor pool with lights in the ceiling in the form of the southern constellations. The food, the parks, the beaches: I can think of a lot worse places in the world to be stuck for protracted negotiations.

The management team at Oz Recycling was a very active bunch, so I was also forced to get in shape. They were marathon runners and triathletes who jogged every day at lunchtime plus swam laps at the North Sydney swimming pool. One time I was visiting and Damien said, "Come on over at lunchtime and bring yer kit"—meaning gym stuff. "We'll do a short jog with some of the guys, swim a few laps, and then we can iron out any open issues over sandwiches. Good chance for you to get to know more people." I grabbed my gym clothes and headed over to their offices. I felt that I could keep up for a "little jog," but I had overestimated my fitness. I was lagging behind, heaving heavily, sweat trickling into my eyes as we climbed the final hill. I felt really embarrassed and weak in front of these guys. I was determined to get myself back into top condition, which I did, signing up for a personal trainer and hitting the jogging track three to four times a week. It was a great wake-up call.

The deal negotiations were now down to the minutiae, and of course the all-important board approval. The experience with Oz Recycling from the start until this stage had consumed about six months.

⸙

Though it would have been a true pleasure to forget about the bad bank in Mexico, we were forced to conduct deals on two separate fronts, Oz Recycling in Australia and Nickelmet in Mexico. The

December 2001 board meeting with Nickelmet had come and gone with no question or comments from anyone, and I was getting nervous. I contacted Max.

"How did the board meeting go?"

"Unfortunately, Steve, consideration of the deal has been postponed as the tolling venture has not been that profitable for us. The board wants to see a road map to profitability before proceeding with a buyout," he offered apologetically.

This was too much.

"Max, Nickelmet is a billion-dollar enterprise. Whether you make or lose a little money in the short term is irrelevant. You've taken control of the market, and are still making millions in Galveston! What else do you want?" I pleaded, hoping for some sympathy.

"I understand your concern, Steve, but some would say you are lucky. You're getting a $20,000 tolling fee every month and doing nothing. Not to mention it seems your Mexican business wasn't so hot in the first place. Calm down, Steve. Wait until March, when the board will review it again."

I had no choice. *Oh well, at least we're getting $20,000 while we wait,* I thought. March came and Max got in touch.

"I have a difficult message for you from our board. We can no longer see the profitability of our 'partnership.' You need to forgo your monthly fee until we can make money or else we may consider dropping out."

Partnership? I was truly postal. I had suggested partnership in the first place and been rejected out of hand. By now most of the key positions at our Mexican company had been filled by Nickelmet employees or people who'd been hired since it had taken over. They knew our suppliers and our secrets. Most of all, they now knew that I had lost the heart to fight them in Mexico.

"Max, there's no way I'm going to forgo the fee."

"Well, perhaps I can extend until June," he offered, "but we're going to have to come to a conclusion by then."

I was home a few months later and set up a meeting with Max. He opened, "We're pulling out of Mexico. Nickelmet will help pay the closing-down costs and maybe we can do some trading together to help you make some money back, but I can't promise anything. My board members have made this very political. It is not my will, but you have no choice at this point," he said.

Nickelmet walked away, and we cleaned up the mess. The lease at Inox Reciclables de Mexico was terminated, and all the employees were dismissed with full compensation owed to them. Once again, we did not run from our employees. Finally the equipment was auctioned, raising less than twenty-five cents on the dollar. Our blood, sweat, tears, and hopes, not to mention about $2 million, lay in the gutter in Guadalajara. I still believe our plan was visionary and would have been a positive development for the Mexican market, but unfortunately it was a complete and total failure. The failure was in the execution and inability to control the situation on the ground. We also lacked an understanding of the power of the big US recycling companies. The Mexican government didn't help much, either.

Max and I, after not speaking for a year or so, overcame our battle wounds and were once again able to share a Bordeaux and a cigar. My view is that if he'd had the personal authority he would have squared my book, but he didn't. It was explained to me later that there had been a catfight between rival board members, and Max had been overruled. I can't hate him for that. After all it was his fax that rolled across my machine back in 1993 on Caine Road, and he did teach me a lot about the scrap business. Who knows, though? Maybe without him, I could have become the Garden Gnome King of America.

I learned a valuable lesson in all this. It is critical not to let your hopes get ahead of your business realities. I had, and ultimately I paid a big price for it. Desperate people tend to be more optimistic, because admitting defeat is a tougher option. This is a dangerous tendency, and one that had left Hartwell very exposed. Our only hope in Mexico had been a bailout by our competitors. That turned out to be wishful thinking. The "bad bank" in North America was now officially kaput, and Hartwell was teetering on the edge. We had burned through all of our investors' capital, and if anything else would go dramatically wrong at this moment we would be in dire straits. I recalled what the Young Entrepreneur of the Year judge had said: "The award is a kiss of death. See you in a year."

⌒⨯⌒

A deal with Oz Recycling would solve everything and set us up for the future. I needed to negotiate well, working toward closure while keeping a cool head and my eyes wide open.

Things slowly chugged along, as one bureaucrat after another took the grand tour of our Asian operations. The waiting was almost unbearable. My nerves were shattered. Psychosomatic rashes broke out on my face, and deep red circles formed around my eyes. At thirty-four years old my hair was now half gray. Though I had something good to offer Oz Recycling and had a creative way of valuing it, in the back of my mind I knew we were low on chips.

During this period of pushing paper back and forth between Hong Kong and Australia, an opportunity came along that was a great honor for both the company and myself, though the timing was a little off. CNBC invited me to be featured in a program called *Asia's Entrepreneurs.* It would be a fifteen-minute spot on television and would be filmed in our offices and at our recycling yard in Hong Kong. I was proud, excited, and terrified at the same time. It seemed positive notoriety always came at challenging moments, making me feel like a fraud. Here I was getting a gushing interview about the success of a young entrepreneur while facing the reality that I had spent the last year unwinding much of the hard work we had done and writing off millions of dollars. I had to smile for the camera and pontificate about our strategies as my insides twisted with anxiety about our future. When I rewatched the video, I could see the strain on my face. It wasn't TV nerves. It was self-doubt. Though my emotions were conflicted, I was proud of the program, as was our team. This moment brought us together and gave us all a new burst of energy.

⌜⋙⋙⋘⋘⌟

Not long after the show aired, I received a call from the English chairman of a global commodities player with whom I had a distant but friendly relationship. I was flattered to hear from such an important man, a billionaire in fact. It gave my morning a lift.

"Alfred," I beamed. "How are you? To what do I owe the pleasure of this phone call?"

"Why don't you come over for a coffee and a chat?" he offered, suggesting he had something interesting to discuss. It was Monday when he called.

"Let's see," I said. "I am free on Thursday morning." *Don't rush over like a starstruck teenager. You're an important CEO, too!* I coached myself.

Thursday morning I showed up at the company's very modern and expensively decorated headquarters. The chairman's smartly dressed secretary led me along a large open trading floor to his office, nestled in the far back corner. *No doubt the best feng shui,* I thought. I felt proud as I walked down the hall, noticing all eyes looking over to see who was meeting with the big boss. Not long ago I would have been grateful to be sitting at one of those desks. Now I was a player, meeting eye-to-eye with the head of the firm. I sat down at the long oval table by the chairman's desk. His secretary offered me a drink.

"Coffee? Espresso? Cappuccino?"

"Cappuccino, please." *Fancy,* I thought. Swiss chocolates were served.

Sitting in his large, posh office among interesting pieces of modern art, I was reminded of the scene in the movie *Wall Street* when Bud Fox, the lowly stockbroker, finally gets to meet Gordon Gecko, the king of Wall Street. The chairman got right down to the point in a rich English accent.

"We would like to buy your business, Stephen. You would continue to run it and at the same time we'd put you in charge of our steel trading division. Send over your books and we'll tell you what it's worth."

Having learned from my Nickelmet experience to keep my cards close to my chest, I replied, "I'm afraid I can't send over our books just yet; they are confidential and I'd need board approval," I bluffed. "But I can tell you we made about $1.5 million last year. How much would you pay for us if we could substantiate that?" This was the "good bank's" earnings.

He seemed a little annoyed and grumbled, "Look, Steve, this is the way we do things. I need to understand more about your business before I can talk valuations."

"Of course, Alfred, but I do have minority investors. I have to talk it over with them and get back to you," I explained.

"Yes, yes. We know KLM well. Our people checked you out. Look, get back to us sooner rather than later. I might change my mind," he said with a wry smile.

I shook his hand, bowing slightly out of habit, and made my exit. I am pretty sure my feet didn't touch the ground as I walked back to the elevators along the trading floor. *Das right. You da man!* I thought, suppressing a grin. I called Peter Bentley in London, and he was very supportive.

"You handled yourself well. But Steve, now's not the time to sell 100 percent. It's time to build."

Though I was tempted by the thought of the money, I knew Peter was right. We had a good plan. I called over to the chairman and thanked him for his interest and time, but did not send over the books.

"Best of luck to you, then. Keep in touch" was his only reply.

This little episode was important. It made me think of the time when Mei and I were helplessly floating in the Flores Sea. When you're out there in the ocean in your life preserver, slowly losing hope, and you see a sailboat coming at you, it's not easy to say, "Thanks, but keep going. I prefer a motor yacht." It took confidence to pass this by, and that was not always easy to muster. My emotions were very volatile, swinging wildly between boldness and sheer terror.

It was December and we were heading into the holiday season—another year. It had been a year of planning but also a year of waiting. I would have preferred a year of action. Oz Recycling had let go of the ROCE or ROCCE formula as a basis for valuations and we now had a solid "heads of agreement," or deal outline, covering all the major issues. We were just waiting for the final sign-off from the board, and it seemed imminent. I felt good actually—tired but good—time for another Christmas with the family in Pennsylvania.

My mother goes all-out for holidays. The house is transformed into a Christmas movie set with candy, cakes, lights and—oh yes—figurines and ornaments made in China. Though life can get hectic when you get the whole family under one roof, including my rambunctious but lovely niece and nephew as well as two big dogs, it is a wonderful time to be together. Mei and I usually stayed in the guesthouse. That way we could get some needed peace and quiet, keep my work organized, and use the phone at night without disturbing others.

Christmas passed with no news from Oz Recycling. *Holiday time. Best not to push. They'll come to us,* I thought. They did. It was around 11 PM on January 1—January 2 in Australia—and we were scheduled to fly back to Hong Kong the next morning. Our bags were packed and Mei and I lay in bed talking when the phone rang. It was Muru, head of international and point man on the deal. He was very subdued and got right to the point.

"I'm sorry, Stephen, but we have made a decision *not* to move forward with Hartwell. Damien gave me the green light to go ahead but made it clear that it is my ass on the line if it doesn't work. I just can't be sure of the future profits. I can't take that risk."

"Is this final?" I replied, my hand shaking slightly as I held the receiver tightly against a sweaty ear.

"Yes it is. Steve, it's nothing personal. Let's grab a dinner next time I'm in Hong Kong and we can talk more," he ended.

Though totally shocked, I replied calmly, "This is your right and I respect your decision. All the best."

"You, too, Stephen," he answered. *Click.*

I nearly dropped the phone. What else was there to say? I wasn't going to plead with him. That would have been of no use anyway.

"Hmmmmmmmmmmmm." A very long deep breath.

"What is it?" Mei said, standing in her pajamas.

"It was Muru. Oz is walking."

"What reason?" Mei demanded.

"No reason. Just chickened out."

I lay down flat on the bed staring at the ceiling and Mei snuggled up with me, her head on my shoulder as we both silently soaked in the reality that was enveloping us. Our whole business plan revolved around Oz Recycling. Now we'd lost everything.

Breaking the silence, I said to Mei, "I'm not ready to go back to Hong Kong and face this. I need a few days to recover. Let's delay our return."

She looked at me gently, understanding my pain, but replied, "No, Steve. This is when you are at your best. It's time to fight. Let's go back in the morning."

I knew she was right. As I was taught by Coach Washburn in high school football my freshman year as a running back, even when you get hit, keep those legs pumping; sometimes you break free.

23

HOOKING
A MARLIN

Still in shock from the previous night's call from Muru, we boarded United Airlines' nonstop service to Hong Kong via Chicago. *It's not really over with Oz Recycling, is it?* I thought numbly. *I was sure we were going to close.* Even worse, all of our employees involved in the deal process were expecting closure. *What should I say to them? How do I explain that we're back to square one?* I glared out the window; we were leaving Lake Michigan behind, heading due north. I felt tired, but couldn't sleep and paced the aisles. We reached the Arctic Circle and turned west, arcing over Alaska and the Aleutian Islands. As we passed over the most beautiful mountains and ice formations, lit softly by a full moon on this very clear night, I realized that Mother Nature was putting things in perspective. This problem, Hartwell Pacific, my life, everything was insignificant in comparison with what I was looking at. *These challenges will pass,* I thought. *I just need to make the most of a difficult situation.* After turning south over Siberia and then China, we finally arrived in Hong Kong around 6 PM. Reality was setting in, and as the wheels touched down I braced myself for what lay ahead. I had a marathon to run, and it started first thing in the morning.

I awoke around 4 AM. Unable to go back to sleep, I took a quick shower and headed to the office. It was still dark as my taxi passed the newspaper workers who congregate in Central to coordinate the morning deliveries, bringing back memories of my childhood paper route. I rattled our office building's metal security gate until a bleary-eyed night watchman let me in. Once I was behind my desk, the sun started to break, lighting the harbor and the loading derricks at Kwai Chung Port—first gray then a soft blue, brightening with every minute. It seemed so calm and peaceful. I love mornings in Hong Kong, the quiet anticipation of the explosion of activity that's about to take place in one of the busiest cities in the world.

As I pondered the beauty of the morning and nursed a coffee, my thoughts veered to the task at hand. *Okay, who's next on your list of possible strategic partners?* There was a company in South Africa and a company or two in Europe and America that I had considered, but I'd felt they would be less aggressive than Oz Recycling. If I could find someone who was keen to get into Asia, I would be negotiating from a position of strength. In a sudden moment of clarity, I recalled something Damien, the CEO of Oz Recycling, had briefly mentioned in one of our conversations.

I had said to him, "We're talking to others and we only want to discuss matters in detail if you guys are serious."

I had been bluffing him, trying to create a competitive atmosphere. He had then immediately called in Muru and proposed hashing out a heads of agreement. Damien had asked in a concerned voice, "Who are you talking to, Smythson Recycling?" Not taking the bait, I replied, "I can't reveal that," even though I'd never heard of them.

The name *Smythson Recycling* was now ringing in my ears as the harbor continued to lighten and the water began to churn with the motion of the day's activity. I turned on my computer, launched Google, and searched for Smythson Recycling. Several hits popped up. The first one said, "Smythson Recycling CEO Wayne Warren sees strengthening markets for steel raw materials." I scrolled down farther and clicked on its Web site. "With our headquarters in Sydney, we are the leading metal recycler in Australia," it bragged. I continued my Internet search and discovered that Smythson Recycling was a division of Smythson Steel Group, a top one hundred publicly listed company on the Australian Stock Exchange (ASX). It was actually a bigger company overall than Oz Recycling, and had about the same market share

in Australia. However, it lacked Oz's international presence in the United States and Europe. This information was playing right into my hands. An international strategy was perfect for these guys. Smythson had the same problem as Hartwell: With 50 percent of the market, there was nowhere to grow. Plus, the Australian competition boards are very strict, making further consolidation in the local market difficult. From Google, I also gleaned that Smythson was a very acquisitive company so would not be shy about doing deals if they made sense. *We would be small fry for them.*

Pulling up Smythson's contact details and noting that Sydney was two hours ahead, I placed a call to Wayne Warren, the CEO, punching the numbers a little harder than normal. Much to my surprise, his secretary put me straight through. Luckily, I had my elevator speech prepared and launched right in.

"My company is Hartwell Pacific, we're based in Hong Kong, and we also operate in Thailand, the Philippines, and Malaysia processing stainless steel scrap for major steel producers. I used to be managing director of Nickelmet Asia, and have been living in Hong Kong since 1993. I have some interesting business ideas that I would like to discuss with you in person," I said smoothly.

"Where are you now?" Wayne responded.

"Hong Kong," I replied.

"Well, I'll be in Hong Kong in late February. Maybe we can get together then," he offered enthusiastically.

It was January 3. February seemed a long way away.

"Actually, the reason I called this morning is that I am planning to be in Sydney this week and also, the matter is fairly time-sensitive," I bluffed, thinking on my feet.

"When are you planning to come?" he asked.

"Day after tomorrow," I responded, thinking that I could take the night flight that evening and would have a day's rest in Sydney before the meeting.

Wayne agreed and asked what time would be good for me.

"First thing in the morning," I requested—*always when the brain is fresh*. I never make big decisions in the afternoon if I can avoid it. We agreed to meet at 9 AM on Wednesday.

I called and woke up Mei, excitedly explaining this dramatic new development.

"That's my Stephen!" she enthused tiredly from bed.

I was now bursting with energy, pacing the office. *That's right! I'm back! Off the mat and standing for an eight-count. Bring it on!* I exploded inwardly with clenched fists. Nobody in the office knew what had transpired over these last couple of days. They must have thought, *What's wrong with Steve? He's just come back from holiday and he's pacing around the office like a lunatic.*

I booked a first-class seat to Sydney to ensure a good night's rest and an ass kicker's attitude in the morning. I checked into my favorite hotel, the Observatory, just in time for an order of blueberry pancakes with sausage—"pigs in a blanket." The extra day was used for working out and creating a plan of attack. It was pretty basic: I would take the Oz Recycling deal as it stood and offer it to Smythson on a silver platter.

The next day, after some morning laps in the pool and another round of pancakes, I headed off to Smythson's headquarters in North Sydney across the harbor bridge. Early as always, I grabbed a coffee and did a few loops around the block to keep my nerves calm. Even when I try to be late, I'm always early. Watching the clock, I forced myself to enter right on time. The receptionist announced my arrival. I was shocked to find that Wayne was a young guy, and we quickly worked out that we were about the same age, thirty-five. He was a good bit shorter than me, follicly challenged, and his body longed for the gym, but he had a positive energy, a salesman's smile, and we hit it off very naturally. Oz Recycling had been very corporate, but Wayne seemed more street smart and aggressive.

"What's the deal then?" he had said within a minute of meeting. *This is a guy I can do business with,* I thought.

"I'm on the verge of signing a JV agreement with a major Australian recycling company." There were only two main players in Australia and I was sitting in the offices of one of them. "The other company's a good fit, but we're getting hung up on some details. Negotiations are dragging on and I'm starting to wonder if they're the right partner. We've been haggling for almost a year over stupid shit," I explained with exasperation.

Wayne then let loose a tirade on Oz Recycling and its management.

"They're a bunch of pussies! I worked for them for ten years. We're kicking their asses!"

Though I didn't hate Damien or Muru, I did appreciate what I was hearing and at the time agreed with the "pussies" comment. Of greater importance, I was realizing that these guys were at each other's

throats in competition. Smythson would like this deal because it was good for the company, but if Wayne believed what I was saying it could also block his competitor from front-running the firm in Asia.

"You guys have a great reputation and I understand you're very aggressive about growth," I said, basing that on some of Wayne's comments on the Internet. "If you can match the price and fix the details, I'm with you guys."

I then laid out the deal. Wayne listened carefully, acknowledging the key points with a nod of his head. After finishing the explanation, I said firmly, "I can give you a couple of weeks to consider but not more than that."

"That won't be necessary," Wayne responded.

My stomach sagged and my heart moved up into my throat. *I thought he'd at least take a closer look.* Then he finished his sentence.

"We'll do it. If you can stick around, I can have my business development guys up here from Melbourne tomorrow. We can hash out a term sheet right then and there."

Yes! In less than a week we'd gone from total despair to a new live deal.

With most of the heavy lifting having already been done, together with Oz Recycling, we were now moving at full throttle. I informed Wayne that my CFO, Mei, was in Singapore and could get to Sydney in time for the meeting.

The heads of agreement was wrapped up easily and amicably over the next few days. As part of the due diligence process, a tour of Asia was scheduled with Smythson's senior management. Thrilled with the pace, I told Wayne, "As long as we keep this up, I'll go quiet with your competitor."

Wayne paused for a moment, and then replied, "Actually, Steve, I don't really care, but I heard from one of my contacts inside Oz Recycling that they have already declined interest in Hartwell."

"They would say that, wouldn't they? They know we're in bed together and are not happy about it. Forget the gossip, let's focus on the deal and the exciting opportunities ahead," I said nervously, regretting that I had brought up the subject. *He who is silent is thought to be a fool. He who speaks out removes all doubt!* Granddad's words echoed once again. Whether Wayne bought my story or not, Smythson was very eager to expand internationally, so things continued smoothly.

As was the case in most of the companies I dealt with, the business leaders were charming and affable—enter the bean counters.

Group CFO Rick Jones was friendly at the outset, but quickly began grilling me on risks, threats, and earnings projections. Next, the lawyers joined in with a laundry list of "reps and warranties," which are contractual terms that basically say: "If any of your claims turn out to be false, we will have your ass in a sling and own your company in the process." The key to negotiating these clauses is to differentiate between committing to the truth and guaranteeing a business outcome. I was of course willing to commit to being truthful but not to guaranteeing their downside risks. At this moment I knew I needed the best lawyer I could afford. Luckily, that lawyer was also a personal friend.

Charlie Compson was a young star and newly minted partner in the Hong Kong office of Lincoln Snopes LLC, one of the most highly regarded Wall Street law firms. He is a brainy and intense Williams grad who was always slightly disheveled and more or less lived in an office that was cluttered with stacks of papers and only half decorated in a *F--- you, I didn't have time to hang the pictures* style. He also shares my love of fine food and red wine, so Charlie would be an excellent addition to our deal team.

During the negotiations and courting period, news started to hit the papers of a new and dangerous disease that was spreading through the region. Severe Acute Respiratory Syndrome (SARS) had killed a few people in China and Vietnam, and it seemed to be rapidly spreading via "super carriers," those who carried the contagious disease and traveled extensively. Soon a large number of people would die in Hong Kong. Those who lived in buildings where there had been outbreaks were quarantined in isolation wards, separated from their loved ones. Citizens of Hong Kong were told to wear surgical masks in elevators, subways, taxis, planes, or any other close-contact situations. It was really eerie and depressing. If someone coughed, people would quickly move away. Everyone opened doors with their elbows and pushed elevator buttons with their knuckles, a habit I still maintain from that period.

I came back to Hong Kong from Bangkok one evening on Thai Airways and found Mei staring at the television set.

"Steve, look. This is your flight, TG 613. A guy with SARS was on your plane. It says if you get a fever to call this hotline." *Shit!* I thought. *This is serious.* Luckily, I'd been in business class, and in fact had chosen to move to a section that was not near anyone else as a paranoid precaution, but I called the hotline nonetheless. The operator informed me that the SARS carrier had been fairly far back in

economy, but if I developed any symptoms in the next ten days I should contact a doctor immediately. I contemplated the image of SARS traveling through the ventilation system, swirling about the business-class cabin as I innocently inhaled. The guy on my flight soon died. Strangely, about seven days into the possible incubation period, I came down suddenly with the worst chest cold I'd ever had. I absolutely panicked and quickly arranged an appointment with a doctor. Thoughts of dying in an isolation ward, unable to say good-bye to my family in America, rushed through my head. No matter what my fears were, I knew the only decision was to turn myself in. I went down to the doctor's office and approached the reception.

"I have a serious chest infection and I was on a flight with a SARS carrier less than ten days ago."

The nurse's eyes bulged and she promptly ushered me in to see the doctor, keeping well away.

He asked me immediately, through a surgical mask, "Do you have a fever?"

"No," I replied.

"Good. Calm down. You don't have SARS," he assured me.

He then took out the World Health Organization specification sheet and showed me that the number one critical symptom was a high fever. My heart slowly stopped pounding and my breathing lengthened. He smiled, which made me feel a lot better.

"Bed rest, lots of liquids, and some antibiotics is all you need," he explained.

I took the prescription and headed home, relieved that I would live to see another day. Though getting healthy, I was still nervous. This was starting to have similarities to September 11 and my Mexican Nickelmet experience. I could just hear it: "We are very interested but want to wait until this whole SARS thing blows over." *What's going on? God must not want me to make it!* I thought.

Smythson had made a rule that nobody who had traveled to a SARS-infected country in the previous ten days could meet with any of its senior executives, so I headed Down Under to Australia and made the Observatory Hotel in Sydney my base of operations. With ten days to kill and Easter weekend approaching, I decided to take Mei somewhere warm and beautiful for a long weekend. We went up to Lizard Island on the Great Barrier Reef to do some fishing and relax. On our first day there, we chartered a boat and cruised out to the

Ribbon Reefs in search of the elusive black marlin. We caught two beautiful blacks, one four-hundred-plus pounds and the other around three hundred, Mei and I each getting our quarry to the boat for a tag and release. A lucky day! We returned to Sydney tanned, rested, and ready for another round of negotiations. I let Smythson know about our exotic weekend with a hidden message that we were not desperate for money and were taking negotiations easy. This could not have been farther from the truth.

A month later, Smythson's quarantine policy ended and SARS eventually wound down, quietly disappearing just as it had entered our world. I never understood how something so lethal could just appear, kill a few hundred people, and go away. I hoped I would never have to live through anything like that again.

The parties were pushing to meet internal deadlines to wrap things up, and I was pleased with the principals' level of commitment. It seemed that it was a done deal and we just needed to finish the paperwork. The main problem, as far as I could see, was that Smythson's newly employed general counsel decided to hire her alma mater law firm to draft the contract. Eager to impress and get in with this new client, the lawyers went overboard and wrote a book of a document that would take ages to get through. Even the Smythson executives privately told me that it was excessive and heavy-handed.

It was decided that the best way to get this done quickly was for my lawyer Charlie and me to fly to Melbourne for an "as long as it takes" session with Smythson's legal team. Charlie agreed, and we were shortly on our way. Charlie had read the cumbersome document and said, "Don't worry, just stay calm, and I'll sort this out. Leave it to me; you're the good guy and I'm the bad guy."

We were invited up to the penthouse offices of Smythson's outside counsel and ushered into a large conference room with sweeping views of the city. The senior partner, Fred, was directing people around one end of the long oval table. Two junior lawyers filed in with Smythson's general counsel and two others from Smythson's business development department.

"Is there anything we can get you to make you comfortable—a cappuccino, some juice, or water?" we were asked.

A nice tray of refreshments arrived, an assortment of biscuits and tea sandwiches. Everyone was smiling, greeting one another, and making small talk. Smythson's general counsel opened the meeting.

"I suggest you go through the document and let us know with which parts, if any, you have issues," he said confidently.

Everyone was seated, each with a set of documents, a notepad, and a company pen in front of them. Charlie had a glass of ice water, which he quickly drained down to the cubes, and opened the first of three documents, nodding gently. As he perused the papers, casually flipping through the pages at a pace that clearly showed he wasn't reading, he started chewing loudly on a mouthful of ice. "Crunch, crunch, crunch." Pause. "Crunch, crunch." He took in another mouthful and continued flipping through the pages. "Crunch, crunch, crunch." *What the hell is he doing?* I thought.

Charlie, satisfied that he had reviewed the document, slowly started in. "Let me see. I do have some comments and concerns." He pulled out a marking pen from his briefcase and crossed out the Smythson name as the contract party. *Hmmm,* I thought. Then he drew a line through a quarter of page two, turned to page three, and drew a big X over the entire page. He continued, turning page by page and crossing out no less than half of each. When he was done, he put the document down and said enthusiastically, "Well, that should do it. I think we are almost done. We can start planning where we want to go for lunch."

Everyone around the table looked a bit confused. Fred, the senior partner, jumped to the defense, "You crossed out more than half of my drafting. You can't do that! You have to explain to me what changes you want for each of those clauses and why! What's wrong with the contract?" he demanded, showing his frustration.

Charlie responded slowly and calmly, "You see, Fred, if things go well, which I'm sure they will because my client is such a good guy, then everything will be fine. But if they don't—" Charlie's voice sharpened and became more voluble with each word, the edge of a New York accent coming to the surface. "—all of these clauses serve one purpose and one purpose only, and that is to f--- my client up the butt! Now, Steve is my client, but he is also my friend and I won't stand by and let you f--- him up the butt! This is the most one-sided, egregious contract I have ever read! It shows a total lack of sincerity or respect and I must advise Steve to move forward with Smythson very cautiously. For starters, you have the contract party as some newly created, one-dollar Hong Kong company! Do you think we are children?!"

24

NEGOTIATIONS GET SERIOUS

Holy shit! What just happened? I panicked inwardly, avoiding the eyes of my future colleagues. The general counsel for Smythson was in total shock.

Charlie then started at the beginning of the document and worked his way through it, citing the most egregious clauses while chewing loudly on ice. All faces around the table were bright red; I am sure mine was crimson as well. This was about to get ugly. When he finished, Charlie asked for a sidebar and suggested we make it a bathroom break. We arrived at the gents and checked that all the stalls were empty. I was very concerned.

"Charlie, what are you doing? You're going to torpedo the deal!"

"No, I'm not. You go in and apologize for my behavior; I'll be in shortly. Steve, this contract is a stinker. We have to kick it hard from the get-go to gain control of the negotiation. I'll get you as far as I can. In the worst case, you publicly fire me and send me back to Hong Kong. By that point I will hopefully have gotten you most of the way there. No matter what, you'll be in much better shape than if you sign that piece-of-shit contract. These piss-ant lawyers don't know who they're dealing with! At Lincoln Snopes we kill for our clients!" he shouted. "You just stay the good guy, Steve. Keep your mouth shut and look

down." I expected him to start pounding his chest. *Charlie's in the house!* I thought. I knew the contract stunk and also had faith in my friend.

I walked back into the conference room and apologized for Charlie's language, but insisted that we needed to have a more balanced contract. The head of business development for Smythson stated firmly, "I just want to go on the record saying that your lawyer is a real asshole."

"Well, he is obviously upset," I retorted. "And I have to admit that makes me concerned. I want a fair-and-square deal that captures the spirit of the principal agreement."

"That's what we want, too, Steve," he replied.

"Good, then I'm sure we will be fine. Let's work to that end. Everyone here wants a fair deal," I ended.

Charlie entered the room and I sat down, wiping my palms with a napkin and pouring myself a cold glass of water. We agreed to calmly go through each clause and discuss it. I stood and planted myself by a window, my back to the assembled group. I wanted to be clear that Charlie represented me on the negotiation of clauses and that I was only to be called on for final agreement. In those cases Charlie would say, "I really don't think you should accept this, but it's up to you." That was our preagreed signal that it was okay.

This went on all day, straight through lunch, and after about twelve hours we had a joint venture contract we could live with. I was pleased and told Charlie that I was relieved that it was behind us. He interjected, "Remember, Steve, this will probably get worse before it gets better. We still have the employment agreement and the share purchase agreement ahead of us. But we're done for today and it was a good one. Let's go grab a pint."

The awkward thing after such a hostile encounter was that Smythson's general counsel had previously invited us out with her husband for a three-hour city-tour trolley ride that included dinner. Obviously this invitation was made in anticipation of a much smoother negotiation. Nobody had the guts to back out, so we agreed to meet at the station at 8 PM. In the meantime, Charlie and I headed for the pub on the corner and grabbed a pint. We then went to play blackjack at the Crown Casino on the Yarra River, where we both won a few hundred dollars. I looked at my watch: seven forty-five, time to go. I would have preferred a root canal. Charlie and I sat there, numbing the pain with red wine, as we chugged slowly along the streets of Melbourne, making small talk with the enemy and her hus-

band for three endless hours. Funnily enough, Charlie was very charming and affable. I marveled at how he could turn it on and off so dramatically. It wasn't personal, just business.

The next day we returned to Hong Kong. There were a lot of negotiations over the next couple of months, some positive and others tougher, but throughout, Charlie was able to maintain his reputation as a real son of a bitch. It was a stressful process, but I was lucky to have a good lawyer. I probably would have been a poor negotiator with my Oz Recycling experience weighing heavily on me.

⤜∝⤛

Negotiations with Smythson drew toward a close and we had pretty much everything ironed out, but I was totally blindsided by what happened next. I prepared a paper for Peter Bentley and the KLM fund outlining all the key details of the deal. I also enclosed a copy of the draft agreement. Peter let me know that he would read through it and get back to me. Up to this point he had been very encouraging and pleased about the developments. The deal as structured had given us "put options"—the right to sell our shares to Smythson at a future point in time on a preagreed formula that was a healthy multiple of earnings. KLM thus had a guaranteed exit—the ultimate goal for any venture capital investor. If there is no liquidity for your shares, you never get your money out.

I was expecting a congratulatory response and a pat on the back but instead received a cold glass of water in the face.

"KLM," Peter wrote, "is not interested in the deal as proposed. The North American strategy was a failure and hurt our returns, and we now want to recoup some of our losses before we approve this deal." When I had mentioned the half-million-dollar write-off due to the closing of South Carolina in our first board meeting, it had seemed like he wasn't paying attention, but it now appeared he had just been biding his time. I knew this was a great deal for all shareholders and felt strongly that he should tell me what was wrong with it or how we could make it better for all concerned.

"I'm open to suggestions," I concluded.

Peter replied that he was not concerned about the other shareholders, as his only interest was in KLM's position. The next thing he wrote blew me away.

"We are happy to persevere ahead without Smythson Steel. We believe in your management ability and unless we improve the economics of the deal for KLM, we will not agree to go along. If you read your contract, you will find that we have the right to block this from going forward."

I was furious. *This is total bullshit.* I got the contract out and found clause 12.8, which covered the sale of shares. KLM did have the right to block, but it said, "Approval is not to be unreasonably withheld." He had to be reasonable. I called Litchfield's, my original law firm, to have its lawyers review the contract. They got back to me with a phone call and explained that though clause 12.8 required reasonableness, clause 4.1 did not, and while the two clauses seemingly contradicted each other, clause 4.1 was the more powerful. Peter could block us for any reason he wanted and didn't need to explain himself. *Doesn't everyone have to act reasonably anyway?* I thought. The short answer was no. Peter owned a small percentage of our company but controlled 100 percent of this decision. I felt totally naked and violated. I ran it by Charlie, who explained gently to me, "Yeah. You're f---ed." Litchfield's saw it from a different angle.

"Don't worry. This is a good deal for him. He's not that stupid. Just rattle his cage. We'll draft a letter stating that we agree with him and that we'll call off the deal."

Rattle his cage? My cage was experiencing a 9.0 earthquake on the Richter scale! I had no appetite for a fight at this stage. I had told Smythson all along that KLM was on board, and I was concerned that a fight with it over the "bad bank" would be damaging to our negotiations. After all, Smythson was only buying into the "good bank" and knew nothing about our problems with the bad one. In some way, I am sure we could have called Peter's bluff, but I was in no mood for high-stakes poker. He didn't have to be reasonable; it was sitting there in black and white in our contract. He held the stick; it made no sense to pretend that I held it.

At the end of the day, we had to cough up $500,000 to KLM to get our deal done. I learned the hard way to never let minority shareholders have absolute rights. At least have a reasonableness clause enabling a third party's involvement to resolve disputes. Without it, there is no adjudication. I also now understood that being the drafter is a power position worth paying for if you can get it, as it puts the burden on the other party to find all the hidden angles and haggle for every change. Little things like the inclusion or exclusion of the word *reasonable* can be critically important.

One last sticking point that was not resolved until the final stages was the obvious conflict of having a husband-and-wife CEO/CFO team. We knew that was not tenable for a public company such as Smythson, and Mei was very excited about stepping out of the business to be more Mrs. Greer than Mrs. Hartwell. She had no desire to be the "Scrap Queen"; "Scrap King," as I was dubbed by the *China Daily,* has a better ring to it anyway. The problem was that Mei played a vital role in the company and Smythson knew that. They had gained a high level of respect for her during the negotiations. Together we came up with a way to ease her out over the next year by making her a consultant and using that time as an opportunity to recruit a professional CFO.

Finally, on June 30, 2003, Symthson's year end and coincidentally my thirty-fifth birthday, just six months after our deal with Oz Recycling had gone down in flames, we had a deal confirmed. Smythson now owned 50 percent of Hartwell Pacific. Mei and I were in Sydney for the closing, staying once again at the Observatory Hotel, dining on fantastic seafood in the evenings, and learning to appreciate the intricacies of the Australian grape varietals. My good friend Bernie McGuire, whose couch I'd slept on when I first arrived in Hong Kong ten years earlier, was now living in Sydney, so I scheduled a celebratory lunch with him at Aria, a great restaurant next to the famed Sydney Opera House with views of Darling Harbor. That morning the local papers, the two national papers, the *Australian* and the *Financial Times,* and the *Melbourne Herald* carried the story. The articles sang the praises of the deal as well as the industriousness of a "young, American entrepreneur." Nothing like blueberry pancakes, a hot cup of coffee, and reading your name in the paper, as long as it's a positive story.

It was a beautiful, crisp, clear day and I chose to walk down from my hotel to meet Bernie. As I strolled along Circular Quay at the Sydney waterfront, my phone rang. It was Muru, the head of international for Oz Recycling, the guy who had rejected us over Christmas.

"Hi, Steve. Just calling to say that I was pleased to see your name in the morning paper. Congratulations on your deal. Well done. I wish you and Mei the best of luck," he said magnanimously. He couldn't have been that happy really. Anyway, I appreciated the call.

I entered the restaurant and there was Bernie with a big smile on his face, a congratulatory hand reached out, and a copy of the *Financial Times* on our window-side table. This is the definition of a good

friend—there for you in the tough times and celebrating with you in the good times. There was nothing but joy on Bernie's face.

⌐◦∞◦⌐

Back in Hong Kong and with the deal under our belt, Mei and I began planning to find a new home more befitting two successful corporate executives. Our property agent called one day and said, "I have a beautiful apartment overlooking Hong Kong Park. It is right in the center of the city within walking distance of Citibank Tower and the Shangri-la Hotel. These are very rare and will likely only be on the market for a day or two." I figured that was a classic sales pitch and noted that it didn't even have a balcony. She insisted that it was worth our while to have a look, so Mei and I drove down to Kennedy Road along the park on a sweltering August day to meet the agent. We took the elevator to the ninth floor of the fifty-year-old, twelve-story building—one flat per floor. The front door opened, and a forty-foot-wide, eight-foot-high wall of windows creating a steady breeze throughout the apartment greeted me. It was love at first sight. I said, "We'll take it."

Mei thought I was jumping the gun, but as I stood at the windows overlooking the park and the city I knew that I had found a home. After ten years of temporary living, shared flats, the coffin, the needle in the sky on Bridges Street, and a passable flat on Conduit Road, I finally felt a sense of permanence, of having my feet solidly on the ground.

⌐◦∞◦⌐

Once the euphoria of finding our strategic partner, clinching our deal, and solidifying our base had settled, it was time to get organized. We created a board of directors for Asia, which included Bill Yardley, CEO of Smythson Steel Group; George Frampton, a member of the founding family; Wayne Warren, the head of the recycling division; and, of course, me. The prickly CFO was also on the board as a non-voting member. My relationship with him had never recovered from the difficult joint venture negotiations in which he'd played the bad guy. It was an open secret that he disliked me, perhaps because a thirty-five-year-old and his smart-ass New York lawyer didn't roll over in the negotiations.

Though my relationship with the CFO was a bit strained, I really loved having an active board to challenge my ideas and put ritual focus on business planning and reviews. I had never had a mentor or any business leadership around; it was just Mei and me, arguing in bed. Nonetheless, on many occasions, the board confessed that our systems were more stringent than Smythson's, particularly with regard to our inventory and cash controls. I was proud to note that for the most part, our organizational structures held up to scrutiny.

There was a great feeling of confidence in the air. Smythson Hartwell Recycling was finally open for business. It was time to blow the dust off our copper and aluminum plan and put it into action.

We first made some important organizational changes, hiring A. K. Yeap, an experienced executive, as our GM for Malaysia This allowed us to change from a family business to a professional corporation down in Johor Bahru with the retirement of Mei's mother and stepfather. We next got Philip Wu, our financial controller, more involved in operations. This gave us a capable executive with a broad understanding of the numbers measuring everything from quality and unit output to consumption of hydraulic oil. Operations would now step up and make marked improvements and significant contributions to the bottom line. I also moved Carrie Woo, a sharp and organized young woman, from the position of finance admin manager over to head of business analysis and risk management. She would filter through all the numbers and give me the critical details I needed to make the important trading decisions. Helen Hon, a hardworking and tough-minded local, became head of trading and logistics. We then hired a new CFO, John Chen, whom we recruited from PepsiCo. With these moves, together with our board's oversight, Smythson Hartwell Recycling would now have a balanced and experienced team to watch over a fast-growing business.

However, we still needed a transfer agent or key executive from Smythson to give us an education on the new product lines. From its Queensland division, Smythson put forward Rob Chapman, a young manager with a can-do attitude. He was a handsome, beefy guy with a bleached blond mane who had been a competitive surfer and raced super bikes on weekends back in Australia. "We'll have everyone trained up in a couple of months and be cookin' with gas on the barbie. No worries, mate!" With Rob in place, all we needed to do was train up our employees, create a work plan, and purchase appropriate equipment.

The training schedule for our key Asian managers would include hands-on experience in Australia. They were quietly thrilled about that. The training went well. My team was aggressive, took learning

very seriously, and was soon very knowledgeable about these new metals. They wandered Smythson's recycling yards with notebooks and pencils in hand, analyzing every detail, strength, and weakness. Most Americans I know would have considered a training trip to Australia to be a boondoggle or chance to hit the beach in the morning and the bars in the evening. On the contrary, my guys don't drink, don't enjoy the beach, and even complained that the training ended at 5 PM, leaving them with nothing to do. They recommended that the training trips be shortened and made more intensive. There were times when I felt it would have been fun to work with people who shared more of my personal interests, but I had learned that these were not qualities to look for when recruiting. I looked for work ethic and a sense of seriousness over congeniality or ability to assimilate with Westerners. Our people ended up being able to do both.

Next, we designed an efficient workflow. Marketing was not going to be a problem, as Smythson handled over ten thousand tons—five hundred ocean containers—per month of copper and aluminum. Whatever we collected, processed, and loaded could be easily plugged into its network of buyers.

Though the training and operational planning had gone smoothly, I was concerned about the equipment procurement. Total investment would be about $1 million. I didn't have a problem with the overall budget but was not pleased with the way we were spending it. All of our vendors were Smythson's Australian or New Zealand suppliers. I understood the instinct to find the easiest option, but I was pretty certain that China, Taiwan, or Korea were lower-cost producers of industrial equipment than New Zealand. In the end, after considerable debate, we ended up with a mixture that kept everyone happy. I realized, though, that I was going to need to push back from time to time or risk losing our low-cost operating culture. *You can't ask people to save money on small stuff, and then blow big money in front of their faces on equipment from New Zealand. Cost control is not a singular action. It's a culture.* At times, Smythson executives thought I was being petty or just trying to show my authority, but the truth was I was defending our culture. Every small breach is a cut, and I was not going to allow a "death by a thousand cuts."

Even though Hartwell was becoming less and less mine, I was happy with our start and could see us morphing into a large professional corporation. We had overcome fraud, failed deals, near death in Indonesia, SARS, a battle with our private equity investors, and millions of dollars in losses, but had somehow come out on top. We were now poised for greatness.

25

A WALK IN THE PARK

The metals markets were hot, particularly for nickel, and profits were up a solid 50 percent year-on-year. We entered year two of our joint venture in a strong position.

Copper and aluminum earnings were now also starting to kick in, but weren't even close to the continued meteoric increase in stainless profits. The nickel market continued its boom, with an increase from around $10,000 to over $35,000 per ton. With this increase in prices and POSCO's continued strong demand, net income went up a whopping 250 percent over the next six months.

Smythson was pleased that it had obviously made a good investment, but now faced a dilemma. As earnings jumped, so did the value of the half of the joint venture it did not own. In fact, because its future buy price would be based upon historical earnings, our record profits were making its acquisition more expensive by the day. No matter what, Hartwell's shareholders were over the moon as they started counting their future winnings. Every dollar in profit growth now had a multiplying wealth effect.

We now started facing increasing pressure from Smythson to invest in capital expenditures and acquisitions, but quickly realized that this was not necessarily in Hartwell Pacific's interest. The more capital investments we made, the less cash there would be available for dividends. Smythson was also stonewalling us on dividend approval, so cash was piling up on the balance sheet. Without their approval, we would be unable to distribute our profits to the shareholders, and would instead just be giving them away to Smythson in the buyout. I spoke to Peter Bentley and Mei about this issue and we all agreed: "No more investment, and we want maximum dividends."

Long speeches were made by Smythson about our mutual interests and goodwill, but the facts remained and the positions were clear. Smythson and Hartwell were joint venture partners with very different interests.

To resolve this conflict, we went back to the negotiating table. Once again, Bill Yardley and Wayne were the good guys and the CFO was the bad guy. Throw in Smythson's legal department and Charlie Compson and we were at it again. The players had been called out and the battle was set to begin. Smythson made the initial approach.

"We want to expand. That's in the company's best interest, and it will obviously require investment. We think we have a solution that will enable us to build out the business and also make everyone happy. We'll buy you guys out early at an attractive number, and you'll remain as chief executive for Asia to help us with our global push," Bill Yardley offered positively.

"This could be interesting, Bill. Hartwell shareholders are listening and we await your firm bid," I replied calmly, having learned over the years to keep my cool.

We were now quickly heading into Christmas with no word from Smythson. I felt the smart way to play our cards was to go quiet and focus on the business. *Keep your distance,* I thought. *Don't come on too strong.*

In the meantime, our now seasoned executives at Smythson Hartwell responded perfectly to the market opportunities that presented themselves. When prices of a commodity don't move, the market situation becomes very transparent; it's then hard to make great profits, because everyone knows the value of the commodity. There are no secrets and no opportunities to bluff and negotiate. The market, however, was currently bouncing around like a yo-yo. Commodity

traders and hedge funds in particular caught whiff of this and jumped in with both feet. These new players utilized sophisticated computer-driven trading strategies that created the volatility companies like ours love. Hartwell now enjoyed the fastest inventory turns, greatest diversity of revenue streams, record sales volumes, and was making in a month what used to take us a year. Smythson's slow acquisition process was costing it millions.

I maintained my calm facade, but inside my nerves were beginning to fray. I knew that with these higher commodity prices and volatility came the need for higher capital commitments to finance the inventory. I also understood that just as you can enjoy the benefits of volatility, you also can get on the wrong side of it. So far our skills had been serving us well, but I knew that a dark day could come and suddenly we wouldn't be looking so cute. I felt strongly that this was a perfect-storm opportunity to push through a great deal for Hartwell's shareholders.

Shockingly, Smythson finally came through with a bid that was a complete lowball. I was told privately and apologetically that this offer was born on the CFO's desk. I responded coolly, "There must be a misunderstanding. We thought you wanted to buy our shares. Your bid is way off the mark. Let's move on, we've wasted a lot of time. We can be an effective joint venture, but we just need to resolve the unintended conflicts that are inherent in our contract."

Wayne quickly got back to me. "The deal's not dead. We'll sort it out with our team and get back to you shortly. You-know-who is being a total pain in the ass!"

"Take your time," I replied with a snicker to myself.

Profits continued to grow.

It was now about March 2005 and a serious offer was put on the table that was more or less acceptable, though we of course did not let on. It was a number that would give the KLM Asia Venture Fund a great return on its investment and set Mei and me up for life. A meeting was held in Hong Kong at a boardroom in the Shangri-la Hotel to finalize the deal. Mei and I sat across the table from Bill Yardley (CEO), Rick Jones (CFO), and Wayne Warren (Recycling CEO), next to a window that overlooked the tea lounge where I had negotiated our initial deal with Peter Bentley and the KLM Asia Venture Fund years earlier—lots of karma in the air.

Everybody stated their financial case as to why this was a good or bad price depending on where they were sitting at the table. The strongest arguments came from the CFO, for whom this deal seemed particularly painful. Bill Yardley and Wayne sat quietly. Calculators were out, and everyone was trying to outmath one another. Tempers flared until finally the CEO jumped in: "I've had enough. This is our final offer." He scribbled it on a piece of paper and handed it to me. "It's valid right now and right now only." The CFO looked down, shaking his head.

The offer was solidly higher than what Mei and I had agreed with Peter Bentley would be our bottom line. I stifled my smile, taking in the implications of what was being discussed, held still for dramatic effect, and then asked if Mei and I could talk about it privately. We all agreed to break for lunch and eat separately. Mei and I had sushi and the Smythson people hit the buffet. We returned to the boardroom after lunch and took our seats.

"There's a small gap in expectations and we should meet in the middle," I opened. I passed a notepad to him with our final counteroffer.

Bill Yardley paused, showing frustration on his face, and then reluctantly said, "Okay. We're done."

I stood, and reached out my hand. "The company is yours."

Bill met my grip halfway across the table and that was that.

The price was fixed, but once again we would have to maneuver our way through the contract details: the reps and warranties, non-compete agreements, as well as my employment contract. Charlie was back on board and the new general counsel in Smythson's office—the old one had resigned—was much more amenable and sensible. This was an easy process compared with the Herculean task we had completed while putting the joint venture together.

The final negotiations were all about me—making sure I would be tied to the business for at least three years. Smythson insisted on a serious financial penalty if I left the company before that time had passed. The haggling got a little nasty, and it was hard at times as it was all personal in nature. Mei got particularly mad when Smythson's lawyer offered up, "What if Stephen gets killed, is incapacitated, or becomes unsound of mind?" As I mentioned, Chinese people don't talk about these things. I was of course flattered that Smythson valued my services so highly, but onerous clauses were offensive and my lawyer Charlie, once again, did not hesitate to go ballistic when these moments popped up.

"You don't own my client!" he'd bark.

March 31 rolled around, and we expected to close that afternoon. We had booked a table for a celebratory dinner at Grissini, a nice Italian restaurant at the Grand Hyatt with beautiful views of Hong Kong Harbor. I had a fine bottle of red picked out in my mind.

We were working in Lincoln Snopes's main conference room, which the firm had generously donated. It had an open view of Hong Kong Park and our apartment.

There were no major business issues left but lots of little, technical legal stuff—contradicting clauses, arguments about word choice and the placement of commas. I had learned the hard way that these can end up being important, so I kept my distance and let Charlie go to work.

It became clear that dinner was not going to happen. People in Australia were getting stressed. They had intended to announce the deal to the stock exchange in the morning, and the press release was ready to go now that the ASX had closed. This was an important transaction, as it was Smythson Recycling's first international investment and signaled its intention to become a global player.

We worked into the evening, consuming plenty of Starbucks coffee and ultimately dining on Domino's pizza. It was getting late and Michael Rawley, Smythson's general counsel in Melbourne, was sleeping with his phone on. We were instructed to call at any hour if we needed him.

Around ten o'clock we hit a snafu, a minor matter of Hong Kong law that required a specialized local lawyer to resolve it. Smythson's very pleasant representative, Kim, explained: "Look. There is no way we can close. We need to tell Australia that this isn't happening tonight."

Charlie took me aside. "This is really bad joss. On closing day, you close. Are you prepared for an all-nighter? If you are, I am, and I'll get some local counsel in here now."

"I'm in," I replied.

Charlie made an announcement. "We came to close, and at Lincoln Snopes we close even if takes all night. Kim, do you have the funds ready?"

"Yes," she answered. "I'm authorized to make the transfer from our account in New York. We have till 5 PM, New York time, to give them the instruction. That's 5 AM Hong Kong time."

"Are you sure? I need funds in our account to close this deal," Charlie emphasized.

"We can do it," Kim confirmed.

"Okay, let's agree to compromise on all the chickenshit that's left with only one mission in mind: closing. Agreed?" Charlie stated.

"Agreed," Kim replied seriously.

"Okay, I'll get Clambert, our local counsel, in here now," Charlie said calmly, with a hint of a threat that if he did this we'd better close.

"Clambert? Who's Clambert?" I asked privately.

"Chris Lambert. I call him Clambert. Or sometimes Clambèr as in Camembert if I'm feeling French," Charlie replied.

Chris is a really nice English guy, and I had a chuckle wondering how it was initially received when this fast-talking New Yorker reduced this Englishman's name to Clambert or Clambèr.

Good as gold, Clambert showed up with his wife in tow to keep him company for the late night. Perhaps she doubted the veracity of his comment that he needed to spend the night out with an important client.

The lawyers got down to business, but things were more technical than we thought. We needed to keep calling Australia to wake up Michael Rawley and finalize details. The hours crept by, and I started smoking cigars to stay awake and to keep relaxed. Charlie got me a beer out of the company fridge.

"Stay cool, babe. We're gettin' there," he comforted.

Mei had gone home to rest. I was to call her if it was going down; she'd bring the champagne.

Two o'clock. Three o'clock. Four o'clock. My eyes were bloodshot and so were Charlie's. It was now just down to printing documents. A Harvard Law grad was the only guy around in the office, and Charlie assigned him the task of printing and collating contracts. There was a quiet ironic joy to a Harvard Law grad being my gofer.

Finally, just before 5 AM, I called Mei to bring the champagne down. Stacks of documents were lined up on the table in the conference room. Everybody got busy signing—share purchase agreements, employment agreements, everything in triplicate. The signing was done, and Kim gave the instruction to the bank in New York to transfer the funds.

"We did it! We're done!" Kim enthused with an exhausted giddiness.

"No we're not. Not until I see the faxed transfer confirmation," Charlie lectured.

Urgent calls were made, and there was a long stressful silence that ended when the document finally slipped out of Lincoln Snopes's fax machine at 5:30 AM. That was it. We popped champagne, lit cigars, my third for the night, and made a toast.

"To Hartwell Pacific and Smythson Steel! Onward and upward!"

I thanked Charlie, Kim, and Clambert profusely. Mei looked at me blankly, neither of us truly understanding what had just transpired.

The offices of Lincoln Snopes were trashed and reeked of smoke. As I walked out to the elevator foyer, I said to Charlie, "Your people will be shocked when they arrive for work this morning."

"No they won't. This is normal. Congratulations, Steve," he replied.

The elevators of Citibank Tower opened and in a confused fog, Mei and I shuffled across the lobby, catching odd glances from the security guards. We then exited the building through the back into Hong Kong Park for the short walk to our apartment. The sun was coming up. Light was dancing off the gleaming office towers and the birds in the park were calling. Mei and I held hands.

Epilogue

Selling the business was in some way a great relief. All of the accumulated stress had taken its toll, and Mei and I were both truly burned out. The good news was that the company, riding the raging commodity boom, continued setting profit records. In fact, our best year ever was in 2006, the year after we sold. I could have suffered from seller's remorse but did not. At the time, I had had serious concerns about the markets being overheated and what could happen to our profitability if they collapsed. I now planned to use the negotiated transition period to recover from twelve breakneck years and to take stock of my life while making a new plan for the future—this time with a healthy nest egg. We had climbed a dangerous mountain and more than anything we now just felt safe.

However, even from that position of safety, in many ways I was lost. The reason I had woken up every day in the past was to make sure that Hartwell Pacific and its people would survive and thrive. Though I would remain as CEO for three more years and honor all my commitments, I now felt that the company we founded and the responsibility for it was in someone else's hands. There was some excitement about working with a larger corporation that could play a bigger investment game, but being a manager isn't the same as being a partner. The final decisions no longer came down to me and the current in my veins just didn't pump with the same vigor. My job seemed to be more analyzing and reporting, than creating a vision and executing it, and the politics and bureaucracy inherent in any large organization began to grate. Nonetheless, I used this period to learn more about the needs of a public company and to take copious notes on how to structure and run a larger, more institutional organization, but there was no way I was looking for a long-term corporate career. I knew I would ultimately need an exciting entrepreneurial challenge to satisfy my expectations. The three years with Smythson and ultimately MegaSteel—which acquired Smythson's business in 2007—were uneventful. We made our profits, provided solid returns to our shareholders, and I smoothly passed the baton to a designated successor.

In the midst of this minor career turmoil, the main personal issue that Mei and I faced was that we had no kids and were struggling with

fertility. The company had been our family, and our apartment now seemed hauntingly quiet. Our solution to this problem was to use every free moment we had to travel. We had some fantastic trips and enjoyed those times immensely, but soon realized that we were in fact running away from the situation. The emptiness we felt threatened to consume us. But Mei and I are fighters and believe inherently that every problem is solvable—and solve it we did. Determined to have a decent-sized family, we applied for adoption, utilized a surrogate mother, and wouldn't you know it, Mei ended up randomly getting pregnant. The void in our hearts was filled by New Age triplets— Hailey, George, and Ashley—all arriving within six months of one another, with an age gap between youngest and oldest of just under a year. That haunting silence has been replaced by a wonderful symphony of chatter and clatter.

In 2008, immediately after fulfilling my tenure with MegaSteel, I joined up with Oaktree Capital, a large distressed debt and private equity firm, as an independent senior adviser. The goal now is to find an acquisition that can be my next vehicle for growth. It may sound counterintuitive, but amidst the enormous pain inflicted by the current recession there is also tremendous opportunity. In some ways, the Asian economic crisis of 1997 was the best thing that ever happened to Hartwell. Asset and wage deflation created a low-cost entry opportunity into just about any industry that held interest, and today that is the case once again. For sure the going will be tough—markets are volatile, credit is tight, and consumers are fearful—but if you can build a business that can survive in this environment, glory will be yours when the economy turns around. And it will. That will be my next adventure . . . but this time I won't be starting from scratch.

Acknowledgments

I must first say that had I known how much work goes into writing a book and getting it published, I probably never would have started. Without the constant support and encouragement of my family and friends, I would not have completed this project.

In particular I would like to thank my editors. A brilliant young gentleman named Matt Huttner put in many hours of work and was extremely helpful when it came to structure, while brutally slashing and burning around five hundred pages of text into what I hope stands today as a cohesive and fast-flowing story. He also relished the debate over word choice as we savored scotches and cigars. His fingerprints are all over this text. Alexandra Shelley, a consummate professional and Yale professor, taught me the painful phrase *killing your darlings* in the ruthless pursuit of eliminating superfluous or irrelevant stories as well as enforcing the maxim *show don't tell*. I fought hard in the beginning but in the end adopted most of her suggestions and admit that she was right.

I would also like to thank my many friends who painstakingly read my early text and offered suggestions and encouragement: Mom, Dad, my brother Andy, Ian Edgar, Justin Kent, John Vargis, Allen Dorcas, Tom Leander, Richard Huttner, Bernie McGuire, George Jackoboice, Mark Walsh, Mary Scott, Bill Duryea, Lisa Siu, James Chen, Raphael Le Masne, William Pfeiffer, Graydon Joseph, and Roy Kuan.

Great thanks and gratitude should be assigned to Jed Lyons, my mentor in this project, who told me early on, "There is a book in here somewhere, but you have a lot of work to do." He was right. That was two years ago. He also generously offered up all of his contacts in the publishing and editing world as well as many sage editorial comments. Again, this project would not have been completed without him, and I am very grateful.

I also appreciate the support and encouragement of my publisher, Peter Burford. Finding the right publisher is a real challenge, and I am confident I found a very good one. Thank you for your confidence.

Finally, I save the greatest acknowledgment for my wife, Mei, who is the lead character in this book, my soul mate, and my biggest fan. Though English is her third language, her commonsense input was uncannily helpful and can be found in most chapters.